DEAD SERIOUS

Breaking the Cycle of Teen Suicide

DEAD SERIOUS

Breaking the Cycle of Teen Suicide

Jane Mersky Leder

2ND EDITION | COMPLETELY REVISED & UPDATED

A Book for Teens, Adults & Educators

Copyright © 2018, 1987 by Jane Mersky Leder

ISBN 978-1-946229-53-3 (Paperback edition)

SUMMARY: Discusses the problem of teenage suicide, its effect on friends and family, warning signals, bullying, LGBTQ teens, peer prevention programs, ways of coping, and methods of helping a friend who is considering suicide. Includes case histories, interviews with teens who have attempted suicide, and a list of places to turn for help.

Editing by Hannah Eason
Front cover image by Amanda Matthews
Book design by Tasha Kenyon
Distributed by Bublish, Inc.
Printed and bound in USA First Printing January 2018
Published by Jane Mersky Leder
Visit www.janeleder.net

Publisher's Cataloging-In-Publication Data
(Prepared by The Donohue Group, Inc.)

Names: Leder, Jane Mersky.
Title: Dead serious : breaking the cycle of teen suicide : a book for
    teens, adults & educators / Jane Mersky Leder.
Description: 2nd edition, completely revised & updated. | [Evanston,
    Illinois] : Jane Mersky Leder, [2018] | First published in 1987 with
    subtitle, A book for teenagers about teenage suicide. | Interest age
    level: 12 and up. | Includes bibliographical references.
Identifiers: ISBN 978-1-946229-53-3 | ISBN 978-1-946229-52-6 (ebook)
Subjects: LCSH: Teenagers--Suicidal behavior--United States. | Suicide--
    United States--Prevention. | Adolescent psychology--United States.
Classification: LCC HV6546 .L43 2018 (print) | LCC HV6546 (ebook) | DDC
    362.280835--dc23

To my brother Robin:

Your suicide changed my life.
Your spirit is with me always.

CONTENTS

FOREWORD 1

I'm Not a Stranger to Suicide 1

Teen Suicide: Dead Serious 1

Here's the Thing.. 2

A Parable: As Told to Me by Scott LoMurray,
    Sources of Strength.. 2

Why a second edition *of Dead Serious?* 3

Middle School Kids... 4

Three Big Takeaways... 5

ACKNOWLEDGMENTS 7

CHAPTER 1: WHEN IT'S SOMEONE YOU KNOW ... 9

Kevin's Story 11

Reactions to Suicide 17

    Denial.. 18

    Blame... 18

    Guilt.. 19

    Anger... 19

    Grief 19

    Search for Answers.................................... 20

    Healing Never Goes in a Straight Line 21

Strategies: Resources 21

CHAPTER 2: BEHIND THE STATISTICS.............. 23

Youth Risk Behavior Survey.............................. 25

The Teenage Brain.. 26

Sleep 28

Don't You Know? It's All Academic.. 29

Homework: The 10-Minute Rule 30

Social Media: 9 Hours A Day... 30

Loss: Death 31

Loss: Divorce... 31

Loss: Support... 33

Moves Are Tough 34

Economic Stress... 35

When Things Go Wrong in Childhood – Sexual/Physical/
    Verbal Abuse 35

The Facts.. 36

Chris's Story... 36

Strategies: Where to Find Help... 40

CHAPTER 3: **ANXIETY AND DEPRESSION** **43**

Anxiety Disorder... 45

Strategies: What Can You Do to Be Less Anxious?......................... 47

Strategies: Some Cool Apps 48

Depression.. 48

Signs of Depression 49

Some Major Risk Factors for Depression 50

What Causes Depression? 50

Professionals Treating Depression 51

Advances in Treating Depression.. 51

Depression on the Rise for Teenage Girls 52

Strategies: What Can You Do to Feel Less Depressed?.................... 54

Self-Harm: Cutting.. 55

Strategies: If You're a Teen Cutter.. 59

CHAPTER 4: **EXPLODING THE MYTHS/ RECOGNIZING THE WARNING SIGNALS 61**

A Quiz 63

Exploding the Suicide Myths 64

Joe and Jeff's Story 64

Ron's Story 67

Tim's Story 67

Jeffery's Story 68

Steve's Story 69

SOS: Suicide Warning Signs 70

  Six General General Warning Signs 70

    Acting Out 70

    Alcohol and Drug Abuse 71

      The Opioid Epidemic 71

      Teens Mix Prescriptions with Other Substances 72–73

    Passive Behavior 72

    Changes in Eating Habits 72

    Changes in Sleeping Habits 74

    Fear of Separation 74

Strategies: Where to Get Help – An Introductory List 75

Specific Warning Signals 76

  Abrupt Changes in Personality 76

  Sudden Mood Swings 77

  Risky Behavior 77

  Decreased Interest in School and Poor Grades 77

  Inability to Concentrate 78

  Loss or Lack of Friends 78

Final Distress Signals 78

  Loss of an Important Person or Thing 78

  Hopelessness 79

Obsession with Death 79

Making a Will/Giving Away Possessions 80

Strategies: What Can You Do? 80

CHAPTER 5: **SUICIDE SURVIVORS.....................83**

Every suicide leaves an estimated six or more "suicide survivors"—people who've lost someone they care about deeply and are left grieving and struggling to understand.

My Mother's Story 85

Bev and Ron's Story.. 86

My Sibling Story 94

Strategies: Join A Suicide Survivors' Group 98

Strategies: Read a Book.. 98

CHAPTER 6: **OVER THE EDGE: INTERVIEWS WITH SUICIDE ATTEMPTERS 101**

Kate's Story 103

Kurt's Story 111

Natalie's Story.. 113

CHAPTER 7: **BULLYING: A POWER PLAY THAT HURTS 123**

What Is Bullying, Anyway? 125

Myths and Facts About Bullying 125

Climbing the Social Ladder 126

What We Know About Bullying and Suicide...................... 127

David's Story.. 128

13 Reasons Why 129

Witnessing Bullying 131

Bethanne's Story.. 132

Callan's Story 134
Cyber Bullying: Nowhere to Run, Nowhere to Hide 135
What's the Solution? 136
Strategies: Ways to Stop/React to Bullying 137

CHAPTER 8: **LGBTQ TEENS: OVERCOMING THE STIGMA WITH RESILIENCY AND PRIDE 141**

An Abridged Glossary of Terms 143
Doing Just Fine, Thank You 147
Milanka's Story 147
"Gender-expansive" Children and Young Adults 148
Not A Level Playing Field 150
    Being Outed 150
    Rejection by Family and Friends 150
    Physical Safety at School and Beyond 152
August's Story 153
    Homelessness 154
Ali's Story 155
    Substance Abuse 156
    Suicide 158
Sky's Story 158
On Being Transgender: It's Not a Disorder 161
Hope 164
Strategies: Valuable Resources 166

CHAPTER 9: **CONNECTIONS 171**

Josh's Story 173
Dylan's Story, Take 2 175
Strategies: Listening 177
Your Friends Are the First to Know 177

Strategies: Mirroring ("Mirror on the wall . . .") 178

Strategies: When A Friend Won't Talk.. 180

Strategies: Paying Attention to Nonverbal Clues 181

Strategies: How to Ask Good Questions 182

Suicide Prevention Programs That Make the Grade 184

Strategies: Suicide Hotlines 185

Fire Within 186

The Trevor Project: "Saving Young Lives" in the
    LGBTQ Community 188

Strategies: Where to Get Help... 188

Sources of Strength: Peers Rule 190

SOS Spinoffs: We Have Your Back 192

What Now?... 193

"You've Got a Friend".. 194

Another six months, I'll be unknown
give all my things to all my friends
you'll never step foot in my room again
you'll close it off, board it up

"Adam's Song" — *Blink 182*

FOREWORD

I'm not a stranger to suicide. My mother's first cousin took her own life, but the cause of her death was listed as an "accident."

Three days before my wedding to my ex-husband, his aunt took her own life. Didn't know whether or not to cancel the wedding. We went ahead.

My brother took his life on his thirtieth birthday. It's one thing to consider the death of someone you love; it's quite another to face the reality that he is gone. Even though it's been years since his suicide, a day doesn't go by that I don't look at his photo on my desk and wish more than anything that he were still here. If only I had known what to *do* or where I could have gone for professional help.

Let's face it: talking about suicide isn't easy. I get that. But the sad reality is that teen suicide is a serious problem: dead serious. The number of teens who take their own lives has mushroomed. In 2015, a new study by the National Center for Health Statistics reported that the suicide rate among girls between the ages of 15 and 19 reached a *40-year high.* Between 2007 and 2015, the suicide rate for those girls *doubled.* For young males, there was a *31 percent increase.*

The statistics don't lie, even if they are just numbers on a page without a story—without the beginning, middle, and end of a friend's, a classmate's, a child's, a neighbor's, even a sibling's life.

We can never know for sure, but the best estimates show that more than 5,240 teens in grades seven through twelve attempt suicide *every day.* (One teen girl who'd attempted suicide a few years earlier said, "Suicide is the bravest thing someone can do!") More than five thousand teens die *every year*—that's more teens than die from cancer, heart disease, AIDS, birth defects, stroke, pneumonia, influenza, and chronic lung disease *combined.* And the news gets worse (as if it could) because the most recent survey reports that suicide attempts are four times greater for LGB (lesbian/gay/bisexual) teens than their straight peers and that these attempts are four to six times more likely to result in medical treatment. Among the starkest findings is that 40% of transgender people have attempted suicide in their lifetime—nearly nine times the attempted suicide rate in the U.S.

HERE'S THE THING: *You and your friends can probably recite the warning signs to look for when someone you know is in crisis, maybe even contemplating suicide. Don't get me wrong: it's important to recognize these red flags, like changes in a friend's personality, eating and sleeping habits, attitude toward school, and on we go.*

But it's even more important to know what to do to prevent these downward spirals from occurring in the first place. Kids usually talk to other kids long before they talk to adults. You and your peers know what's up. So, why wait until someone you know is in crisis? Doesn't it make more sense to get ahead of the curve and figure out how to operate from a position of strength? When things get tough for a friend (or you), networks of peers and trusted adults will be in place. You'll have solutions up your sleeve and will be ready to hit the ground running. (More about this in Chapter 9.)

A Parable as Told to Me by Scott LoMurray, Sources of Strength

It Goes Like This:

There's a man who lives along the bank of a river near a waterfall. One day while out walking, he sees a kid caught in the current, about to go over the waterfall. The man dives into the water, pulls the kid to safety, performs CPR, and saves her life. This scenario happens over and over again. Sadly, not everyone is saved. It's a losing proposition. Then he has an idea and walks upstream, away from the waterfall and the heavy current. He figures it might be better to hang out where there is less danger. In a safe place, the kids can learn how to swim and how to avoid the potential disaster of falling over the waterfall in the first place. And if they do somehow get close to the edge, they will have the tools they need to find a way to avoid the fall and make it to shore.

You're smart. You get the point. This suicide prevention thing starts upstream, where things are not in turmoil. You hang out with your friends. Right? Maybe you have a new song or cool app you'd like to share. Maybe you talk about some stupid thing you did and how it feels bad. If you are failing chemistry and may have to go to summer school; if you are smoking too much pot or drinking too much; if you're having trouble getting out of bed in the morning and the rest of the day is a struggle, chances are either you'll speak up or your friends will suspect something is going on. Good friends hang together and help each other out. You are each other's first line of defense.

...

Why write a second edition of *Dead Serious* all these years later? The world teens inherited in 1987, the year when the first edition of *Dead Serious* was published, looked nothing like it does today. There was no Internet. No social media. No cell phones. No texting. For the most part, gays and lesbians were in the "closet"; certainly, there was little, if any, discussion about gender identity. Academic pressure was real but hadn't reached today's fever pitch. Music, art, and gym were an integral part of the school day and gave students a break from academics. When there was a need for information, kids went to the school or public library (imagine!) where they had to read books or squint to read newspapers and magazines on microfiche. Talking about sexual abuse, self-harming

TODAY, THE BIGGEST SURGE IN SUICIDE RATES IS AMONG YOUNG KIDS BETWEEN THE AGES OF TEN AND FOURTEEN.

behavior, and suicide was taboo. And while bullying has always been a problem, kids went home after school where they were "safe," free from the nonstop barrage of social media. In the late '80s, the number of youth suicides had begun to drop and continued its downward trend until the late '90s. Today, the biggest surge in suicide rates is among young kids between the ages of ten and fourteen.

...

No one knows for sure why more middle school kids are having a rougher time—why they are more anxious, more distressed, more drawn to suicide as a way to permanently solve their angst. Experts do have some possible explanations: academic pressure; the onset of puberty at a time when technology and social media have changed the way they (we) live; online bullying; the scary world around them with fears of terrorism, political upheaval, economic recession. Middle school kids are overexposed. They do not feel safe; they do not feel secure.

The second edition of *Dead Serious* reflects the changing social and cultural landscape, with a focus on stories and strategies to help you (and adults) prevent problems many young people face before things mushroom out of control.

Dead Serious is not a book about doom and gloom. It's an intimate look at the lives of today's teens, like you, the pressures you face, and the many possible combinations of reasons why a teen with her whole life ahead of her falls over the "waterfall." Yes, some of the stories are sad. But there is always a suggestion or two about what could have been done upstream to prevent the tragedy long before a depressed, troubled teen teetered on the edge of the abyss. *Dead Serious* is a book about hope and empowerment. It provides tools and strategies to help break the cycle of teen suicide.

Three Big Takeaways

1. Talking about suicide does **not** make matters worse. What makes matters worse is **not** talking. That may sound counterintuitive. But more than anything, a person struggling with suicidal thoughts wants someone to listen, to show that they care and that they "get it." They want help, and you can be the conduit between a friend and a trusted adult.

2. It is **never** your job to *save someone* but to connect with a trusted adult who can secure professional help.

3. It **is** your job to break the code of silence if a friend tells you not to tell anyone else. Better to have an angry friend than no friend at all.

So I'm passing the baton to you. You will run the final lap. Become part of a team of your peers and adults that makes the grade. Wins the race. Helps to break the cycle of teen and middle school suicides. And if you are ever depressed and think that life is not worth living, you'll know where you can get help 24/7.

National Suicide Help Line:
1 800 273-TALK (8255)

With hope and gratitude

ACKNOWLEDGEMENTS

I always feel like I'm accepting some award and thanking all the people who helped me receive such an honor. As so many authors write, there is no way to mention everyone who contributed to their book. It's true. So, let me first give a shout out to all the teens and young adults who shared their stories with me. It often takes a brave person to tell the truth, particularly when some of the experiences are filled with hurt, disappointment, even shame. And to the experts on subjects ranging from bullying to depression, from LGBTQ teens to suicide prevention programs: I couldn't have written this book without you. I know your time is valuable, and I'm appreciative that you were willing to spend some of it with me. And before I get the hook and the TV commercial begins, let me thank Kathy Meis, Founder/CEO of Bublish, Inc. Kathy is the kind of Renaissance woman all authors want in their corner. She is wicked smart and passionate about publishing the best books around. And to my agent, Berenice Hoffman, who is no longer with us but who urged me to write a second edition of *Dead Serious* more than twenty years ago. Better late than never. Finally, this book is dedicated to my brother, whose suicide rocked my world and changed everything. His death sent me on a journey that continues to this day.

Some of the names in this book have been changed in cases where the people referred to would prefer to remain anonymous.

CHAPTER ONE | # WHEN IT'S SOMEONE YOU KNOW

Like a comet
Blazing 'cross the evening sky
Gone too soon

Like a rainbow
Fading in the twinkling of an eye
Gone too soon

Shiny and sparkly
And splendidly bright
Here one day
Gone one night

Like the loss of sunlight
On a cloudy afternoon
Gone too soon

Like a castle
Built upon a sandy beach
Gone too soon

Like a perfect flower
That is just beyond your reach
Gone too soon

Born to amuse, to inspire, to delight
Here one day
Gone one night

Like a sunset
Dying with the rising of the moon
Gone too soon

Gone too soon

"Gone Too Soon" – *Michael Jackson*

10

KEVIN'S STORY

Kevin's history book was open and sitting upright on his desk. He couldn't concentrate, not after last night's scene. He wondered whether Brad had gone straight home or walked the streets brooding over Olivia and her new boyfriend. Never mind. He and Brad were going to have a great summer. Camp out on weekends. Work at the grocery down the street during the week and make some big bucks. Maybe take a trip to the Rockies at the end of the summer. Brad would forget all about Olivia.

He closed his eyes. Thinking about his summer plans with Brad made him even more anxious for the school day to end.

When Kevin opened his eyes, he saw his counselor, Ms. Davies, standing over him.

"I need to talk to you," she said quietly.

What had he done now? He picked up his books and followed Ms. Davies into the hall.

"Something terrible has happened to Brad," she said. "His mother found him in his car in the family garage last night." *So, that's where he went.*

Ms. Davies took a deep breath. "Brad is dead. He took his own life."

"He's not dead. We're playing cards tonight."

"There's a detective in Mrs. Lyons's office waiting to talk to you. He wants to ask you some questions."

...

Kevin slammed the car into reverse and screeched down the driveway. He and his parents had been arguing all morning. His mother was worried sick that he'd "drive off a cliff." His dad had ordered him not to drive to the funeral alone. They were upset. He didn't care.

Why hadn't Brad talked about it? Kevin would have listened. They told each other everything. Now he wasn't so sure. Maybe Brad hadn't wanted his help. Maybe he hadn't wanted anyone to change his mind. Kevin swiped at the tears running down his cheeks. He wasn't going to get all choked up. Not again. Brad hadn't talked to him, so why should he care?

...

The funeral was supposed to be small, but there were hundreds of people, people Kevin had never seen before. He hated all the strangers. Brad would have hated them too. He was the shy, quiet type who loved being by himself, taking things apart and putting them back together. Why couldn't he have gotten his life right?

Kevin walked closer to the casket. He could see Brad's mom surrounded by a ring of people. She looked so tiny. Kevin had always thought of her as much taller. He remembered the night Brad had come home drunk. Mrs. Brogan had told Brad what a fool he was. If he wanted to be a fool, she'd said, he could be one on his own time. But he had better not be a fool in front of her again or she'd knock him around the block and back. Mrs. Brogan had seemed very tall that night.

Kevin wanted to talk to her. He wanted to tell her how sorry he was and how, even though Brad never touched a cigarette in front of her, he chain-smoked when he played cards with the guys. If only he could reach out and hug her and make everything like it had been. But he could barely remember the last time he had hugged his own mother.

The knot in his stomach tightened. Brad had had a few problems. Who didn't? Olivia, his first girlfriend, had started dating someone else. And he hadn't been able to decide what to do after high school. Being a cook in Miami sounded cool. "Asshole idea," his dad had said.

When people started out to the parking lot, Kevin sat up, adjusted his tie, and nodded at the other three pallbearers standing near the casket. He had never understood funerals. His mother had told him that they make a permanent picture in your head that the dead person is gone. He didn't need a funeral to do that.

···

Why had Brad taken his own life? *Someone* was responsible.

Not Mrs. Brogan. She had always been there when Brad needed her. And sometimes when he didn't. He remembered the time, years before, when she'd marched Brad back to the grocery store and made him admit to the checker that he'd lied when he said the eleven pop bottles were his. What he had

WHY HAD BRAD TAKEN HIS OWN LIFE! *SOMEONE* WAS RESPONSIBLE.

done was dishonest, and Mrs. Brogan had wanted her son to accept the consequences. At the time, Brad had hated his mom for being so principled. Later on, he realized she'd done the right thing.

Kevin tried not to blame Mr. Brogan, but it wasn't easy. Brad's father worked, slept, and drank beer. That was it. When Brad had been younger, his dad had come to watch him play football. But when Brad had quit the team, his dad had been angry. "You're just like me, only worse," he'd said. Brad wasn't anything like his dad. When his dad got angry, everyone paid. When Brad got angry, he got quiet and withdrawn. He was the only one who paid.

···

Kevin's best friend was dead, and there was no reason. If he'd died from a disease or an accident . . . But he had taken his own life. What could have been so bad? It made no sense.

If only he had known Brad was so unhappy. If only he had seen the signs. But what signs?

Kevin remembered the night back in seventh grade after the roller-skating party. Brad and another friend, Dave, had decided to walk home instead of riding the bus. They didn't have far to go. Besides, maybe they'd stop at McDonald's for something to eat. As the boys approached the restaurant, Brad challenged Dave to a race. Brad took off across Madison Street with Dave on his heels.

They talked about the accident only a couple of times. Brad told Kevin the car swerved to miss him but hit Dave instead. There was nothing the paramedics could do; Dave was dead on arrival at Good Shepherd Hospital.

Brad hadn't been the same after that. He had seemed to crawl into a shell. He got headaches that made him vomit, and his skin turned white. He got pimples all over his face. Kevin figured Brad had to work it out on his own; he didn't know what else to do.

If only he had done something then, maybe Brad would be alive now. If he had made him talk about it. But Brad had said he didn't want to talk, and Kevin hadn't pushed. Anyway, Brad couldn't have taken his own life because of an accident so many years ago. He had to have forgotten all about it.

A sharp guy like Brad doesn't kill himself for no good reason. That would be crazy. Brad might have been confused, but he wasn't crazy. Maybe his dad had finally gotten to him. Mr. Brogan was a cop who worked the shift from three in the afternoon to eleven at night. And on weekends, Mr. Brogan sat in front of the TV, drinking beer and doing crossword puzzles. If he drank too much, and he often did, he'd either fall asleep or leave the house without telling anyone where he was going.

One night, the phone rang late, and it was someone from the hospital telling Mrs. Brogan that her husband had been in an accident and that she better come right away. Brad told Kevin one side of his dad's face looked like it had been mashed in a blender. He was cut up so badly he stayed in the hospital for almost a week.

"That's not good enough," Kevin screamed. "You couldn't have killed yourself because of your old man. You could have moved out, gotten your own place with some other guys. You go off and kill yourself without letting me know, without letting me help. Okay. So you wanted to keep it to yourself. Fine. Keep it all to yourself. I don't care. Just don't expect me to waste my tears over you." Tears streamed down his face.

Maybe this was all Olivia's fault. She and Brad broke up every other week. They broke up, then got back together. Again and again. They went steady off and on for two and a half years.

Brad and Olivia would be going separate ways after graduation. So why not get it over with? Brad didn't care. At least that's what he said.

During a card game with Kevin and some other guys, Brad had talked about his future.

You're lucky," he'd said to Kevin. "You know what you want to do. You've got your art. You want to be an artist. I've got nothing."

Kevin had felt uncomfortable. He'd known Brad was having a hard time. "You'll get it together," he had said.

...

Brad had made one more attempt to win Olivia back. When that had gone south, Brad had stormed off. He'd insisted on walking home. "Just go. Take my car and go."

"I can't take your car," Kevin said.

"Take it." He shoved the keys in Kevin's hand.

"Come on, this is nuts." Kevin tried to give the keys back. But Brad had already turned around and begun walking away.

Frustrated, Kevin got into the car, turned the key, and then slowly backed down the driveway. *Okay*, he thought, *I'll cruise around the block a few times and stall for time. Brad needs to cool off.* After wasting several minutes, he drove by Brad walking slowly toward home.

"Hey, jump in. You're crazy to walk. Besides, this is your car."

"I want to walk. Just park the car in the driveway and leave the keys in the mailbox."

No use arguing. When Brad made up his mind to do something, he did it. No point in trying to stop him.

...

A month after Brad took his own life, Kevin halfheartedly agreed to play poker with some of the guys. He had to get out of the house. Kevin waited anxiously to see Brad again. He had so much to tell him. He was going to art school in the fall. The high school baseball team had taken the league championship. Olivia and her boyfriend had broken up.

Brad never reappeared. But Kevin thought about him a lot. Some days he thought he understood why Brad had killed himself; other days he had no idea. He could never remember how long it had been since Brad had died. Sometimes it seemed like years, sometimes only a few days.

Time was meaningless to Brad's mom too. She and Kevin talked a lot. Every time he saw her, she cried. Not right away. She pretended she was fine at the beginning. Then she'd ask Kevin if he remembered a certain incident, such as the time she'd marched Brad to the grocery store to return the bottle money. And then she'd cry. At first, Kevin felt funny talking about Brad. He thought the less he talked, the sooner the pain would end. But it was just the opposite. Talking made him feel better. Sometimes it made him laugh. More often, it made him cry. The letting go felt good. But the searching for answers never stopped.

Now, the knot in Kevin's stomach often loosens. His younger brother tells a dumb joke about the chicken crossing the road and he laughs. The wounds are starting to heal. And sometimes things are almost as they were. He forgets all about Brad. The pain is gone. Then, like a ghost, it reappears. When he's playing baseball on a hot summer afternoon, or when he opens a bedroom dresser drawer and finds an old shirt he once loaned to Brad. How could he ever forget?

Reactions to Suicide

It's been many years since I interviewed Kevin (not his real name) about the suicide death of his best friend. In many ways, his reactions to Brad's death mirrored my own and those of the majority of others who have lost a friend or family member to suicide: the denial, the blame, the guilt, the anger, grief, search for answers, and the healing that never goes in a straight line.

Take a look at the following quotes and decide which reactions to suicide they each represent.

one:

"He's not dead. We're playing cards tonight."

two:

"There must have been a reason Brad killed himself. *Someone* was responsible."

three:

"If only he had done something then, maybe Brad would be alive now. If he had made him talk about it. But Brad had said he didn't want to talk, and Kevin hadn't pushed."

four:

"You go off and kill yourself without letting me know, without letting me help. Okay. So you wanted to keep it to yourself. Fine. Keep it all to yourself. I don't care. Just don't expect me to waste my tears over you. Tears streamed down his face."

five:

"He wasn't going to get all choked up. Not again. Brad hadn't talked to him, so why should he care?"

six:

"But the searching for answers never stopped."

seven:

"The wounds are starting to heal. And sometimes things are almost as they were. He forgets all about Brad. The pain is gone. Then, like a ghost, it reappears."

one: Denial

When Kevin was first told that Brad had taken his life, he refused to believe it. The truth was too hard to bear. How could his friend

DENIAL IS A SHORT-TERM DEFENSE MECHANISM AGAINST DEATH . . .

do something like that? It didn't make sense. And it was easier to deny that his best friend wouldn't be at

the card game that night, or any other night, than to accept that his friend was dead.

Denial is a short-term defense mechanism against death— death by suicide or by any other means. "I can't believe that this has happened, that he won't be around anymore."

two: Blame

Kevin did his best to find someone to blame for Brad's death: Maybe it was Mr. Brogan, Brad's father. He hadn't been the most supportive of dads. Or maybe it was the friend who was hit by a car in front of Brad and later died. Then there was Olivia, who broke up with Brad and broke his heart. Or maybe it was Brad himself; he didn't have a clue what he wanted to do after graduation.

Truth is there is never one reason why someone takes his/her own life. And never just one person to blame.

three: Guilt

Friends of those who have taken their own lives, such as Kevin, feel they could have prevented the suicide if only they had known how unhappy their friend was. In some cases, they did know their friend was suicidal but didn't tell anyone, probably because they were sworn to secrecy. Secrecy is *never* an option. If you sense or know that a friend is severely depressed, find a trusted adult who can help your friend get the professional help needed. Better to break a friend's confidence than to lose him forever.

four: Anger

Anger is part of the grieving process. We usually get angry when feeling hopeless, helpless. You get angry at the friend who took his life. Angry at the fact that he didn't bother to talk to you about his problems, that he didn't even say good-bye. Angry at yourself for not seeing the writing on the wall. While anger is a natural reaction to suicide (to any painful loss), it eases over time. Most often, the anger morphs into sadness and forgiveness.

five: Grief

Everyone reacts differently to suicide. Some people scream and cry. Others, like Kevin, try not to get emotional but waver back and forth. But sooner or later, they're forced to accept the truth: a friend is dead, and the death was not a mistake.

There are no right or wrong ways to grieve. You can take all the time you need, even when people say things like, "Well, you've got your life back on track, right?" or something more direct: "It's time to stop feeling sorry for yourself." Life is not a TV show in which characters "get over it" in thirty minutes to an hour. It takes time to grieve. For many, the pain never goes away; it becomes a dull ache.

six: Search for Answers

For Kevin and everyone who has lost someone to suicide, the search for answers can be confounding. If someone dies in an auto accident, there is a cause, a reason. If someone dies from a disease like cancer, there is a reason. If someone dies of old age, the death is understandable. But suicide? There are only guesses as to why.

Some survivors, like me, find comfort in talking to everyone who knew the person who took his life in an attempt to find clues or, in some cases, to find support. The act of *doing something* can be helpful. I wrote a book. Now I'm writing a second one. I've learned a lot about my brother and about the way other people remembered him. But after all these years, I still have many questions that will never be answered.

But I'm still certain that my brother visited me after he died. I know I wasn't crazy when, a few days after my brother's funeral, he appeared in my bedroom in the middle of the night. I sat up and turned on the light, and there he was—dressed not in some white, angel-like getup but in a pair of faded jeans and a work shirt. I was terrified and had no idea what to do or say. For three nights, my brother showed up after dark. On the third night, I managed to tell him how much I loved and missed him but that I understood he'd made a decision to move on to whatever was next. He nodded, turned, and walked through my closet.

I've retold this story many times. And more often than not, people look at me like I'm crazy. They think I've gone off the deep end with grief. But I know what I saw was real. I know that my brother needed my permission to leave this earth plane and that, as his older, beloved sister, he'd come to me to cut the cord.

seven: Healing Never Goes in a Straight Line

There are days—even weeks or more—when the grieving stops. Your life goes on. Then you hear a song or see an old friend or attend a family event, and the pain returns. Usually, the grief doesn't last as long as it used to. The truth is: it never goes away forever but leaves a dull ache that comes and goes.

Strategies:

Resources

If you know someone who has died by suicide and feel that you need help or information, contact any of the following people or organizations near you:

- **Local support group** – You can use support group directories from, among others, the American Foundation for Suicide Prevention (Afsp.org/find-support/ive-lost-someone/find-a-support-group) and Suicide.org (Suicide.org/suicide-support-groups.html).

- **School counselor or teacher** whom you trust

- **Private counselors** – Ask your school counselor or doctor for recommendations.

- **Clergy**

CHAPTER TWO | **BEHIND THE STATISTICS**

All the kids that I can't compare to
making friends like they're all supposed to
you will never come close to how I feel

"Solitude Is Bliss" — *Tame Impala*

Youth Risk Behavior Survey

The most recent survey by the Centers for Disease Control and Prevention (CDC) of teenagers in grades nine through twelve, in both public and private schools, found:

- 17.7 percent of students reported seriously considering suicide in the previous month!

- Of those, 14.6 percent had made a plan as to how they would attempt suicide

- 8.6 percent had attempted suicide at least once

- 2.8 percent had made a suicide attempt that led to poisoning, injury, or an overdose

No complete count is kept of suicide attempts in the United States; however, each year the CDC gathers data from hospitals on nonfatal injuries from self-harm. And that estimate, say many experts, is low. Why? There's a big stigma around suicide. You know, it's one of those

THERE'S A BIG STIGMA AROUND SUICIDE.

hush-hush subjects that gets pushed under the rug. People don't like to talk about suicide. And they don't want to report it.

It may surprise you (or maybe not) that females attempt suicide three times more often than males. But males are four times more likely to *die* by suicide.

> **"Sophomore year was rigorous academically. I just gave up."**— *J., 18*

> **"It's hard trying to figure out my outside interests."**— *M., 13*

> **"We just try to be our own person but we don't know how to cope."**— *Lily, now 20*

Even in the best of times, you and your peers are faced with an avalanche of changes and expectations. Parents expect you to become an independent person, capable of making your own decisions and taking care of yourself. Teachers and parents expect you to decide what to do after graduation and how to do it. Your friends expect you to fit in. As if that's not enough, your body has no idea what to expect. One day you're up; the next day, you're down. And dare we throw in the political climate with all its tension and mistrust? It can get rough out there. Some authors have even called the world you're living in the "age of anxiety."

> **"What's happening now will determine our future. I worry about social and environmental justice. I work as an intern for Planned Parenthood because they provide such important basic health care. And I worry that it will be defunded. That's why I want my voice to be heard."** — *Lia, 16*

According to the CDC study referenced above of seven thousand high school students, one out of every five teens reported severe problems with self-esteem, feelings of failure, alienation, loneliness, lack of self-confidence, and thoughts of suicide.

The Teenage Brain[*]

I am not a neurologist who specializes in adolescent brain development. I'm not a neurologist. Period. I've read a lot about the teen brain, though, and can summarize what I've learned. If you're a teen, I don't have to tell you how wacky your thinking and actions can get. (At least, that's what we adults think.) If you're a parent— well, having a teen in the house may make you wonder how you'll survive and get along with this "new" person who has invaded your home. You suddenly have no idea who this child of yours has become. The good news: this transformation generally lasts only a year or two. So, hold on!

---

[*] www.npr.org/templates/story/story.php?storyId=124119468

Without getting technical, the experts tell us that adolescence is the "most tumultuous time" for the brain since birth. The area right behind the forehead, called the frontal cortex, thickens and continues developing. This is the thinking, planning, strategizing part of the brain, and it is still not "on board". So, teens often don't make the most responsible decisions. Duh! As Frances Jensen, a pediatric neurologist at Boston Children's Hospital commented, "It's the part of the brain that says: 'Is this a good idea? What is the consequence of this action?' It's

THE EXPERTS TELL US THAT ADOLESCENCE IS THE 'MOST TUMULTUOUS TIME' FOR THE BRAIN SINCE BIRTH.

not that they [teens] don't have a frontal lobe. And they can use it. But they're going to access it more slowly." The nerve cells that connect teens' frontal lobes with the rest of their brains move as slowly as when they get out of bed in the morning.

The frontal lobe affects mood and risk taking. This may explain why teens take risks like experimenting with drugs and/or alcohol, driving like Indy 500 racecar drivers . . . the list goes on. (BTW, my then sixteen-year-old son did the racecar-driver thing, totaled his dad's car, and broke his back. I've lived this nightmare.) The sluggish frontal lobes make it more challenging for teens to correctly read feelings. One study showed that three-quarters of teens were unable to read fear in others' faces. If they can't see fear, for example, in their peers, they are perhaps more likely to be involved in risky behavior. Teen brains don't take in and organize information the same way adult brains do. Still, adolescence is a time when the connections teens make with people in their lives can make a huge difference as they move toward young adulthood. Contrary to what teens say, they are "yearning" for more time with their parents. But it's hard for teens to own up to their needs when their "job" is to become independent. Message to parents: your kid still needs you. They will eventually come around. And message to teens: it does get better. All those crazy things you do are part and parcel of a brain that is still forming. You might think of it as a growth spurt; eventually, you grow into your brain the same way you grow into your body.

Sleep

"Sleep is the golden chain that ties health and our bodies together." – *Thomas Dekker*

What we know about neurology and learning sciences is that you can't possibly be 100 percent receptive and engage 24/7 without breaks, without time to sort and process information and reflect on it. Getting enough sleep is one way to get the breaks you need. Teens need on average nine-plus hours a night. Most get 7.5 hours. You're not filling up your tank

> **TEENS NEED ON AVERAGE NINE-PLUS HOURS A NIGHT. MOST GET 7.5 HOURS.**

but building a huge sleep debt. It's no wonder that you are often exhausted in first period. Look around at the sea of sleeping faces. Experts say you should still be in bed sleeping. Maybe starting the school day an hour later would help. And getting enough sleep is one of the best ways to keep up with what's going on in and out of school. Sleep affects your mood, your ability to think, to perform (yep, on tests, for example), and to react in ways that make sense.

So, how many hours do you get? Are you up texting and posting on Facebook into the wee hours of the night? Do your parents have a clue? For those of you tied to social media as if it's an umbilical cord wrapped around your neck, it's a good idea to give your body and your brain some much-needed rest. Sleep deprivation is linked to all kinds of bad stuff: depression, anxiety, car accidents, obesity, bullying. . . . Bottom line: catch up with your "friends" in the morning and mine as much energy as you can during a good night's sleep.

You'll need it, because most schools are programmed to make you sprint from class to class with few breaks. You want to hang with friends. No time. You are hungry. Well, no food until lunch period. You want to get a jump on your homework, but there's no time during the school day. So, you've got all this homework after school, not to mention extracurricular activities that often last all year, instead of just during, say, baseball or football season.

With more double-working parents in nearly half of U.S. homes, moms and dads, concerned about how their kids (you) spend their unsupervised time, overschedule extracurricular activities. It's a Catch 22: parents need to know that you are safe, while you need time to chill. You are overscheduled, tired, and stressed. It's a vicious cycle that creates big-time anxiety.

Don't You Know? It's All Academic!

You don't have to be depressed or suicidal to feel stressed out. So, what's different today than, say, thirty years ago when your parents were your age?

You are beginning to face pressures like getting good grades, good test scores, being accepted by a good college *much earlier.* A nonprofit organization called Challenge Success surveyed thousands and thousands of kids in schools where the majority go on to college. "They're not talking about girlfriend and boyfriend strife," says Denise Clark Pope, senior lecturer at the Graduate School of Education, Stanford, and the cofounder of Challenge Success. "They're not talking about the stress of their parents getting a divorce or being alcoholics. The thing that comes up the most is tests, grades, and getting into college. It's all *academic.* And this pressure begins in middle school, sometimes even earlier." (Organizations like Challenge Success are now getting requests to consider working with elementary schools.)

What might be some of the suggestions to parents? According to Pope, one of the basic ones is "Don't flash card your kids to death. Let your kids play. Encourage them to make right choices without helicoptering over them." In other words, give them space to enjoy childhood and let them make mistakes from which they can learn.

> **"A good way to think about homework is the way you think about medications or dietary supplements. If you take too little, they'll have no effect. If you take too much, they can kill you. If you take the right amount, you'll get better."** — *Harris Cooper, Duke University psychology professor*

Homework: The 10-Minute Rule

Here's the amount of homework recommended for teachers to assign. Teachers should add ten minutes of homework as you progress from one grade to the next, beginning with first grade. For example:

- **first grade** – ten minutes
- **second grade** – twenty minutes
- **fifth grade** – fifty minutes

Okay, so you get the picture. A high school junior would be assigned one hour and fifty minutes of homework; a high school senior about two hours. Any more than two hours is usually not going to improve your grades. So, how does your homework load stack up?

Social Media: Nine Hours a Day

No, not nine hours a day of homework. Nope, we're talking about nine hours a day the average teen spends on social media, watching TV, and listening to music. That's more time by far than you spend sleeping and more time than you spend with your teachers during the school day and your parents at home. Hours in front of a computer/cell phone *may* change your brain to affect things like memory and concentration. (The jury is still out on the negative effects computers and smartphones have on the teenage brain.)

Nine hours a day on social media eats up a lot of homework time—and a lot of time for anything else. It's no wonder that you are feeling pressured to keep up socially *and* do well on tests, get good grades, and be accepted by a good college.

Yes, academic pressure is at the top of the "stressed to the max" list. But there are other reasons why some teens struggle with how to build the tools that can help them be strong and resilient in the face of challenges.

Loss: Death

Many young people who suffer from anxiety or depression—and even attempt or complete suicide—suffer the loss of someone or something very important.

When Brad's friend was hit and killed by a speeding car, Brad seemed to crawl into a shell. As Kevin put it, "He just wasn't the same after that." Brad lost interest in everyone and everything. Mrs. Brogan suggested Brad see a counselor; Mr. Brogan refused. Brad was left to come to terms with his friend's death alone. And although no one will ever know for sure, it is quite possible that he never really accepted what had happened. Brad had told Kevin that the car swerved to miss him and hit Dave instead. Maybe Brad felt that he should have been the one to die—a case of what experts call "survivor's guilt."

Loss: Divorce

"I had a nasty family life. My parents got divorced."
— *Angie, 18*

While it is no longer true that the divorce rate in the U.S. is rising (it has been declining since 1980) or that half of all marriages end in divorce (a young couple marrying for the first time today has a lifetime divorce risk of 40 percent), the fact remains that the loss of a family unit affects millions of American kids. Some responses from children of divorce:

"I was so upset. Why was this happening to me?"

"It was overwhelming going back and forth between my parents."

"My parents divorced when I was seven. My dad and I were best buddies. Then he wasn't around as much."

If your parents have divorced, you know how hard it can be. For many young people, divorce is harder to accept than death. In "Dear Mom and Dad," a young boy reads a letter written by Monica Epperson who experienced five divorces during her childhood. Epperson is the founder of The Child of Divorce: *thechildofdivorce.org.*

She writes about being heartbroken and a child who lost her sense of security. She urged her parents not to think that she was resilient. She was not. She was, she wrote, being taught that she came from a person who is unlovable and wrong. Her belief that love is unconditional was taken from her; it was hard for her to love for fear of being hurt again. Epperson's eloquent expression of how divorce affected every part of her belief system and self-worth is a haunting description of the devastation divorce can have.

Adult children of divorce are more likely to have seriously considered suicide than their peers from intact families, suggests research published in 2011. The study found that men from divorced families had more than three times the odds of considering suicide in comparison to men whose parents had not divorced. Adult daughters of divorce had 83 percent higher odds of suicidal ideation than their female peers who had not experienced parental divorce.*

---

* *www.huffingtonpost.com/2011/01/24/divorce-and-suicidal-idea_n_812456.html*

A reminder: The vast majority of children of divorce have never been suicidal. It's just one factor among many.

My IQ is 142

My mind is diseased. That I know

I am going to kill myself. What a relief it was

I am so much better now

You cannot do wrong when you are dead

Time is infinite. You are at the beginning — *Ted, 18*

Loss: Support

In the last weeks of his life, Ted, a senior in high school, drew fantasy cartoons and recorded his thoughts in a secret code that only a close friend could decipher. "My choices are to run away or to commit suicide," one message was decoded to read.

Ted, the son of a retired lieutenant colonel in the US Army, was thoughtful and articulate. He loved long debates about evolution versus creation. He impressed his friends with his understanding of things such as how speed affects time. Even though he got *B*s and *C*s, Ted's aptitude scores put him near the top of his class. Because of this promise as a student and as a future officer in the armed forces (he was active in his high school's ROTC program), Ted received a presidential nomination to compete for admission to West Point.

But the pressure of trying to improve his *B* and *C* grades to apply to West Point made Ted extremely anxious. He confided to a friend that he didn't know if he could live up to his parents' expectations. It was clear they wanted him to attend West Point; Ted wasn't sure he belonged there. Slowly, he just gave up on his studies. He stopped doing homework and, four days before his death, did poorly on an important test. It really hurt him to fail, and he told a friend after he got his grade that he needed psychiatric help. The friend didn't think Ted was serious. He just laughed it off.

Stuffed in his locker at school, police investigators found a strange story Ted had written. It was called: "The Push . . . the Fear . . ." In it, Ted was talking about his good and bad traits. One was "fear of failure." Next to it he wrote: "Oh, hey, you coward." With the pressure to succeed and fulfill his parents' wishes overwhelming him, Ted gave up.

Moves Are Tough

"When my mother lost her job, we moved to four different cities in four years. I eventually gave up on school. At the beginning of my junior year, I tried to commit suicide." — *Kurt, 18*

With so many Americans on the move, neighborhoods and schools are different from the way they used to be. Fifty or sixty years ago, most Americans lived in rural areas and stayed put their entire lives. The community was strong. People cared for each other. The roots were deep.

Today, almost 81 percent of Americans live in cities. It's not unusual for folks not to know their neighbors. While Americans are not moving as often as they did in the past, more than 11 percent moved in 2016, most often because they wanted a better home or apartment. A move can be tough. It often means you have to leave good friends behind and make new ones. Your new school will be different—harder, easier. Believe it or not, if you move in middle school, your chances of receiving a high school diploma by early adulthood are cut in half.

No need to panic! Talk to your parents and siblings about a possible move. Express your concerns. Work together as a family to check out your new home and neighborhood before you move. Maybe take a tour of your new school. Sign up for an afterschool activity that will put you in touch with other kids who share similar interests. Once you're in classes, get tutoring right away if you are floundering. Nip things upstream before the current gets too strong. (If there is a peer-tutoring program in your school, check it out.) And keep in touch with your old friends. It's a lot easier than it used to be. No snail mail required.

Economic Stress

Some experts suggest that economic downturns may be yet another factor that affects teens and their families and that can create tremendous stress and anxiety. The Great Recession that began in late 2008, for example, impacted millions of Americans. More than 7.5 million jobs were lost. The unemployment rate doubled. Maybe one of your parents lost a job, and money was tight. Your parents couldn't afford that new computer you'd coveted or the second-hand car they'd promised for your sixteenth birthday. Maybe your family had to downsize—to move to a smaller home or into an apartment. No one was happy. Your parents were under a lot of stress (maybe they still are). And when parents are anxious, there is no way of hiding it from you and your siblings. Again, economic pressure and the instability it causes can be one of many factors that contributes to a vulnerable teen's decision to take her own life. Statistics do show that when times are tough, suicide rates go up. Conversely, in times of economic stability, suicide rates go down.

WHEN THINGS GO WRONG IN CHILDHOOD: SEXUAL/PHYSICAL/VERBAL ABUSE
*Research has shown that the experience of childhood trauma and the risk of the individual who suffered it attempting suicide in later life (as a teenager or as an adult) are **extremely strongly correlated.***

The Facts

1. One out of five girls are sexually assaulted as children.

2. During the age range of twelve through seventeen, females have the highest incidence of forcible and nonforcible sexual abuse.

3. Research by the Crimes Against Children Research Center suggests children are most vulnerable to sexual abuse between the ages of seven and thirteen.

4. One out of twenty boys suffer the same abuse (some studies place that number much higher, more like one out of six).

5. The perpetrator is most often someone a sexually abused girl or boy knows and trusts.

6. Sexual abuse creates an overwhelming sense of powerlessness, worthlessness.

7. The risk of suicide becomes greater as the length and frequency of abuse increases.

8. Among adolescents, suicide attempters report more sexual abuse than those who do not attempt.

CHRIS'S STORY

Chris was eight or nine when a neighbor whom he liked and trusted sexually abused him. But it took more than twenty years for him to begin to understand how devastating that abuse was and the problems it caused.

"I remember having a nightmare where a clown stepped out of a picture and loomed over my bed. I woke up screaming. Neither of my parents came to soothe me. That first memory sticks out for me and underscores feelings of being afraid and unprotected. And that set the tone for my whole childhood. I don't remember my parents ever telling me they loved me or hugging and kissing me like other parents."

Chris's parents, he said, didn't know how to take care of themselves, let alone take care of him. Chris describes living in a house that was always in "survival mode." There was food on the table but no love lost. His parents tolerated one another but nothing more. If they were in the same room, they were either watching TV without saying a word or screaming at each other. Chris had no model for what a healthy relationship looked like.

His parents did eventually divorce, but the damage to Chris and his worldview would rear its ugly head throughout the rest of his childhood and into adulthood. "There was no one I could go to for protection or support. There was a complete lack of trust."

Chris's on-off switch was not working at home or in school. His nickname in kindergarten was "Mt. Saint Anderson" (his last name), a play on "Mt. St. Helens." Mt. St. Helens was and still is an active volcano in the state of Washington that "blew its top" big time in 1980. Just like the volcano, Chris erupted in temper tantrums and spent a lot of time in the principal's office. Chris got the message that he was emotionally unstable. Other kids got the message too and picked on Chris because he was out of control, had weird parents, and had a house that was a mess. (His mother was a hoarder.)

Things changed when Chris was around eight or nine. A new kid moved into the neighborhood, and he became a friend. The new friend's "father" (Chris was never sure exactly who he was) treated him with attention and respect—something Chris had never experienced from other adults. Chris started spending a lot of time at the man's house. "For the first time, there was this adult who cared about me." The two loved to talk about wrestling and wrestling luminaries like Hulk Hogan. Sometimes his friend would be there, sometimes not. Chris figured maybe the parents were divorced and that there was joint custody or something like that. He never knew for certain.

One day, things turned ugly. Chris says he knew in his gut that something wasn't right, but he didn't have the emotional strength to do something about his intuition. He got himself in an uncompromising situation and was raped by this man in whom he had placed his trust and respect.

ONE DAY, THINGS TURNED UGLY.

The summer before high school, Chris moved in with his aunt, uncle, and young cousin. To this day, he doesn't know who made the decision or why. Life in his new home was normal and functional, which, Chris says, probably saved his life. But the move was tough. He went from a small school of four hundred to one with approximately 2,200 students. It took him about an hour and a half to go to and from school by bus. He had little or no time to participate in school activities and to make new friends. He felt isolated, dislocated, and alone.

"Eventually, I just started fantasizing about killing myself because I didn't know what the future would lead to. I didn't think that the situation I was in was a permanent one and I didn't feel worthy of the good things that were starting to occur for me. So in my thirteen-year-old mind, I think the idea of killing myself started to make sense because it seemed like the easiest thing for everybody. I wouldn't be a burden to my parents anymore. I wouldn't be a burden to the rest of my family. I wouldn't have to go through shame and the pain and all of the things that I was feeling that I didn't see any solution to."

As Chris relates his story, he realizes that, with all the work he's done over the years to deal with and overcome the sexual abuse, he has never spent time putting things in the context of suicide. Yet during college—with the pressure of doing well academically and the problems he had connecting on a social level with other students—he slipped back into a deep depression with thoughts of suicide for the second time. His grandfather had made him sign a contract that required Chris to maintain a 3.0 GPA, get a job right away, reapply for financial aid, write a letter home every month, and give up the possibility of having a car as an undergraduate. His grandfather cancelled their contract two months before he was to make the first tuition payment. Fortunately, Chris's application for financial aid was approved, and he able to stay in school.

"Somehow I was still alive and still pushing through. But all the bad stuff and trauma had piled up, and I thought, 'Maybe the only way to stop the pain is to stop being.' I think what saved me was that, by then, I had a support system of people I trusted who respected me and took the time to listen. And I was stubborn. I wanted to build a life for myself."

After graduating from college, Chris checked off all the boxes: He started his career, he got married, bought a home. He was, he thought, living the American Dream. But the pain never went away. "I had never really processed the sexual trauma; I was trying to escape." His marriage ended in divorce. It was, Chris says, a very "dark period." And that's when he took the plunge and began what has been a ten-year odyssey to reclaim his life by addressing the sexual abuse and the many ways it led to feeling powerless, depressed, and, at times, suicidal.

Chris is a survivor. He is happily remarried. He helped found the National Organization on Male Sexual Victimization: *www.malesurvivor.org.* He is one of the world's leading experts on trauma and its impact on men specifically. His mantra guides him and all the survivors of childhood trauma, male or female.

You are not alone.

It was not your fault.

It is possible to heal.

It is not too late.*

---

* *www.malesurvivor.org/seeds-of-hope/*

Strategies:
Where to Find Help

- **Therapist Directory** – MaleSurvivor's Therapist Directory is a listing of hundreds of mental health professionals from around the United States and elsewhere who work with male survivors of sexual abuse.

- **Resource Directory** – Links to international resources and websites of partners in the work of healing.

- **RAINN** – National resources for sexual assault survivors and their loved ones (www.rainn.org/national-resources-sexual-assault-survivors-and-their-loved-ones)

- **Women's and Children's Health Network** (www.cyh.com/HealthTopics/HealthTopicDetails.aspx?p=243&np=293&id=2358)

- **GoodTherapy.org** (www.goodtherapy.org/blog/best-of-2013-goodtherapyorgs-top-10-websites-for-abuse-survivors-1220137)

CHAPTER THREE | **ANXIETY AND DEPRESSION**

It's like forgetting the words to your
favorite song

You can't believe it

You were always singing along

It was so easy and the words so sweet

You can't remember

You try to move your feet

Eet, eet, eet, eet

Eet, eet, eet eet . . .

"Eet" — *Regina Spektor*

Depression is on the rise, particularly among teen girls. Between 2004 and 2015, the risk of depression sharply increased as young people transitioned into adolescence. Six percent of boys and as high as 15 to 16 percent of girls were depressed. That works out to about a half million more depressed teens—three-fourths of whom were girls

Some fifty years ago, the medical profession as a whole did not believe that children and teens got depressed. While anxiety was recognized, it was relegated to the back burner and considered something most kids (and adults) experienced—physical symptoms like sweaty hands, a racing heart before a big game or important date, stomach butterflies before a test (particularly if you were unprepared). Today, extreme anxiety is recognized as a disorder, as is depression. Sometimes they go hand in hand, sometimes not. What's key is to learn about the characteristics of both disorders and, in working with a therapist, determine which one fits most closely with your experiences.

Anxiety Disorder

We all get anxious. It's part of the human condition. And it's often a good thing to be concerned, even to worry. But when the worry begins to dominate your life for two weeks or more and you can't stop, you may have an anxiety disorder. Check for the following signs:

- Desire to be "perfect"
- Need for constant approval and reassurance from others
- Easily fatigued
- Difficulty concentrating or mind going blank
- Irritability
- Muscle tension
- Problems with sleep

"If high school is about educating students for a future life, then why is it causing such anxiety that there is an increasing number of hospital admissions for teenage suicide attempts? Why do we have to think about our adult life every day as a teenager? I'm a junior in high school, and sometimes I forget that I'm supposed to have a life as a teenager. I can't sleep at night; all I do is stay up thinking and planning. Why are more American teenagers than ever suffering from severe anxiety? It's because we get it into our heads that school is what's going to make things better; we live for the future instead of actually just living." — *Natalie Jew, 16**

In student surveys, teens identify academic pressure as the number-one cause of their anxiety. Some teens can manage the pressure, and while they get nervous and worry about a test or a final grade, their anxiety does not continue at a fever pitch. For other teens, the anxiety can be overpowering and spin out of control, affecting more than the classroom. You may suspect that you fall into this second group but aren't sure. Or you may be sure but don't know what to do. The best thing you can do is make an appointment with a mental health professional who has the training and experience to diagnose what's going on and who may suggest some kind of therapy. The good news here is that, with early intervention, anxiety disorder can be treated, and you can look forward to a much less anxious, more productive, and happier life.

The sad fact: 80 percent of kids with a diagnosable (and treatable) anxiety disorder do NOT get treatment. That number has not changed. What's going on? Often—particularly in rural, underserved areas—trained professionals who treat adolescents are few and far between. And there's the stigma around admitting that a teen has a disorder that many don't believe exists or that they feel is

---

* https://goo.gl/9GUScH

nothing more than a lack of willpower or just a "phase." You know the line: in time, teens get over whatever is "ailing" them. After all, their parents did. (Maybe or maybe not.)

Strategies:

What Can You Do to Be Less Anxious?

On your own or at the suggestion of a therapist, here are some things you can do:

- **Be more mindful.** Sit quietly and focus on your breathing. Inhale. Exhale. Don't change the pace. Just concentrate.

- **Meditate.** There are many schools of thought and different ways to meditate. For me, the first thing I do is find a quiet spot. Turn off my phone. Shut the computer. Take a break from the outside world. I sit in a comfortable chair with my feet flat on the floor and my head unsupported. Then I choose a word. Any word. I close my eyes and repeat the word over and over in my mind. I don't say the word out loud. At first, your mind is going to wander. Accept that as something that happens to everyone and then get back to repeating your word. You may want to try this for five minutes at first and then build up to twenty minutes or more.

- **The "Plexiglas" Box** – One expert on adolescent anxiety and depression offers this message that has worked with many of his patients, including a fourteen-year-old who thinks that everyone is judging him—and not favorably. The psychiatrist suggested that his patient put himself in an imaginary "box" made of Plexiglas. The patient could see out, and his peers could see in. This "box" was coated with rubber, so when someone hurled an insult or said something that hurt the boy's feelings, it would bounce off the rubber. The patient felt safe and protected. The doctor reported, "This imaginary shield worked wonders. After a few tries, the patient felt less anxious. He had trained himself to repel the perceived negative judgments he assumed other were making about him."

- **Focus on the good things in your life.** As humans, we are hardwired to remember negative events and experiences. You might try writing down the good stuff that happens to you during the day. This has been shown to increase your sense of well-being and reduce feelings of anger, anxiety, and depression.

- **Try a little humor.** Early studies of humor and health showed that humor strengthened the immune system, reduced pain, and reduced stress levels. A good laugh can do wonders.

Strategies:

Some Cool Apps

There's an app for just about anything, right? And there are some apps you can download to your cell, computer, or other device that guide you through some relaxation techniques or help you practice positive thinking.

There are exercises, games, charts, even places to journal.

- t2health.dcoe.mil/apps/breathe2relax
- my.happify.com
- www.thinkpacifica.com

Depression

Just as it is normal to worry, it is also normal to feel down, sad, even worthless. The key is for how long: An hour? A day? A week? Most mental health professionals set a two-week time frame. If after two weeks you or a friend has been having a "bad case of the blues" or barely functioning under a "black cloud," you may be suffering from depression. You don't need to be told that being a teen sometimes feels like you're on a roller coaster of moods. You're up, you're down, you're nowhere at all. But depression is constant; it never seems to go away. You have trouble getting out of bed in the morning. You don't want to talk to anyone, even good friends. Your life feels worthless with no escape to something better. As you check out the following list, you'll see that many of the warning signs for depression are similar to the warning signs for anxiety disorder and for suicide. That's not an accident: most people who are thinking about suicide are depressed or suffer from other mental disorders.

Signs of Depression

1. Change in appetite: eating less

2. Sleep disturbance: taking a long time to fall asleep and waking early

3. Loss of interest or pleasure in activities

4. Loss of energy, fatigue

5. Feelings of self-hatred, guilt, and worthlessness

6. Inability to think or concentrate

7. Inability to do much of anything

8. Recurrent thoughts of death or suicide

In 2015, according to the National Survey on Drug Use and Health Report, an estimated three million adolescents aged twelve to seventeen in the United States had experienced at least one major depressive episode (MDE) in the past year. That's 12.5 percent of the population in that age group. Untreated, depression,

UNTREATED, DEPRESSION CAN LEAD TO SERIOUS HEALTH RISKS.

in combination with other factors, can lead to serious health risks, including suicide. However, as with anxiety disorder, getting effective treatment early can make a huge difference.

Some Major Risk Factors for Depression

- Trauma (sexual/physical/verbal)

- Previous episodes of depression

- A family history of depression

- Another untreated disorder, such as anxiety, drug and/or alcohol addiction, antisocial behaviors

Teens suffering from depression are at higher risk for all kinds of problems: substance abuse, a smaller group of friends, trouble at school, risky sexual behavior that leads to higher rates of pregnancy and sexually transmitted diseases, and a much higher risk of suicide—up to twelve times that of teens who are not depressed.

What Causes Depression?*

It's not known exactly what causes depression, but a variety of issues may be involved:

1. **Biological chemistry.** Neurotransmitters are naturally occurring brain chemicals that carry signals to other parts of your brain and body. When these chemicals are abnormal or impaired, the function of nerve receptors and nerve systems change, leading to depression.

2. **Hormones.** Changes in the body's balance of hormones may be involved in causing or triggering depression.

3. **Inherited traits.** Depression is more common in people whose blood relatives also have the condition.

4. **Early childhood trauma.** Traumatic events during childhood, such as physical or emotional abuse or the loss of a parent, may cause changes in the brain that make a person more susceptible to depression.

---

* *Mayo Clinic*

5. **Learned patterns of negative thinking.** Teen depression may be linked to learning to feel helpless—rather than learning to feel capable of finding solutions for life's challenges.

Professionals Treating Depression

For many young people, a combination of psychotherapy—talking alone with a psychologist or psychiatrist—and family therapy is successful in treating depression. For others, a combination of drug therapy (antidepressants) and talk therapy seems to work better. The key, say the leading psychologists, is flexibility. If a month or two go by and talk therapy isn't helping, it may be time to try drugs. Often talk therapy can help young people who are taking antidepressants recover even more quickly.

Lia, sixteen, has been diagnosed with both anxiety and depression. She suffers headaches, loss of appetite, and trouble going to sleep even when she's exhausted. "Everything felt like work. Getting up in the morning was work. Being around other people was work. I had negative thoughts all the time." And her anxiety? "You know things like if I don't get this assignment done, the whole class will know. I'll get a letter from my teacher and then I won't be able to go to college." But life for Lia is improving. She talks with a therapist on a regular basis and takes a small dose of an antidepressant. "It's the combination that works for me."

Advances in Treating Depression

When I wrote the first edition of *Dead Serious,* the antidepressant Prozac had just been introduced. Since then, a wealth of antidepressants (many of them combinations or different doses of existing drugs) have been approved by the Food and Drug Administration (FDA). But in 2003, the antidepressant Paxil was shown to cause thoughts of suicide in a small percentage of patients. The FDA released a black box warning for all antidepressants. But after the data had been analyzed and reanalyzed, some researchers disagreed and found that there were no additional suicides or suicide attempts due to the medication. Still, the use of these drugs decreased significantly, and the suicide rate went up! And when doctors began prescribing more antidepressants again, the number of suicides went down! Clearly, antidepressants do work; still, some physicians are reluctant to prescribe them or prescribe them more cautiously. And that's not a bad thing. As with any other medication, the person who takes an antidepressant needs to be monitored regularly for any unpleasant side effects and for the success of the drug.

For psychologists like Deborah Serani, an expert in the treatment of depression, another important part of working with teens is psychoeducation. What's that, you ask? "It's teaching a client the reason why they're struggling with a particular illness. The more a client knows, the more empowered she will feel." In the case of depression, Serani says, it's important to separate myth from fact. For example, being depressed is not a weakness in character; there are biological and environmental factors—not just psychological—at work. Also part of psychoeducation with teens (and adults) is diagnosing and differentiating between mild, moderate, and severe depression. For those with milder depression, talk therapy alone may be effective in reducing the symptoms. But for others, who are in a bad place—even a dangerous place—a psychiatrist would be asked to join a team of other professionals and decide whether to prescribe an antidepressant.

Depression on the Rise for Teenage Girls

"I always smile and look real happy when I'm depressed. I make everybody think that I'm just fine. That way, they'll leave me alone." — *Kate, 19*

Anyone can get depressed: girls, boys, high achievers, low achievers, whites, African Americans, Native Americans, Hispanics, Asians, rich and poor. But studies have now confirmed that teen girls are more than two times more likely to get depressed than boys. Catherine Steiner-Adair—clinical psychologist, school consultant, and author of *The Big Disconnect: Protecting Childhood and Family Relationships in the Digital Age*—says that we know girls define themselves in comparison to others. Many of her patients tell her that they get their "entire identity" from their phones. They constantly check to see the number of "tags," "likes," Instagram photos, and Snapchat stories. "We live in a culture of huge gender inequality," says Steiner-Adair. "Girls are still getting the message that what you look like, how much you weigh, and how pretty you are is the primary source of their power. This makes them very vulnerable." For middle school girls whose bodies mature early, the going is even rougher.

MEN ARE STARING AT GIRLS LONG BEFORE THEIR BRAINS ARE DEVELOPED ENOUGH TO HANDLE THE UNWANTED ATTENTION. IT'S SCARY AND CREEPY.

"It's the Wild Wild West out there," Steiner-Adair says. "Men are staring at girls long before their brains are developed enough to handle the unwanted attention. It's scary and creepy."

Steiner-Adair and others point to the role social media play and how the experience of teen girls today is very different from their mothers'. Back in the "day," girls came home after school, talked on the phone, and watched TV, or listened to records. If there were problems with other girls, they didn't have to deal with them 24/7. They had a safe place in which to disconnect and recharge. Not so today. On the one hand, technology provides 24/7 help with everything from homework to depression. On the other hand, technology can be "really bad." Away from teachers and parents, girls (and boys) experience a world in which the values they've been taught no longer apply. Being "snarky," starting rumors, hacking, pretending to be people that are not often negatively affect friendships, self-confidence, and connection with others. Girls lose their filter and do and say things they'd never dare do or say face to face. "There's a lot of mean-spirited stuff online," Steiner-Adair says. "Girls take the brunt."

Are there solutions? Yes. Schools need to be proactive and incorporate units in every grade that focus on what it's like to be a young person in the technology age and the effects their online behavior can have on themselves and on others. Feelings of being "left out" or judged should be addressed. And teachers, parents and physicians need to pay more attention to the teens they live and work with and pick up on signs of anxiety, depression, and suicidal thoughts much earlier and, if necessary, intervene.

Strategies:

What Can You Do to Feel Less Depressed?

Lia talked about taking care of her physical health as well as her mental well-being. "I exercise and try to eat well. I do things to make me happy. I'm involved in theater and work in front of and behind the curtain. I watch TV, go for a walk, eat chocolate." She laughs. "And I call or text my friends. Usually, when I'm depressed, I'm not going to put myself out there to be super social. But making an effort really does help."

Here are some other healthy actions that can put depressed teens in a better place:

- Listening to music
- Playing an instrument
- Reading
- Writing/Journaling/Blogging
- Playing sports

- Playing video games
- Add your own self-care activities here

For the millions of teens who, like Lia, suffer from depression, there are support groups and numbers to call. Here are just a few:

- **Anxiety and Depression Society of America**
  www.adaa.org
- **American Foundation for Suicide Prevention**
  1-800-273-TALK
- **Depression and Bipolar Support Alliance**
  www.dbsalliance.org/site/PageServer?
  pagename=home
  1 800-826-3632
- **Families for Depression Awareness**
  www.familyaware.org
  1-781-890-0220

Self-Harm: Cutting

Back in 2005, National Public Radio aired a fascinating segment on *Morning Edition* called "The History and Mentality of Self-Mutilation." You can listen to the entire program by visiting www.npr.org/templates/story/story.php?storyId=4697319. What follows is an edited version.

ALIX SPIEGEL reporting: In the late nineteenth century, two American doctors—George Gould and Walter Pyle—documented something they saw as a strange medical phenomenon. They reported that women all over Europe were puncturing themselves with sewing needles. In fact, this practice was common enough that European doctors had developed a name for the supposedly hysterical women who practiced this form of self-torture. They were called needle girls. However, according to psychiatry professor Armando Favazza, this was not the first time or place that the behavior had surfaced.

Professor ARMANDO FAVAZZA (University of Missouri): Self-mutilation spares no social class. It spares no gender. It spares no ethnicity.

SPIEGEL: Favazza, who works at the University of Missouri, has spent years studying self-injury and has found ample evidence of the practice in all kinds of settings. It's a problem in monasteries and nunneries, as well as modern-day prisons, and could even be found, he says, in ancient Greece. It's difficult to understand why anyone would deliberately harm themselves. Most of us, after all, spend our lives trying to avoid pain. But after years of research, Favazza says this behavior is best understood as a form of self-help, albeit a morbid form of self-help. For people whose emotions are hyperreactive or for those raised in an emotionally chaotic environment, it often seems like the best way to silence a swirl of pain and anxiety.

PROF. FAVAZZA: They describe it as popping a balloon. All the anxiety just seems to just go away.

Ms. Rebecca Raye (practices self-mutilation): Part of me almost feels like I am—that all the things that are really hurting me at the moment are just kind of leaving me, along with the blood.

SPIEGEL: This is nineteen-year-old Rebecca Raye. A series of fresh inch-long cuts climb Rebecca's arm like a ladder, sixty neat parallel lines. She made these cuts five days ago after realizing that her financial situation was not what she hoped it would be. . . . Before she cuts, she says her mind is exploding. But once she feels pain, there's a kind of peace.

MS. RAYE: I'll just be really calm and my thoughts will finally kind of be making sense, instead of them like racing through my head and nothing quite clicking. Just kind of centralizes my thought on one thing.

SPIEGEL: This is common, says Armando Favazza. He points out that people who harm themselves don't experience pain in the usual way.

PROF. FAVAZZA: And the fact is that most self-mutilators do not feel pain when they mutilate.

SPIEGEL: You say cutters, particularly people who have been abused in some way as children, frequently respond to stress by dissociating, a mental state which, in a sense, protects them.

PROF. FAVAZZA: What's being done is being done to their body, but it's not being done to them because they're kind of floating out there away from their body.

...

Sadly, the number of young people who cut (more girls than boys) has mushroomed since this program aired. Statistics on teen cutting are hard to come by because there have not been many studies done. It's estimated that one in every two hundred girls in the U.S. between thirteen and nineteen, or one half of 1 percent, cuts regularly. And those numbers are on the rise. Why do teens cut? Most researchers and mental health professionals agree that cutting is a way to deal with anxiety and depression. And

MOST AGREE THAT CUTTING (AND OTHER FORMS OF SELF-HARM) IS NOT AN ATTEMPT AT SUICIDE . . .

most agree that cutting (and other forms of self-harm) is not an attempt at suicide but, rather, an unhealthy way of relieving stress.

Cutting makes kids feel better and gives them a sense of control in lives that, otherwise, feel very out of control. Some cutters feel numb; they don't feel real. Cutting makes them feel alive and brings them into their body. Other cutters feel *too* much and use cutting as a way to discharge all those feelings—feelings that most people don't find overwhelming. Some cutters report a kind of "rush" or "high" similar to the "rush" runners often report when they've pushed themselves to the max. The jury is still out on what happens in the brain and body when someone cuts and how cutting releases "feel good" opioids.

In her article "Teen Depression and Anxiety: Why the Kids Are Not Alright," author Susanna Schrobsdorff reported that of the dozens of teens she interviewed, every single one knew someone who had engaged in self-harm (most often, cutting) or had done it themselves. A Seattle Children's Hospital study that tracked hashtags used on Instagram to talk about self-harm showed a dramatic increase from 1.7 million search results in 2014 to 2.4 million one year later. Schrobsdorff writes that it's hard to know why self-harm has surfaced now. "It's possible that we're just more aware of it now because we live in a world where we're more aware of everything."

> **"IT'S POSSIBLE THAT WE'RE JUST MORE AWARE OF IT NOW BECAUSE WE LIVE IN A WORLD WHERE WE'RE MORE AWARE OF EVERYTHING."**

Or, says Janis Whitlock, director of the Cornell Research Program on Self-Injury and Recovery, there may be a cultural element. Starting in the late 1990s, the body became a kind of billboard for self-expression—that's when tattoos and piercings went mainstream. "As that was starting to happen, the idea of etching your emotional pain into your body was not a big step . . ."

...

Strategies:

If You're a Teen Cutter

Tell somebody—a sibling, a friend, a parent or relative, anyone you can talk to. Overcoming your shame and admitting your problem is often the hardest part of getting help.

- **Identify what triggers your cutting behavior.** This can be difficult to do on your own. You'll probably need to work with a mental health professional.

- **Stay with it.** Breaking your cutting habit can be challenging. But with treatment, teens who cut themselves can and do successfully learn more healthy ways to deal with stress and negative emotions.

- www.teenhelp.com/physical-health/cutting-statistics-and-self-injury-treatment/

CHAPTER FOUR | **EXPLODING THE MYTHS/ RECOGNIZING THE WARNING SIGNALS**

Every night I just want to go out, get
out of my head

Every day I don't want to get up, get
out of my bed

"Every Night" — *Paul McCartney*

Take a quiz and answer "True" or "False" to the following statements.

1. Joe and Jeff told a group of their friends that they were going to kill themselves by "flying off a cliff." Because they talked about killing themselves in front of friends, they were just looking for attention and wouldn't actually go ahead with their plan.

2. Once Ron made up his mind to kill himself and said good-bye to his friends, nothing anyone could do could stop him.

3. Jeffrey tried to kill himself by swallowing thirty-five aspirin tablets. He got sick and had a ringing in his ears for four days. After the discomfort and fright he felt, Jeffrey probably wouldn't attempt suicide again.

4. Steve's depression seemed to have lifted. All his problems appeared to be behind him. He was back in school and studying hard. He was out of danger.

5. Anna, Janie's best friend, knew Janie was depressed and thinking about suicide. But Anna talking to Janie about suicide would only give her ideas and make things worse.

6. People who kill themselves are crazy.

Guess what? The correct answer to every statement is FALSE. Yep. Every single one is a myth—not true. So, let's take them one by one.

Exploding the Suicide Myths

MYTH: *When people talk about killing themselves, they're just looking for attention. Ignoring them is the best thing to do.*

REALITY: The truth is that most people who take their own lives do talk about it. Eighty percent of adolescent suicides make open threats before they kill themselves.

JOE AND JEFF'S STORY

Joe and Jeff, both sixteen, had been best friends since sixth grade. Back then, Joe had needed a buddy badly. His parents had argued constantly ever since he could remember and had finally separated when Joe was in fourth grade. That's when he started talking back to his teachers and picking fights. By sixth grade he'd become a loan shark, loaning money to his classmates and doubling the debt if they didn't pay him back the next day. Jeff looked up to Joe as a "real cool operator." In seventh grade, Joe started drinking and smoking pot. He'd go to school stoned and would fall into bed at six-thirty every night. His mother didn't seem to notice. One month before Joe turned thirteen, his mother remarried. Eight months later, she left the house and joined her new husband in another city, 120 miles away. Joe's life came undone.

Joe's father returned to raise him and his two brothers; things went from bad to worse. As far as Joe was concerned, his father cut him down every chance he got. Nothing he did or said was right. Joe hated his life at home and started spending as much time as he could with Jeff and Jeff's family.

After their cattle ranch ran into hard times, Jeff's family moved into town. Jeff's mother got a job as a police dispatcher; his father sold cars. And then their life started to go wrong. Jeff's father worked long hours and drank heavily. He had little time left for his family. Then he got involved with another woman. Jeff's parents separated, then got back together. But things were never the same.

Jeff's behavior at home started to change. He became withdrawn and started smoking pot and drinking. Both he and Joe were increasingly unhappy. They fought with their fathers and saw the little town where they lived as a prison where nothing would ever change.

The first time they talked about suicide, the boys fantasized about going to Pole Creek, where they'd swallow some sleeping pills and lie down on the grass to die. But they weren't really serious . . . not then.

The two friends talked about suicide again, only this time there was a new plan: they could drive off the cliff at Dead Man's Curve. The boys still hadn't set a date, but both agreed that killing themselves that way would probably be painless.

One Monday morning, Jeff and Joe skipped school. They got drunk, talked, and drove around town. Maybe this was the day to try out Dead Man's Curve. Close to dinnertime, they picked up a friend and drove her around. Jeff told her they were going to fly through the air off a cliff. He also said they would come back alive. The friend didn't believe him. On their way to the high school, Joe stepped on the accelerator, hit ninety, lost control of the car, hit a fence, and spun off the road into the ditch. No one was hurt.

Later at the town library, standing around with a group of kids, Joe turned to Jeff and said, "Let's go kill ourselves." "Yeah," Jeff said. "Let's go." The others laughed.

"We're serious. We're going to fly off the cliff," Joe said as he got into his car with Jeff. One of the boys who had heard all this tried to push his way into the car.

"Stop it," Joe said. "We don't want to be responsible for your death."

"Screw you," the boy said. He still didn't believe they were serious.

Jeff and Joe got out of the car one more time. They shook hands all around.

"I'll bring flowers to your grave," one of the girls said, laughing.

Joe took off a cap he was wearing and gave it to another girl. "You'll never see me again. Keep it for memories." Still, no one thought they were serious.

"You don't believe us," Joe said, "but we're going to do it. You can read about it in the paper tomorrow."

When he regained consciousness, Joe saw paramedics kneeling over him. "What happened to my friend?" he asked. "What happened to Jeff?"

Three days later, Jeff was buried. The grave was marked by a simple stone that read:

Loved Son and Brother

Jeffrey Scott Allen Westerberg

July 7, 1964–November 17, 1980

Gone Fishing

Joe and Jeff repeatedly told their friends about their plan. Unfortunately, no one believed them.

MYTH: *Once a person has decided to take his/her own life, no one can stop him/her.*

REALITY: Not true. On the contrary, suicidal people are often ambivalent about living or dying. Many "signal" their intentions or talk openly about their plans. It is not your responsibility to save someone from taking his/her own life. But you can listen, watch for warning signs, and consult with a trusted adult who can then get professional help.

Ron's Story

Ron Neal was probably hoping that his friends would rescue him at the last minute. Otherwise, his parents ask, why did he leave every door in the house unlocked? Why had the automatic garage door opener been unlatched, so that the door could be opened by hand from the outside? And why was the door between the garage door and the house kept open by a dog cage with a barking dog inside?

Unfortunately for Ron, his friends arrived too late. As they drove up the driveway, they saw the garage lights on and heard a car running. They rushed to the garage where they found Ron's limp body slumped behind the wheel. He was already dead.

In Francine Klagsbrun's book *Too Young to Die,* the author wrote about a young woman who spent weeks planning her suicide. She jumped from her seventh-floor apartment window, but a tree broke her fall. She survived. Later, she talked about her feelings as she jumped. "As I began to fall, I wanted more than anything to be able to turn back, grab hold of the window ledge, and pull myself up."

Tim's Story

Tim was fifteen when he decided that life just wasn't worth the hassle. He'd gotten into a fight at school earlier in the day. The night before, he and his girlfriend had had a big argument. His friends were mad at him too, and he didn't know why.

"I was just really mixed up . . . I was making the people around me miserable too, so I thought the best thing for me to do was kill myself."

Tim was saved by his older brother, who came home unexpectedly in the middle of the day, broke into the house through the back window, found Tim unconscious, and immediately called 911.

"I guess I'm pretty damn lucky," he says now. "Being in the hospital kind of cleared my head. Before, I'd walk around either so stoned or so confused that I didn't know what I was doing a lot of the time. It made me learn to take things much easier."

On the second anniversary of Tim's suicide attempt, his friends gave him a party.

He announced, "I'm glad my brother came home early that afternoon."

MYTH: *Once a person tries to take his/her own life and does not succeed, the pain and shame will keep him/her from trying again.*

REALITY: In fact, just the opposite is true. Within the first three months to a year following a suicide attempt, people are at the highest risk of a second attempt—this time perhaps succeeding.

Jeffrey's Story

Jeffrey's story is a perfect example. He had thought about suicide every day for six months. He hated who he was—"just ordinary." He didn't get the praise he needed from his parents and felt that they paid more attention to his brothers and sisters.

The first time he attempted suicide, Jeffrey waited until his family had left for the day. Then he swallowed thirty-five aspirin tablets, one by one. He drank a beer and lay down to die. Then he started to get really sick. His ears rang for four days. He told some friends about what he'd done. They didn't seem to believe him.

Six weeks later, Jeffrey decided to try again. He drank Jack Daniels until he got up the courage to use the handgun he had put on top of his bedroom dresser. But he was too drunk to get up. Instead, he passed out.

Luckily, Jeffrey didn't get a chance to try a third time. Before that could happen, a friend read a journal he was keeping for one of his classes. It was filled with thoughts of death. The friend told the school social worker, who met first with Jeffrey, then with his parents. Jeffrey was rushed to a psychiatrist, who insisted he be hospitalized immediately. Jeffrey spent the next four months in the hospital, where he gained a new lease on life. If his friend hadn't stepped in, chances are that Jeffrey wouldn't be around today. His advice to other suicidal teens: "Don't do it."

MYTH: *When a suicidal person's depression appears to have lifted and he/she seems better and happier, he/she is out of dancer.*

REALITY: Depression can be most dangerous just when it appears to be lifting. When a person is severely depressed, she/he may want to die but may lack the energy and power to carry out a plan. But when she/he feels a bit better, it's easier to carry through with a suicide.

Steve's Story

The psychiatrist who saw Steve wrote a letter to the marine recruiting office saying that he was severely depressed. He had stopped eating. He couldn't sleep. And he had threatened to cut off his big toe.

After Steve got out of entering the marines, the depression seemed to lift. He started classes at a junior college, got a part-time job, and made plans to take out a girl he liked. Three months later, he was dead.

When a fifteen-year-old suburban Chicago boy killed himself, his family was shocked. "Things seemed to be going so much better for him. He appeared to have adjusted to our move to a new school district. And he had made plans to go fishing."

MYTH: *Talking to a troubled person about suicide will just give him/her ideas.*

REALITY: Another common mistake. You don't give a suicidal person ideas about suicide. The ideas are already there. Talking about them honestly and openly will help, not hurt. Most troubled people really want to talk about what's bothering them. It's a relief to get their pain out into the open, as long as they know their feelings will be taken seriously and with understanding. One of the biggest mistakes people make when talking to a troubled young person is to deny the problems or to tell him or her that the problems aren't really serious and will pass. Again, the best way to help someone thinking of suicide is to immediately tell a trusted adult who, in turn, will connect with a professional who will take over from there.

MYTH: *People who kill themselves are crazy.*

REALITY: Most suicidal people are not insane. Many who try to kill themselves suffer from severe anxiety, depression, or other conditions like post-traumatic stress disorder (PTSD), often a result of sexual/physical abuse.

SOS: Suicide Warning Signals

There are warning signals—some clearer than others—that indicate something is wrong. What's important is that you recognize these warning signals, talk to your friend (or, if you have a peer-to-peer program in your school, contact a mentor who can serve as a connector between the friend and a trusted adult.) It's important to remember that you are not responsible for a friend's problems and cannot solve them on your own. But you can be the first line of defense and begin the process of making connections.

And it's been awhile since I can say that I wasn't addicted. And it's been awhile since I can say I love myself as well.

"It's Been A While" — Staind

Six General Warning Signals

1. Acting Out: Aggressive, Hostile Behavior
If you or your friends have problems, what do you do to blow off steam? Drink? Use drugs? Drive like maniacs? A lot of young

people who feel angry and unhappy do those things. Some go a step further and get into fights, shoplift, or even run away from home. Acting out to the extreme can mean that someone is anxious, unsettled, or uncomfortable with the internal and social pressures of adolescence.

2. Alcohol and Drug Abuse

When it comes to alcohol and drug abuse, there are a wealth of studies. Here are the results of a few of them. Where do your experiences fall?

- In 2015, 32.8 percent of students in grades nine to twelve drank at least one alcoholic drink at least one day during the thirty days before the survey.

- 17.7 percent drank five or more drinks of alcohol in a row within a couple of hours on at least one day during the same thirty-day period. (This number decreased to 20.8 percent in 2013.)

- 18 percent binge drank.

- 8 percent drove after drinking.

- 20 percent rode with a driver who had been drinking.

The Opioid Epidemic: You can't pick up a newspaper, watch TV news or check out an online news site and not hear about the opioid epidemic. The current numbers are staggering. Drug overdoses are now the leading cause of death among Americans under 50.*

What does this mean for teens? They are ending up in the ER in greater numbers from opioids and heroin overdoses. In 2015, the most recent year of a study reported in the journal Pediatrics, 8 percent of adolescents reported abusing prescription opioids, and the majority of them had been prescribed opioids previously by a physician for medical reasons. Later, they began taking the drugs for "nonmedical" reasons—abusing them.

---

* https://www.nytimes.com/interactive/2017/06/05/upshot/opioid-epidemic-drug-overdose-deaths-are-rising-faster-than-ever.html

Teens are also mixing prescription opioids with other substances. Check out the following statistics from the National Institute on Drug Abuse.*

Teens Mix Prescription Opioids with Other Substances: Nonmedical use of prescription (Rx) opioids by teens remains high, and a new study shows that 7 out of 10 teen nonmedical users combine opioid medications with other drugs and/or alcohol. This puts teens at much greater risk of overdose.

7 out of 10 teen nonmedical users combine Rx opioids with other substances. The substances most commonly co-ingested were: marijuana 58.5%, alcohol 52.1%, cocaine 10.6%, tranquilizers 10.3%, amphetamines 9.5%.

Teens who reported co-ingestion of Rx opioids with other drugs were: 8X more likely to report abusing marijuana, 4X more likely to report being drunk more than 10 times

3. Passive Behavior

Do you ever feel that you just can't get moving, that it's too hard to do anything, and that there's not much worth doing, anyway? That's passive behavior, and many depressed/suicidal young people feel that way most of the time. "It's like being wrapped in Saran Wrap, trying to get through but never making it past the plastic," said one suicide attempter. Kate, another attempter, described her passivity as feeling nothing, having to burn herself with an iron just to know that she was alive. Passive young people are afraid to let their anger and frustrations show. If they did, they might get carried away: all the rage they've been keeping inside might fester and explode.

4. Changes in Eating Habits

Mary grew up feeling that she wasn't as good as everyone else around her. She set very high standards for herself and never

---

* www.drugabuse.gov/related-topics/trends-statistics/infographics/
teens-mix-prescription-opioids-other-substances

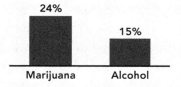

Percent of teens that usually or always combine Rx opioids with marijuana or aclohol*

24% Marijuana
15% Alcohol

Also alarming is the fact that abuse of prescription drugs affects young adults more than any other age group.**

PAST-YEAR USE

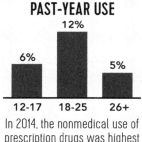

12%
6%
5%

12-17 18-25 26+

In 2014, the nonmedical use of prescription drugs was highest among young adults.

MOTIVATIONS FOR USE

Most young adults say they use Rx drugs to:

concentrate • study
get high • **increase alertness**
relieve pain • deal with problems
have a good time with friends
relax • **loose weight**
feel better • sleep

- In 2015, more than one million youths between the ages of twelve and seventeen met criteria for problem use or dependence on illicit drugs or alcohol.

- Overuse of drugs and/or alcohol increases risk for suicide and homicide.

- Nearly 10 percent of teens who were taken to a hospital emergency room with a drug overdose had attempted suicide.

- Drug abuse can lead to memory problems, changes in brain development, accidents, school and social problems.

- Girls are more likely than boys to be depressed, have eating disorders, or be sexually and/or physically abused. All these factors can increase the likelihood of substance abuse.

- Girls using alcohol and other drugs are more likely to attempt suicide.

- Substance use can lead to abuse and addiction more quickly for adolescent girls than boys, even with the same amount or less of a particular substance.

* www.drugabuse.gov/related-topics/trends-statistics/infographics/
teens-mix-prescription-opioids-other-substances
** National Institute on Drug Abuse – 2017

thought she measured up. Her home life didn't do much to make her feel better. Her parents always seemed on the verge of divorce. By the end of eighth grade, her parents separated, and Mary, who weighed 135 pounds, almost stopped eating. "It seemed like everybody hated me, and it was kind of like my way of getting my parents back together and getting back at people who make fun of me and to scare them." She lost forty-seven pounds over the next year, shrinking down to a mere eighty-eight pounds.

While most suicidal teens don't become anorexic like Mary, they may change their eating habits dramatically. Healthy eaters may start nibbling at their food or not eating at all, while picky eaters may start eating as if there's no tomorrow.

5. Changes in Sleeping Habits

In the months before nineteen-year-old Teri F. killed herself, she stopped sleeping. The books that used to calm her down and eventually put her to sleep didn't help anymore. Because of her lack of sleep, Teri was tired all the time and started showing up late to her part-time job. She eventually lost that job and a second one because of tardiness.

On the other hand, someone who may have slept normally or too little may start sleeping too much. After Mark took his life, his parents tried to uncover what unrecognized signals he might have given. Mark's father remembered: "During the last week he seemed to be sleeping more. He'd go to bed early and then he'd get up late and go off to school, so that we never really had a chance to talk to him."

6. Fear of Separation

Do you remember how you felt on the first day of kindergarten or your first night away from home? Leaving your parents and home can be difficult. But for someone who is troubled, such separation can be traumatic. If a friend suddenly seems uncomfortable about sleeping over or having his/her parents go away, it may mean trouble is brewing.

Strategies:

Where to Get Help – An Introductory List

National Suicide Prevention Hotline
1-800-273-TALK (8255)
TTY: 1-800-799-4889
www.suicidepreventionlifeline.org
Twenty-four-hour, toll-free, confidential suicide prevention hotline available to anyone in suicidal crisis or emotional distress. Your call is routed to the nearest crisis center in the national network of more than 150 crisis centers.

SAMHSA's National Helpline
1-800-662-HELP (4357)
TTY: 1-800-487-4889
www.samhsa.gov/find-help/national-helpline
Also known as the Treatment Referral Routing Service, this helpline provides twenty-four-hour free and confidential treatment referral and information about mental and/or substance use disorders, prevention, and recovery in English and Spanish.

National Institute on Drug Abuse for Teens
https://teens.drugabuse.gov

American Society of Addictive Medicine
asam.ps.membersuite.com/directory/SearchDirectory_Criteria.aspx
Search Membership Directory to find a membership physician.

American Academy of Child & Adolescent Psychiatry
www.aacap.org/AACAP/Families_and_Youth/Resources/CAP_Finder.aspx

American Addiction Centers
http://americanaddictioncenters.org/rehab-guide/teens/

Drug Rehab Programs

Smart Recovery
www.smartrecovery.org/community/calendar.php
Online Meetings

Specific Suicide Warning Signals

The first group of six warning signals sets the stage for trouble. The next six indicate a loss of control and balance. You or someone you know can no longer hide the pain.

1. Abrupt Changes in Personality
Teri had always been quiet and shy. She had trouble making friends and, from the time she was a toddler, seemed content to play by herself. When she turned sixteen, her personality changed abruptly. She started hanging out with a wilder group of kids, whose main goal in life was to have a good time. The phone rang all the time. Teri always had something to do and friends to be with. Once a good student, she now stopped studying. Teri's parents weren't happy about the drop in grades but felt that she'd finally come out of her shell. Less than two years later, she was dead.

Sudden changes in personality can be a sign that a friend, son, or daughter has become preoccupied with suicide. The problem is that most youth aren't settled about themselves and their place in the world, and changes in personality occur often, even in those who are not depressed. The key is whether the changes are different from the usual pattern.

Amy had been an outgoing, happy fifteen-year-old who had many friends and participated in a lot of school activities. Suddenly, she started spending more and more time by herself. She stopped all her outside activities, choosing instead to sit alone in her room for hours at a time. She attempted suicide but survived.

2. Sudden Mood Swings

Who hasn't had days when they feel great one minute and down the next? Moodiness is part of being a human, particularly part of being a teen. But if these sudden mood swings continue for long periods, they're not normal.

Adolescence is a time of extreme changes in mood. One day you're up, the next day you're down. Sometimes, it only takes a matter of minutes before things change. Melissa was somber and withdrawn. She stopped spending time with her friends, choosing instead to spend all her free time alone in her bedroom with the door locked.

> **ADOLESCENCE IS A TIME OF EXTREME CHANGES IN MOOD.**

Then, one evening, she got dressed and went to a friend's party. She danced, sang, and talked a blue streak. She was the "life of the party." But the next day, just as suddenly as her mood had seemed to improve, she was back in the dumps, refusing once again even to talk to her friends.

3. Risky Behavior

Ted felt like a failure and flirted with death several times before actually taking his own life. One of his friends remembers the afternoon after an ROTC parade when Ted got behind the wheel of his car and started driving like a maniac. He pulled out right in front of a huge truck, scaring his friend half to death. When Ted got back to school and parked his car, he turned to his rattled friend and said, "Somebody could really die in a car." His risky behavior could have alerted his friend that Ted was ready to take big chances with his life and those of others. But it's easy to overlook such boasting and talking big, because such behavior is part of trying on adolescence.

4. Decreased Interest in School and Poor Grades

Because school is a major part of your life, it is also one of the best measures of your or someone else's mental health. If a friend's or your grades fall dramatically, the chances are good that something isn't going well.

Studying came easily for Dale. He got A's all through junior high school. But when he started high school, he seemed to lose interest in his schoolwork. He'd drift off or read a book instead. His grades fell to mostly D's. Dale made his first suicide attempt toward the end of his freshman year.

5. Inability to Concentrate

In this world of technology, passwords, and 24/7 news cycles, it's hard to focus, to concentrate. But when you or someone you know can't concentrate long enough to read a paragraph or remember what you did five minutes before, it's time to take a harder look at what's going on.

6. Loss or Lack of Friends

Many young people who end up suicidal never had friends to lose. Justin was one of those kids. He never fit in very well. He was very critical of kids his own age and often cut them down. He would rather read science fiction or listen to Beethoven than do the "common" things everybody else was doing. Justin took his life on Valentine's Day, maybe because, as his mother explained, he felt that everyone else in the world was in love or had somebody except him.

Several studies have found that many youth who took their own lives didn't have or didn't feel that they had a close friend. There wasn't one special person to whom they could turn. They were disconnected and focused only on themselves and their problems.

Final Distress Signals: Impending Doom

1. Loss of an Important Person or Thing

For a young person who is already troubled and unable to hide the pain, death, divorce, or breakup with a boyfriend or girl-friend can be the last straw.

Remember: there is never just one reason why someone takes his/her life.

Natalie had always thought about suicide. Her mother was mentally ill and her father was a strict disciplinarian who had trouble showing love and support. But Natalie had joined a street gang and found, at least temporarily, a substitute family. School wasn't going well, but Natalie had a boyfriend. That was all that mattered. When he broke up with her, her world collapsed. She made her first suicide attempt soon after the breakup.

"He was the happiest little boy you ever saw," Charles's mother said. He loved music and could play the cello before he could read. When Charles was eight, his father had a serious heart attack. And that's when Charles stopped being happy. Though his father eventually recovered, Charles blamed himself for his father's illness. As he grew older, he became withdrawn and more and more depressed. He took his life in his parents' home.

2. Hopelessness

Jeffrey was a very active kid. But suddenly everything got to be too much for him. He quit his part-time job at a pizza place. He stopped doing his homework. And he dropped a new girlfriend because she'd only be "another burden." Life appeared hopeless, and Jeffrey decided he was more trouble than he was worth.

Nothing makes a hopeless young person happy—not food, friends, activities, or accomplishments. "I might as well be dead," wrote one teen in a suicide note.

3. Obsession with Death

Vivienne L. had been obsessed with death long before she walked into her mother's studio and took her life. For Vivienne, death meant an end to pain. She wrote about death constantly: "Death is going to be a beautiful thing." And she talked about death with a friend. "I knew from what she told me that she was very, very serious about suicide . . . Sometimes she'd tell me that she'd tried to strangle herself." Vivienne rehearsed her suicide many times. She worked to overcome her fear of it by experimenting. By the time she actually took her life, death had lost its horror.

4. Making a Will/Giving Away Possessions

Before Mary attempted suicide for the third time, she gave pictures of herself to friends so that they would have something to remember her by.

Before Jeff tried to kill himself, he wrote a "will," leaving his record collection to a friend and his sports equipment to his younger brother.

Young people who are getting ready to die often give away some of their possessions to a sibling or a friend. They are, in a sense, executing their own wills. Making a will is perhaps the most serious sign of a potential suicide.

Strategies:

What Can You Do?

Teens who are thinking seriously about suicide will need professional help to work out their problems. While you may be tempted to try to make things better, your best strategy is to listen and then tell a trusted adult. To assume the burden of "saving" someone is both unhealthy and unreasonable. But you can:

1. Recognize the warning signals

2. Listen actively

3. Be supportive

4. Tell a trusted teacher, counselor, parent, coach or other adult

NEVER KEEP SOMEONE'S SUICIDAL FEELINGS A SECRET.

CHAPTER FIVE | **SUICIDE SURVIVORS**

Understand the things I say,
don't turn away from me,

'Cause I've spent half my life out there,
you wouldn't disagree.

Do you see me? Do you see?
Do you like me?

Do you like me standing there?
Do you notice?

Do you know? Do you see me?
Do you see me?

Does anyone care?

— The Cranberries

Every one of these deaths leaves an estimated six or more "suicide survivors"—people who've lost someone they cared about deeply and are left grieving and struggling to understand.

MY MOTHER'S STORY
(AS WRITTEN IN A LETTER)

"Time heals all wounds," they say. "Life goes on," they add. Cold comfort for a mother whose son has just killed himself—who is in a state of shock—living in a nightmare. A mother filled with unanswered questions and self-doubts, who prays for strength to survive this ordeal, to keep her husband and children from falling into an abyss of unbearable grief and guilt. A mother who is screaming and sobbing wildly inside, but who cannot shed a tear. A mother tormented by the anguish of her son's pain, which she was unable to stop.

After four years, the nightmares still occur, but not as often. A calm has settled over all. Her husband and children have gone on with their lives. The self-doubts have all but disappeared. The tears flow easily when touched by memories.

No, time does not heal all wounds. Time softens pain; time dulls grief. Questions remain unanswered.

Yes, life does go on and life is good. It is lived with the memory of a dearly beloved son.

—Shirley Mersky

PARENTS' STORY: BEV AND RON

Bev and Ron couldn't wait to start a family. They weren't trained to be parents. They just jumped in and learned by trial and error. This is their story.

Ron and Bev were married just two weeks before Ron began his stint with the US Army, where he was stationed outside of Boston. Bev stayed behind in Chicago to finish her nursing degree. But the newlyweds saw each other whenever they could during the four months they lived apart. And as soon as Bev graduated, she joined Ron on the army base. She was three months pregnant. Bev wanted a son. She had the name Steve picked out from the beginning. Ron didn't care much whether he had a boy or a girl, as long as the baby was healthy.

Patricia was born in the army hospital in January. Her sister Susan was born in the same hospital ten months later. Then Christine. And a year and three days later, Steve, the boy Bev had always wanted, was born.

When they were young, all four of Ron and Bev's children got along well. The girls, particularly Susan, were good to their baby brother. Because she and Steve looked so much alike—the same size and reddish hair—they were sometimes mistaken for twins.

Susan and her older sister, Patricia, were outstanding students—bright, responsive, and hard working. Steve, on the other hand, never seemed to know what he wanted to do. He didn't show any real interest in working with his hands, as Ron had hoped he would. And he didn't excel in any subjects at school. He did like scouting, though, and played Little League baseball for a couple years. He was a good player but seemed to shy away from competition. It was as if he didn't want to be disappointed in himself or let others down.

Around the time he turned twelve, Steve started having trouble in school. The junior high principal called his parents several times. Steve was pushing kids in the lunch line and fighting with other boys. When Bev asked Steve what was going on, he said a big kid was pushing some other little kid and that he had stepped in. Bev passed that story on to the principal, hoping he would see Steve's side of the story. He didn't. Kids weren't supposed to fight in school. Period.

Steve's grades started falling. He was always looking for an excuse not to go to school. By the time he started high school, he had a truancy problem. Bev was worried. She was spending what seemed like her whole life on the phone calling in and making excuses for Steve. After each call, she vowed

STEVE'S GRADES STARTED FALLING.

not to lie for him again. But she just couldn't stand letting him suffer the consequences of his truancy.

Ron didn't go for excuses. As far as he was concerned, every kid was supposed to know what he was doing with his life by the time he was fifteen or sixteen. Either you took up a trade after high school or you went to college. For a while, Steve talked about driving a truck. But he changed his mind. He didn't feel like doing that or anything else. Ron was furious. He took out his anger by yelling. Steve hated the yelling. He felt like hitting his dad sometimes, but he never did. He punched holes in his bedroom wall instead.

Ron says he worried that something wasn't quite right with Steve but never thought about getting professional help. Steve was a loner. He spent hours by himself in his room. Ron didn't like that; it bothered him that Steve couldn't make or didn't want friends. But Steve liked his privacy and used his time alone to good advantage. He collected coins and could tell you where each coin came from and how much it was worth. He was a trivia buff too and read things like *The Book of Lists* and *The People's Almanac* from cover to cover. When he was sixteen, Steve asked his parents for a Bible.

Steve's apparent interest in God and religion was a good sign. Ron went out and bought Steve a Bible.

If Steve had found religion, he kept it to himself. But his near obsession with physical fitness was common knowledge. On school nights, he went to bed around nine. That way, he could get up early enough the next morning to work out before school. His parents usually awoke to the sounds of weights clanging and Steve grunting. Steve was a well-built kid who responded to the personal challenge of making his body even stronger. Still, he shied away from attention. When physical fitness tests were held in school, he would stand on the sidelines as everyone else cheered on the school jock to do still another push-up. Then he'd lie down on the gym floor and do more push-ups than two of the jocks combined. Quietly, he'd finish his set, get up, and walk away.

Steve worked a variety of part-time jobs all through high school. He was an usher at a local theater. He delivered papers. And he worked at a 7-Eleven store. Much to his parents' chagrin, he never stuck with one job very long. Just when it seemed that he had a good thing going, he would quit. With all his moving from job to job, Steve still managed to save enough money to buy a 1971 Chevy sometime after his sixteenth birthday. That car was his pride and joy. He was always washing or polishing or doing something to it. He loved that car. No one—not even his sister, Chris, who helped herself to everything else—could have it. It was his.

With Sue and Patricia off at college, Steve was left at home with Chris. He resented her going into his room without permission and helping herself to anything she could get her hands on. He couldn't stand the mess Chris left in her room and around the rest of the house. He hated her constant arguing with their parents. Things got so bad that Steve went out and bought a lock for his bedroom door. If he couldn't keep her out of the house, he could at least keep her out of his room.

Steve didn't have many friends . . . two guys across the street and a guy named Jeff. He didn't date either. If he went out at all, he went with a group of kids. Maybe they'd go to a party or maybe they'd drive up to Wisconsin, where the drinking age was eighteen. Steve looked a lot older than he was. He got served without any problem. His father knew about the Wisconsin drinking trips but wasn't bothered. He'd done the same thing when he was a teenager.

> **STEVE DIDN'T HAVE A LOT OF FRIENDS . . . TWO GUYS ACROSS THE STREET AND A GUY NAMED JEFF.**

But everything came to a head at home during Steve's senior year. Chris backed down the driveway without looking and crashed into Steve's beloved Chevy. As far as Chris was concerned, Steve shouldn't have parked his car there. When Steve arrived home later that day, he was heartbroken. He had had his car for less than a year and loved it more than anything else in the world.

In January of his senior year, Steve turned eighteen and signed up to join the marines as soon as he finished high school. Ron wasn't against his enlisting. He just didn't like the recruiters coming into the schools and "brainwashing" the kids to sign up. He felt they were worse than used car salesmen with all their fast talk.

Steve spent a lot of time over the next two or three months trying to interest other guys in enlisting. He had been promised a private first class (PFC) status, one step above a private, if he could find two people who would actually sign up. He talked up the marines and eventually got two guys to enlist. When he was told that one of the two had been recruited earlier by someone else, he was furious. He knew that he had been taken for a ride. The marines had no intention of making him a PFC.

By June of his senior year, Steve announced to his parents that he wasn't going into the marines. Ron was flabbergasted. What did he mean he didn't want to go? He had signed up. Steve said he had changed his mind. He didn't explain. His only concern now was how to get out. He talked to people and discovered that if he were accepted by a college, the marines would let him go. Steve quickly applied to a local two-year college and got in. He was relieved, certain that he'd beaten the marines at their own game. But when he showed his acceptance papers to the recruiting officer, his request was denied. The rules said he had to attend a four-year college.

It was now the end of June, and Steve had to try to weasel his way into a four-year school—not an easy task at such a late date with his mediocre grades.

Steve applied to the University of Illinois–Chicago and was accepted. Armed with his second set of acceptance papers, he went back to the recruiting officer, who continued to give him a hard time. Steve was a mess. The marines had him trapped. There was no way out. That made him crazy. He stopped eating. He couldn't sleep. He told his parents that he was on the edge of a nervous breakdown.

Desperate, Steve found out that if he got a letter from a doctor saying that he was in no mental condition to join the marines, the marines would let him out. Bev worked in a medical clinic and made an appointment for Steve to see one of the doctors. The physician examined Steve and agreed that he was showing signs of a nervous breakdown. The doctor said that he would be happy to write a letter but felt it would sound more convincing coming from a psychiatrist. Bev agreed and hurriedly scheduled an appointment with one of the psychiatrists at the clinic.

The pressure was unbearable. It was only a matter of weeks before Steve was supposed to start basic training. Steve talked to the psychiatrist. A week later, he had the letter. It said that he was in a severe state of depression.

The psychiatrist did not recommend treatment. That surprised Bev, but she figured once Steve had the mess with the marines settled, everything would return to normal. To be safe, Bev made several copies of the psychiatrist's letter. She had this awful feeling that she would never see Steve again. The marines were going to kidnap him and keep him forever.

The letter worked. Steve got out of the marines in late August and decided to attend the local two-year college where he had been accepted in June. He signed up for the fire science program and loved it. He came home, did his homework, and talked about his psychology class with his mother. Steve also worked two or three evenings a week as a security guard at a store in a large shopping center. He would take his books and sit in the back room of the store and study. Bev and Ron couldn't believe the turnaround. Steve seemed to have forgotten all about the trauma with the marines. He was calm, happy, and excited about college. The signs of "severe depression" had miraculously disappeared.

...

The phone rang at two o'clock Sunday morning. It was a police officer calling to say that Steve had been picked up for speeding, running a red light, and driving "under the influence." He was alone at the time. Ron dragged himself out of bed and made it to the police station in fifteen minutes. When he arrived, he found that Steve had been locked in a cell under constant observation. The arresting officer was worried. Steve had made some remark about not being in court the day his case was to be heard. "Why not?" asked the officer. "You going on vacation?"

"No," Steve said. "You'll read about it in the paper."

The police had impounded Steve's Chevy, but he got it back sometime on Monday. He didn't go to school that day or the next. He said he'd start classes again on Wednesday. Ron left for work Wednesday morning at six; Bev left the house two hours later. Ron got home from work a little later than usual that afternoon. He was a bit surprised to see Steve's car in the driveway, but then, he could never keep up with Steve's schedule. He figured that Steve was in his room doing homework or getting ready to go to work.

Ron went into the kitchen, got supper started, and then walked toward Steve's bedroom. In late November, it starts getting dark around five. Steve's bedroom light usually shone under the door. It was dark. Ron was puzzled. Where the heck had Steve gone? Ron had a weird feeling. Something wasn't right. He ran into Steve's room and flicked on the light. There was Steve lying on his bed. Ron's .22 caliber gun lay on the floor. The Bible Ron had bought for Steve was there on the bed, with a suicide note folded inside.

I am tired. Tired of everything that has happened to me from seven years ago to now. Everything that has happened has taken its toll on me and my mind. I am tired of fighting. You might ask why. But that cannot be answered by anyone, because there is no one who knows the real me. There isn't just one reason but many reasons for my downfall. But I am taking that all with me now . . .

...

The first year after Steve's suicide was a nightmare. Bev and Ron managed to go to work, but that was about all. Bev says she wouldn't have eaten if it hadn't been for Ron's coaxing and good meals. She felt tired all the time, as if someone were pushing her down. Her back and shoulders ached constantly; her heart hurt. Either she fell asleep and then woke up a few hours later, unable to go back to sleep, or she couldn't sleep at all.

Ron and Bev drew closer together after Steve's suicide. Unlike many parents of children who take their own lives, they didn't blame each other for what had happened. They talked more than they had in years, sharing their grief and their unanswered questions: Had Steve decided to kill himself after he was arrested? Was that the last straw? Or had he decided to live it up one more time on a wild weekend because he knew it would be his last? They read and reread Steve's suicide note for clues. They went through all of Steve's books and papers. Maybe he had underlined something in his psychology book or in his Bible. Why had he done it? What had happened seven years ago? Who was the "real" Steve, and what were the reasons for his downfall? They talked to Steve's friends. The search continued.

Bev and Ron joined two groups during that first year—Compassionate Friends and LOSS. Compassionate Friends helps parents cope with the death of a child. LOSS serves survivors of suicide—parents, spouses, siblings, and friends. Between the two groups, Bev and Ron attended three meetings each month. Slowly, they began to work through their grief. They learned how to share their feelings with others. They started paying more attention to their own needs, especially at stressful times like Steve's birthday and holidays. Both Bev and Ron tried to believe that someday they would come to accept what had happened.

Maybe three years after Steve's suicide, Bev and Ron stopped searching for clues. They stopped going to the cemetery every week. Steve had made up his mind to kill himself for his own reasons—reasons they would never understand. But the pain still comes. Bev's voice wavers and her eyes fill with tears when she talks about Steve's having nothing of his own to wear at his own funeral. She cries every time she hears "Amazing Grace." And she still needs to stay home from work on the anniversary of Steve's death. (The anniversary of a suicide is often the most difficult time for parents and other family members. It brings back the nightmare of the suicide, forcing survivors to relive all the emotions that overwhelmed them when they first found out.) Bev goes to an early mass, visits Steve's grave, and usually goes shopping with a friend.

Late autumn is the hardest time for Ron. That's when it starts getting dark around five. The darkness reminds him of the light that should have been on in Steve's bedroom. Parents like Ron and Bev would give anything to be able to talk to their kids one more time. If only they could. Then they could ask all of those unanswered questions. They could find out why . . . why their children decided that life was more painful than death.

MY SIBLING STORY

I didn't actually see the physical mess: I smelled it. The minute I crept into my brother's bedroom, the noxious smell of what I realized later was a Shakespearian potion of blood and paint oozed from every piece of drywall, wood windowsill, plank of laminate floor. The company my mother found to clean up the mess (who in the hell does this sort of thing?) clearly didn't have a clue about removing the stench of death. Instead, they tried to cover it up like a frazzled cook who has just burned a steak and sprays a half can of air freshener in a desperate attempt to remove the odor. I gagged but didn't dare mess things up all over again.

My brother took his life on his thirtieth birthday.

And I'd lost my best friend in my family. My ally. The brother who made me feel important, validated, and loved. He was my safety net. I could tell him anything. He kept my secrets and supported my choices.

I'd dreaded this day for years because, though I prayed it would never come, I knew in my gut that it would. My brother went about his suicide with more thought and precision than he'd applied to just about anything in his life—even basketball and the guitar. No "Happy Birthday." Maybe for the best: my mother couldn't carry a tune. And I couldn't carry the grief and guilt that tasted like one of those three-day-old sheet cakes sold at a discount grocery store. Time for my brother had run out. The alarm clock rang, and I wasn't there to turn it off.

The night of my brother's funeral, I camped in my room. That is, I stayed until my mother banged on my closed bedroom door. "These people have come to see you. You're being rude. It doesn't look right." Rude? How about my brother? Talk about rude. Where the hell had he gone? Out of our lives, that's where. Poof. Just like some magic trick where the girl squeezes into a wood box, curls up in the fetal position, and waits there until the top is lowered and secured by a lock with a chain the size of an Anaconda. Thing is: the girl somehow escapes and reappears. My brother would never see the light of day.

...

Following my brother's suicide, the attention was focused on my parents. I understood all of that and now, as a parent, I understand even more.

Still, I was my brother's sister and I needed comfort too.

I didn't get enough.

I think relatives, in particular, didn't know what to say, how to act. People patted me on the back as if we'd just struck a business deal that would make us all rich. Your brother was a wonderful man, they said. With time things will get back to normal. They were wrong. I'd never accept my brother's suicide or the fact that he didn't even bother to say good-bye.

Didn't he care about how devastated I (and the rest of our family) would be? Was he so selfish and self-absorbed? Okay, so he was in a lot of pain. But we loved him and did all we could to let him know that. He'd been addicted to drugs but was "clean." He was seeing a psychiatrist who'd put him on an antidepressant for what was diagnosed as serious depression. He'd gone to work at my father's company and seemed to be tiptoeing back to a happier life.

> **"DIDN'T HE CARE ABOUT HOW DEVASTATED I (AND THE REST OF THE FAMILY) WOULD BE!"**

We were wrong: dead wrong. Yes, he had more energy and more focus, concentration. He used that boost to plan his suicide. And all the while, he duped us into thinking he was getting his life in order when, in truth, he was planning his traumatic exit.

I blamed myself and struggled with guilt for a long time. Why hadn't I saved my brother? There must have been something I could have done. Why did I kick him out of my house the time he got thrown off an airplane for making a scene? Why didn't I write or call more often? Shouldn't I have recognized the warning signs and not been fooled when everything looked like he was back on the right track? But I wasn't a therapist. There were no suicide prevention programs when I went to school.

> **"I BLAMED MYSELF AND STRUGGLED WITH GUILT FOR A LONG TIME."**

But we tend to see what we want to see and believe what we want to believe. I wanted my brother back, so I thought I could will his return to sanity, calm, even happiness.

I felt all the emotional reactions after a loved one dies: guilt, overwhelming sadness, denial, anger—all of it. And I felt confused. I needed definitive answers as to why he took his life, but there were none. There will never be. I even wished that he'd been hit by a car or died because of some horrible disease. At least, there would have been a cause, a reason.

Like my mother wrote, life does go on. The pain diminishes, but the ache never goes away. There are those times when I hear a song or feel his spirit or look at my adult son and wish that he had an uncle in his life—it's at those times that I tell Robin what a dummy he was for bowing out and how much I miss his buck teeth, his Cheshire smile, and the joy he brought to my life.

...

There's a black and white photo of Robin and me taken in the living room of our summer home on the Canadian side of Lake Erie. The clapboard cottage sat on a bluff overlooking the lake. On good days, the beach below was wide and welcoming. We'd run down the trampled grass path on the side of the cottage, throw our towels and other paraphernalia on the sand, and race to see who would be the first to jump face down into the lake. On windy summer days or days after a storm, the beach seemed to disappear. The putrid smell of dead fish and the tangled necklaces of seaweed, broken shells, and fish spines forced us inside where we played "Uncle Wiggly" or "Shoots and Ladders."

In the photo, Robin squints into the sun streaming in through the row of windows facing the lake. I'm sitting on a chair with one foot on the seat. Robin is perched on the arm of the chair, his left arm draped over the back. He's wearing a pair of blue jeans and a white t-shirt that accentuates his tanned arms—arms not yet sculpted by years of playing basketball and other sports. My rolled-up jeans showcase a leg with an imperceptible ankle that resembles a channeled Doric column. Not sure why I'm wearing a long sleeve checked shirt, but the bandanna wrapped around my head pushes enough of my brown hair away from my face and accentuates my high cheekbones, eyebrows not yet tweezed, and an angular shaped face with a chin not quite pointed but almost. Robin's front buckteeth remind me of Howdy Doody's bright white choppers. I stare straight ahead and, without my glasses to hide my crossed eyes, the right eye heads a bit too far to the left. But there we are—brother and sister, maybe nine and twelve, best buddies who could never have anticipated Robin's troubled future and my eternal sadness at not being able to turn it around.

…

Many suicide survivors find great comfort in groups with other survivors. One study reported that every survivor who had the opportunity to talk one on one with another suicide survivor found it beneficial.

No one can tell how long the grieving process will take. It is different for everyone. There are support groups in most major cities across the country. If you or someone you know would like more information about the suicide survivors' support groups in your area or about books targeted to survivors, you can check out the following list provided by Harvard Health Publications, Harvard Medical School.

Strategies:

Join a Suicide Survivors' Group

American Association of Suicidology
202-237-2280
www.suicidology.org (Click on "Suicide loss survivors.")

American Foundation for Suicide Prevention
888-333-2377 (toll-free)
www.afsp.org (Click on "Surviving Suicide Loss.")

Read a Book

After Suicide Loss: Coping With Your Grief, 2nd Edition, by Bob Baugher, Ph.D., and Jack Jordan, Ph.D.

Aftershock: Help, Hope, and Healing in the Wake of Suicide, by Arrington Cox (B & H Publishing, 2003).

Dying to Be Free: A Health Guide for Families after a Suicide, by Beverly Cobain and Jean Larch (Hazelden Foundation, 2006).

My Son... My Son: A Guide to Healing After Death, Loss, or Suicide, by Iris Bolton and Curtis Mitchell (The Bolton Press, 1995).

No Time to Say Goodbye , by Carla Fine (Main Street Books, 1999).

Silent Grief: Living in the Wake of Suicide, by Christopher Lukas and Henry Seiden (Jessica Kingsley Publishers, 2007).

Understanding Your Suicide Grief: Ten Essential Touchstones for Finding Hope and Healing Your Heart, by Alan D. Wolfelt, Ph.D. (Companion Press, 2009).

NOTE: Many of the books are available as ebooks

CHAPTER SIX | **OVER THE EDGE: INTERVIEWS WITH SUICIDE ATTEMPTERS**

I have done it again

I have been here many times before

Hurt myself again today

And the worst part is there's no one
else to blame

"Breathe Me" — *Sia*

Do you know anyone who has attempted suicide? If you do, you're not alone. What are these suicide attempters like? What problems did they face? Was there a final straw that pushed them over the edge?

Talking to young people who have attempted suicide is one good way to begin answering these questions. While they may be unsure of themselves and confused, they can help shed some light on why suicide has become an accepted "way out" for so many young people.

KATE'S STORY

Kate was hospitalized the first time because her family therapist was sure that she was going to take her own life. The following interview was recorded toward the end of her second hospitalization. She was nineteen.

INTERVIEWER: Tell me about your hospitalizations.

KATE: I was in the hospital the first time from May 27 to October 5 of last year. After ten months at home, I came back again.

INTERVIEWER: What led to your coming into the hospital the first time?

KATE: My family and I were seeing a family therapist. The more I talked about the things that were bothering me, the more depressed I got. I decided that after I graduated from high school, I was going to kill myself. I was going to graduate because my parents wanted me to. Then I was going to kill myself. I had a lot of problems. I wasn't getting along with my dad. I wanted his approval and wasn't getting it. And I broke up with my boyfriend. I couldn't handle that at all. I was totally lost without him. I was also scared about going to college. I didn't feel I was made for college. And then I started thinking about my abortion. I felt real guilty about that.

INTERVIEWER: When did you have the abortion?

KATE: I had it the year before I decided to kill myself. But I had totally put it out of my mind. I tried not to think about it.

INTERVIEWER: And the breakup with your boyfriend and the therapy stirred it up again?

KATE: Um-hm.

INTERVIEWER: Did you talk to any of your friends about your feelings?

KATE: Yes, I talked to three or four friends. They didn't believe me. They thought I was joking when I said I wanted to kill myself. To them, it looked like I was having a good time. That's because I was drinking a lot. But I was using the drinking to cover up my feelings. So my friends didn't take me seriously.

INTERVIEWER: How were you going to take your own life?

KATE: I was going to graduate, which I did, and then that Sunday at a graduation party I was going to tell all my family good-bye. And then that Monday I was going to kill myself by carbon monoxide poisoning in the garage with the car. That's how I was going to do it.

INTERVIEWER: Did you ever know anybody who had taken her own life in that way?

KATE: No. I think I read it in the newspaper.

INTERVIEWER: If you hadn't come to the hospital, do you think you would have done it?

KATE: Yes, because I had tried before. I had taken pills, like speed, and then drank a lot. I was real sick many times.

INTERVIEWER: Did you talk to anybody at school? A teacher? A guidance counselor?

KATE: I talked to one of my teachers and to my counselor. She was the one who recommended this counseling place for my whole family.

INTERVIEWER: Do you think she knew you were going to take your own life?

KATE: I don't think so. I think she thought I was really sad and depressed, that I needed time away from people.

INTERVIEWER: And you never told her that you wanted to die?

KATE: No. I did tell some of my friends but not the counselor or the teacher.

INTERVIEWER: What did you accomplish during your first stay in the hospital?

KATE: The first month I was happy and everything, trying to make everybody think I was fine. And then I got real depressed. I started talking about a lot of my secrets that I had kept inside.

INTERVIEWER: Like the abortion?

KATE: Like being molested when I was seven and raped twice when I was in eighth grade. And that I was still angry at my father.

INTERVIEWER: Your father wasn't the one who molested you, was he?

KATE: No, it was a friend's father.

INTERVIEWER: And the rapes? Were those people you knew?

KATE: Yeah, I knew them in grade school. I was so scared of them after it happened that I went to a different high school. I was terrified.

INTERVIEWER: Did your family know about these things?

KATE: No, not until I got into the hospital. I finally told my parents everything.

INTERVIEWER: What was their reaction?

KATE: They felt real badly for me. At first, they didn't know how to feel or what to say. My dad was real angry, especially about my abortion. And they were real upset that I didn't feel I could go to them and talk to them. But I felt they had certain values, beliefs. I didn't feel they would like me if I went and told them this stuff. They would really hate my guts and wouldn't want me as a daughter.

INTERVIEWER: And you started to feel like taking your own life again after letting all this out?

KATE: Yeah. I just didn't want to feel any more pain.

INTERVIEWER: Where would you be if you weren't in the hospital right now?

KATE: In my grave.

INTERVIEWER: You would be dead?

KATE: Yeah.

INTERVIEWER: You would have succeeded in taking your own life?

KATE: Right.

INTERVIEWER: Other young people who read this might think you're just a regular kid who doesn't really sound that depressed. How do you do that? How do you appear so together when you're actually so desperate inside?

KATE: It's my cover. I always smile and look real happy when I'm depressed. I make everybody think that I'm just fine. That way, they'll leave me alone.

INTERVIEWER: But people here aren't leaving you alone. Does it help that they're taking you so seriously?

KATE: At first, I wished they didn't take me so seriously. I was obsessed with killing myself. But after a few weeks, I was told that I had to start working on my anger and letting negative feelings out. I started feeling less tense or something. I don't know exactly what.

INTERVIEWER: You let it out?

KATE: Yeah, I started to do that. But I have a whole lot more to do.

INTERVIEWER: So, before you would cover up the anger with a smile?

KATE: I still do that sometimes. But now I can tell when I'm doing it and try to change it.

INTERVIEWER: Are you learning how to turn things around so that you're not feeling so depressed?

KATE: No, I haven't learned how to do that yet, but I've learned how to tell people that I'm feeling a certain way.

INTERVIEWER: What happened after you left the hospital the first time?

KATE: I went home, and things were going fine for the first three months. Then I started drinking more and taking speed. I felt I was too fat. I still think that. Then it seemed like I was seeing less and less of my friends. I'd call them up, and they didn't have much desire to talk to me or to go out. They knew I'd been in a psychiatric hospital, and that scared them away. It was real hard for me because some of the friends I thought were really close to me and cared about me deserted me when I got home. I couldn't take that.

INTERVIEWER: What were they afraid of?

KATE: I think they were scared of the fact that I was in a psychiatric hospital with crazy people. They didn't know how I was going to act and didn't want the burden of me going nuts on them or killing myself while I was with them. It was really hard. In a lot of ways, I felt I knew more than they did. I felt more grown up. I found out a lot more about myself and other people at the same time.

INTERVIEWER: So you started to feel lonely, not having your old friends. Was that the primary thing that was getting you depressed?

KATE: That was the start of it.

INTERVIEWER: You were in counseling as an outpatient, weren't you?

KATE: Yeah.

INTERVIEWER: And were you able to talk about these feelings in counseling?

KATE: Some of them. But I wanted everyone to think that I was doing well. When I left the hospital, I was this great patient, someone that people would remember as real positive. I didn't want anyone to see that inside I was starting to fall apart again.

INTERVIEWER: What else was going on that got you more and more depressed at home?

KATE: I had just started college and was having a hard time. I didn't know how to make new friends. All my old friends had just left me, and I was supposed to make new ones. I started a job at a nursery school and had a real hard time working with little kids because of my abortion. And then my father and I started getting along worse and worse. We started arguing and got to the point where we didn't even speak anymore.

INTERVIEWER: Did you try to take your own life when you were home between hospitalizations

KATE: I got to the point where I wasn't feeling anything. It was like I pushed all the pain away. I just didn't want to deal with it anymore. Then I started thinking about killing myself. But I wasn't feeling anything so I tried to feel pain. I burned myself with an iron a couple of times.

INTERVIEWER: Were you alone when you did that?

KATE: Yes, I was alone. I knew what I was doing but I did it, anyway. And then I did real risky things, like use the hair dryer with the water running. If I got electrocuted, I got electrocuted. And I started driving like a maniac when I was alone in the car.

INTERVIEWER: If you had died, people would have thought it was accidental.

KATE: That way, my parents wouldn't have felt so guilty.

INTERVIEWER: How do you think they would feel if you died?

KATE: Pretty sad, I guess. I don't know. If I did it intentionally, they would feel they didn't do enough for me or they weren't around when I needed them. But it's not that way. That's why I thought about writing a letter and telling them it wasn't their fault. It was just me. I couldn't find something that kept me happy, something I wanted to live for. I had given myself eight weeks to see if I could be happier. If I couldn't do that, I told the counselor that I was going to quit seeing him. Then I started talking about doing things like the hair dryer stuff. I mentioned writing a will and a letter explaining why I wanted to die.

INTERVIEWER: How did you feel when your counselor said you had to go back into the hospital?

KATE: I was shocked. And I couldn't change his mind. He said I could sign myself in or he would do something to put me into the hospital. I signed myself in.

INTERVIEWER: What have you done in the hospital this time?

KATE: I learned how to be assertive. I'm working on my anger and trying to find new ways of dealing with my problems.

INTERVIEWER: How do you feel right now about hurting yourself or taking your own life?

KATE: I think about it, usually when something is real hard for me to handle. I get impulsive and feel like strangling myself or something like that. Last night, I was drawing pictures and I drew a picture of a hanging man and a broken heart. I wasn't doing it consciously. I was just drawing. But that's a side I have to deal with. Maybe once or twice a week I feel really good. But it's rare, and it seems like those times only last for a little bit. The bad times last so much longer.

INTERVIEWER: What do you think your chances of surviving are?

KATE: I think they're better now than a month ago.

INTERVIEWER: What do you think of death?

KATE: I drew a picture of death once. I picture it as peaceful and happy and content.

INTERVIEWER: You don't see it as painful?

KATE: I think life is painful.

INTERVIEWER: What do you think your funeral would be like?

KATE: I don't picture many people coming . . . just my parents, grandparents, a few other relatives, and some friends I grew up with. But I do picture the dress I'll wear. And I know that I want one yellow rose with me. That's my favorite flower.

INTERVIEWER: It's almost like someone visualizes a wedding.

KATE: I always get yellow roses on good occasions. My funeral would be a good occasion.

INTERVIEWER: Are you worried that you have to be in a hospital all the time in order not to hurt yourself?

KATE: It scares me. I wonder whether I'm always going to be like this or whether there's going to be a time when I'll finally be able to be independent and on my own . . . to have good times and enjoy them.

INTERVIEWER: Does talking help? Does talking about your feelings help?

KATE: It hurts a lot, but it helps.

Yes, Kate is confused. But she sheds light on how it feels when friends don't take you seriously or when they abandon you. She was sexually abused and raped. She suffers from depression and talks about not feeling anything in order to escape her pain. She took all kinds of risky behaviors like driving way too fast. She wrote a will. And her view of death is a romantic one—"peaceful, happy, and content." Yet underneath all her pain is a willingness— albeit erratic—to work on her anger, to feel happy, and to regain (or maybe gain for the first time) self-confidence and a sense of direction. What do you think of her chances?

KURT'S STORY

INTERVIEWER: You told me that you moved to four different cities in four years.

KURT: I was born and raised in Houston. My mother lost her job, and eventually we ended up in Chicago where my mother had family.

INTERVIEWER: How did you do there?

KURT: Freshman year I got good grades but was depressed. I began using drugs. I saw no future. Sophomore year I lived with my aunt and uncle and went to a new high school. It was very competitive, rigorous. I gave up academically.

INTERVIEWER: How did living with your aunt and uncle go?

KURT: I don't have a father. I hoped my uncle would take his place. It didn't work out. I resented him and my aunt acting like parents. Eventually, my uncle kicked me out.

INTERVIEWER: How did that affect your depression?

KURT: I had a plan to take my life but, at the last minute, didn't go through with it. But I was sitting on the train tracks and got up when the train was about twenty yards away. I was taken to the emergency room at a local hospital and then transferred to a psych ward. I was locked up with "crazy people."

INTERVIEWER: How did that make you feel?

KURT: I was filled with rage. I actually choked another patient. I was given drugs to calm me down. That was a big mistake because it led to more addiction. Later, I signed myself in as an outpatient in a drug rehab facility and was drug free for five months. But then my girlfriend broke up with me, and I started using again, sold drugs, and got addicted again.

INTERVIEWER: That must have been a disappointment.

KURT: I was young and sad.

INTERVIEWER: Did things get any better?

KURT: I'm now a senior and about to graduate. I live with my mom, which is good. But she's not working, and we have to rely on unemployment.

INTERVIEWER: What's your drug situation now?

KURT: I don't sell drugs anymore. I don't like the "slimy underworld."

INTERVIEWER: What about using?

KURT: I smoke some weed but don't do the hard stuff anymore.

INTERVIEWER: How's your mental health?

KURT: I'm generally depressed and anxious. I always see things in the worst way. I am working with a therapist two times a week. It's helping. But I still feel stuck. I don't talk to my friends about my problems because some things are better kept to myself.

INTERVIEWER: What's your plan after graduation?

KURT: I'm thinking of moving back to Houston. I'm like a salmon. I need to go back to where I came from. I still have friends there, and the weather is better. I may go to community college.

INTERVIEWER: How do you see your future?

KURT: I don't think of killing myself. But I'm sad on a daily basis. I wake up in a bummer mood.

INTERVIEWER: Do you do anything to make you feel better?

KURT: Yeah, I try to distract myself. I go to the gym. I have girl-friends. But I recently realized that I'm bisexual. I've chosen to keep it on the hush. I'm comfortable in the closest. I don't see a need to discuss my sexuality or even to ponder it. I just keep the idea in the back of mind and only go after girls.

NATALIE'S STORY

Natalie was fourteen when she attempted suicide. She has been hospitalized twice. Her father admitted her the first time; a year later, she checked herself in. This interview was recorded toward the end of her second hospitalization.

INTERVIEWER: What was it like growing up in your house?

NATALIE: I have a sister and I don't like her. She's nineteen now. She moved out of the house five months ago. I really dislike her. That's a big part of why I'm in this hospital. I refuse to get along with her. She's close with Papa, and I guess that hurts.

INTERVIEWER: Have you always had problems with her?

NATALIE: For about five years . . . since she started getting interested in boys. My parents would go out on bowling nights, and she would have parties. If I called my parents and told them what was going on, she'd beat me. She grabbed my hair and scratched the back of my neck with her long nails. I still have scars.

INTERVIEWER: Your sister is out of the house now?

NATALIE: Yeah, but she comes home every weekend to get money from my father. It seems as if he likes her more than me. He always bails her out. She has her own apartment. He pays for part of the rent, the insurance, and for all of her good clothes.

INTERVIEWER: And that makes you angry?

NATALIE: Yeah, because I don't get it. I don't get half of what she does.

INTERVIEWER: Material things?

NATALIE: Material things and love. He's always liked her better.

INTERVIEWER: Have you ever talked to your dad about your feelings?

NATALIE: I said that he liked her more, and he denied it.

INTERVIEWER: Where does your mom fit in?

NATALIE: My mom's a manic-depressive. She just falls between the cracks.

INTERVIEWER: Is she on medication?

NATALIE: Yeah, she's on lithium. And she's been like this ever since I can remember. People tell me that's why I'm unhappy. The first time I was hospitalized, I was really angry with her. But not anymore. I don't think my mother is the problem at all.

INTERVIEWER: What's it like when she stops taking her medication?

NATALIE: It's hard for the whole family. She does stupid and crazy things. She got angry once when my father was working a lot, so she went and cut up all of his money. Then she parked the car under a broken garage door. The door slammed into the car.

INTERVIEWER: How many times has she been hospitalized?

NATALIE: Countless. I can remember missing at least two or three Christmases because she was either in the hospital or very sick. When she gets sick, she hates the family and tells us that we're not up to her level. I almost hit her a couple of times. But I didn't. My father would beat me. Besides, I knew she wasn't in her right mind.

INTERVIEWER: It must be hard for all of you . . . your dad too.

NATALIE: My father knew what he was getting into when he married her. She had already been in the hospital at least twice. He's a rock, anyway.

INTERVIEWER: He doesn't show his emotions?

NATALIE: He gets annoyed, but he doesn't break down and cry. It just doesn't seem to bother him that much.

INTERVIEWER: When were you in the hospital the first time?

NATALIE: Around this time last year.

INTERVIEWER: Did you try to take your own life?

NATALIE: Yeah, I tried twice. I took my grandmother's pills, something for depression.

INTERVIEWER: How many pills did you take?

NATALIE: Around twenty the first time. My father found me in the morning. I couldn't stand up. He took me to the hospital to have my stomach pumped. Then he took me to my aunt's house. That was on a Monday. I slept the rest of the day and all day Tuesday.

INTERVIEWER: Why did he take you to your aunt's house?

NATALIE: Because he had to work, and my mom was in the hospital. I tried to kill myself again on Wednesday. I took the rest of my grandmother's pills. Then I drank milk of magnesia, Liquid Plumber, and peroxide. I passed out. My father and aunt brought me here to this hospital.

INTERVIEWER: Why did you try to take your own life?

NATALIE: My boyfriend had broken up with me. And my best friend was away. I had no way of reaching her.

INTERVIEWER: How did she react when she found out about your suicide attempt?

NATALIE: She was real mad at me. She doesn't know how to show emotions, but she almost hit me. I'm not saying she doesn't listen to me. But she takes my unhappiness personally. She thinks I don't believe that she cares about me. I don't mean to make her feel that way. None of this is her fault.

INTERVIEWER: Did you tell anybody you were thinking of taking your own life?

NATALIE: No. I always thought about suicide. But I was never serious about it until then. My parents believed I was serious too. But my sister said I was just trying to get attention. The more I talk about her, the more upset I get. It makes me want to leave this room.

INTERVIEWER: Did you think about what death would be like?

NATALIE: I know that I'd go to hell.

INTERVIEWER: Are you religious?

NATALIE: No, but I believe in heaven and hell. I'm not sure people are going to cry when I die. I don't think my life is worth as much as the next guy. I do nothing with my life. I go to school . . . fool around. I'm a good listener, but that doesn't mean I know the right answers. Most of the time I don't.

INTERVIEWER: Did you want to be saved?

NATALIE: No, I thought I had it planned. Both times. But I made a mistake. I left a pill somewhere the first time, and my father found it. The second time, I threw everything up. My father tried to get me something to eat on the way to the hospital. I couldn't eat but I still wanted to kill myself. I went into the washroom and tried to slash my wrists on the metal edge of the sink. That didn't work either. What's strange is that I hate the sight of blood. It makes me totally sick. I must have been out of it because I'd never try to kill myself that way.

INTERVIEWER: Do you like school?

NATALIE: I like going to school to see kids. I get along with them. My problems are with adults. And I feel really ignorant in the classroom.

INTERVIEWER: Are there any subjects that you like?

NATALIE: I like reading. I like scary books by Stephen King.

INTERVIEWER: What kind of grades did you get when you were younger?

NATALIE: Not bad. But I do remember getting yelled at often because I goofed around and didn't know how to spell my name. That was the only problem I can remember until fifth grade. Then I sloughed off. Work started getting harder and harder. I don't have the attention span for it.

INTERVIEWER: What was your father's reaction?

NATALIE: He was mad and got very, very strict with me. I had to be in earlier than all the other kids. I rebelled against my father a lot.

INTERVIEWER: Did you have a grammar school yearbook?

NATALIE: No.

INTERVIEWER: If you had, what would have been written under your picture?

NATALIE: "The most blunt."

INTERVIEWER: You mean, saying what you really feel?

NATALIE: Right. I don't like to "B.S." If I don't like someone, I'm not going to play kissy face with them. I don't like to play games.

INTERVIEWER: What else would have been written about you in the yearbook?

NATALIE: That I know how to take care of myself on the street.

INTERVIEWER: Where did you learn how to be streetwise?

NATALIE: From my girlfriend and my father. My father is the same way I am. He doesn't take anything from anyone. He's a real fighter. So is my girlfriend.

INTERVIEWER: Is she the one who was away the day you decided to take your own life?

NATALIE: Yeah.

INTERVIEWER: Have you been friends for a long time?

NATALIE: For four years. When we first met, I was a wallflower. I stayed in the house all the time. I was scared of everybody and everything. I had gotten in a fight with a girl, and she beat me. I was embarrassed. And I stayed in the house for a year. Then I met Karen. She didn't like my style at all. She taught me how to fight.

INTERVIEWER: Is that something you need to know how to do?

NATALIE: I feel I do. I'm in a gang.

INTERVIEWER: A street gang?

NATALIE: Yeah.

INTERVIEWER: Why do you belong?

NATALIE: I don't consider it a real gang. We don't go around shooting people. We just defend our neighborhood. All my good friends are in it. We're known as real troublesome kids. My parents tell me I've changed. They said I used to be nice and lovable but that now I'm cold, too independent, and too mouthy to adults. They're right about the adults. I have a real problem with them. But I get along fine with my friends. I feel I'm a decent person as far as my personality goes. But I don't like myself at all in other areas.

INTERVIEWER: What don't you like about yourself?

NATALIE: I'm fat. I think I'm ugly. And I don't have my own mind with guys. They hurt me and make me feel like I have nothing left to live for.

INTERVIEWER: That's what set things off a year ago?

NATALIE: Yeah.

INTERVIEWER: Why were you hospitalized this second time? Did you attempt suicide again?

NATALIE: No. I was going to, but I wasn't alone enough. I was on the run, living with my friends. I didn't feel right having one of my friends find me dead. What would they do? Besides, my father would probably kill them.

INTERVIEWER: Did you run away from home?

NATALIE: Yeah. I ran away because I was unhappy. The day before I left, my father beat me. I lost ten dollars and was about ten minutes late coming home. My father dragged me off the bed and punched me in the face. Then he hit me with something and kicked me once. I was bleeding all over the place.

INTERVIEWER: All because you lost the money and were late?

NATALIE: A couple of days before, I was five minutes late, then I was late again. It all built up. My father decided I needed a beating. I think he thought that would put me in my place.

INTERVIEWER: But it had the opposite effect.

NATALIE: Right. I ran away.

INTERVIEWER: How did you get back in the hospital?

NATALIE: I checked myself in. I'd been on the run for eight days. I was thinking of killing myself but didn't want to lay that on my friends. I decided I needed help.

INTERVIEWER: How are you feeling now?

NATALIE: I still feel like killing myself sometimes. But I don't know how to say that to people here in the hospital without losing their trust in me.

INTERVIEWER: But soon you're going to be out of here and on your own. What's going to happen the next time you have a fight with your father or a problem with a boyfriend?

NATALIE: I'm not sure. I don't like lying and saying I'll work it out on my own. I don't know if I'm ever going to try to kill myself again. I really don't know.

If you were to make a list of possible reasons why Natalie attempted suicide several times, what might be on your list?

- Parental abuse
- Mentally disabled mother
- Parental favoritism
- Poor self-image
- Previous suicide attempts
- No one to talk to when boyfriend broke up with her
- Risky behavior: in a gang

What is encouraging is that Natalie, Kurt, and Kate have gone for help. All three realized that they were in trouble and needed professional care.

There is no way of knowing what the future holds for these suicide attempters. The odds are in their favor.

Depressed/suicidal youth who get effective help have a better than 80 percent chance for a full recovery.

...

I finally wanna be alive
I finally wanna be alive
I don't wanna die today
I don't wanna die . . .
"1 800-272-8255" — *Logic*

CHAPTER SEVEN

BULLYING: A POWER PLAY THAT HURTS

You, with your words like knives and swords and weapons that you use against me

You have knocked me off my feet again got me feeling like I'm nothing

You, with your voice like nails on a chalkboard, calling me out when I'm wounded

You, pickin' on the weaker man

"Mean" – *Taylor Swift*

"I moved in middle school. Some girls started to bully me online. They called me a 'monster.' All my friends turned against me. I didn't know what to do. I had to make all new friends." —*Haley, 17*

Haley's story is a common one. The girl who bullied her in middle school was considered the "queen." She was the leader and had the power to call the shots. Because all of Haley's friends wanted the "queen" to like *them,* they turned against Haley—afraid that maybe they'd be the next victim.

What Is Bullying, Anyway?

Bullying is unwanted, aggressive behavior that involves a real or perceived power imbalance (as in Haley's case.) The bullying is repeated, or can be repeated, over time. Making threats, spreading rumors, attacking someone physically or verbally, and excluding someone from a group on purpose are all considered to be bullying. **One out of three teens said they have been bullied in the last thirty days.**

Bullying can lower a victim's self-esteem, create a lot of anxiety, and affect academic performance, and it may lead to depression and body aches and pains. Ouch!

Myths and Facts About Bullying

MYTH: *Most kids who bully are poor students, aren't good at sports, and/or come from dysfunctional homes.*

FACT: Many bullies are the smart kids, the popular ones, the athletes, who have power.

"They can pick out the kids that no one is going to rescue. The kids who bully are generally liked by adults. They know how to turn charm on and off. It is social suicide to go against this kind of bully for fear that, if you do, you might be the next victim." — *Dorothy Espelage, professor of psychology, University of Florida*

MYTH: *Cyber bullying is worse than face-to-face bullying.*

FACT: Nope. Face-to-face bullying is still more prevalent than online. However, bullying in school often spills over into social media after school. There is no place to run, no place to hide.

MYTH: *Bullying causes suicide.*

FACT: We don't know if bullying directly causes suicide-related behavior. We know that most youth who are involved in bullying do NOT think about/attempt/complete suicide.

MYTH: *There is nothing kids can do to stop bullying.*

FACT: Wrong. Anti-bullying programs in schools can be effective. Kids need to help create an environment in which bullying is not tolerated and know what to say and do, if and when they witness a peer being bullied.

MYTH: *Bullying has no long-lasting effects.*

FACT: Children and teens who are bullied have a greater risk of low self-esteem, poor grades, depression, and an increased risk of suicide. They are often less engaged in school, and their grades and test scores decline. As adults, victims of childhood bullying suffer more than others from anxiety, panic attacks, and depression.

MYTH: *Bullying does not affect many children and youth.*

FACT: Bullying in school affects between 18 to 31 percent of students. Cyber bullying victimizes between 7 to 15 percent. These estimates are even higher for some groups like LGBTQ teens and teens with disabilities.

Climbing the Social Ladder

Bullies are often described as the "coolest" kids, but they can be the most hurtful. The perpetrator (the person who bullies) is popular because she/he is powerful, has lots of friends and calls the shots when it comes to style, music, dating, and anything else that seems important. She/he wants to hold on to the position at the top of the social ladder and will do whatever it takes, whether or not that means mowing people over in the process—spreading gossip in school and via social media, convincing people you thought were friends to turn against you. Why would these supposed friends do that? On the surface, it makes no sense. But think about it: these "social strivers" are jockeying for a higher position on the social ladder. They may not reach the top but can get closer. The last thing they want is to find themselves on the bad side of the bully for fear that *they* might be the next victim.

In the past, the word *bully* evoked images of boys entangled in a physical fight. Girls were left out of the equation. But things have changed: today, there's a lot of talk about girls and bullying. Girls don't usually get into physical fights. Their bullying is all about feelings and relationships. Instead of punching someone out, girls can gossip, spread rumors, form cliques, and use social media to "take down" their target. It's always been hurtful not be invited to a party or other event. It's even worse now with invitations splashed all over Facebook and Instagram. And during the party there are those selfies of people smiling and laughing and having the time of their lives. It's like an unending TV commercial that screams fiesta, happiness, fun, possibly romance.

With all this talk about power and climbing the social ladder, it should be noted that a popular girl who should, by all accounts, be the belle of the ball can be bullied too. Why? Well, because other girls are jealous and think she's "too" swag, "too" smart, "too" high and mighty for her own good. So, the shoe fits on the other foot in this scenario, and the "too swag" girl gets the boot.

What We Know About Bullying and Suicide

Tragic stories about teens' suicides linked in some ways to bullying are nothing new. National magazines and local newspapers are filled with them. So, what do the studies show? Bullying behavior and suicide-related behavior are closely connected. Translation: young people who've been bullied are more likely to report high levels of suicidal thoughts or suicide attempts than their peers who have not been bullied. *However*, what the experts don't know is whether bullying directly causes suicide or suicidal behavior. Most young people who are involved in bullying do *not* consider or attempt suicide. But it is correct to say that bullying, along with other risk factors, increases the chance of suicide.

> **. . . WHAT THE EXPERTS DON'T KNOW IS WHETHER BULLYING DIRECTLY CAUSES SUICIDE OR SUICIDAL BEHAVIOR.**

DAVID'S STORY

When David Beres was five, his family moved from Ohio to Michigan. As the new kid on the block, he was picked on by the other children. Some of the bigger kids threw pebbles at him. He would run home crying but stopped just before he walked in the front door. He told his dad that he felt sorry for a child that others were picking on. He never said that he was that child.

When David started high school, he was bullied again. One upperclassman apparently said, "I'm going to kill you." And another boy, the day before what was called "Nerd Day" at school, told David, "You don't have to dress like a nerd tomorrow because you are one." Later the next day, David took his life. Police investigators listed "peer teasing" as one of the *possible* precipitating causes of his suicide.

The word *possible* is important.

Remember: experts don't know whether bullying directly causes suicide or suicidal behavior.

13 Reasons Why

The popular Netflix series *13 Reasons Why* first aired in spring 2017, and it launched a national conversation about suicide. Teens have been glued to their TV or other devices to watch every episode about a girl named Hannah who, in effect, comes back from the grave with thirteen tapes she has left behind. Each tape focuses on a different classmate—some supposed friends—who, she says, factored into her suicide. But as many critics have written, it's not possible to figure out exactly why someone takes her own life and to be able to guard against it happening to others. But, writes Mike Hale of the *New York Times*, the beleaguered school counselor may have it right when he tells Clay, one of the main characters, that you can "just never tell."

Chat rooms and sites like Facebook have been ablaze with comments from teens and adults who have watched the show. Their opinions vary from those who love the show and feel it has important messages to those who found it disturbing and dangerous for vulnerable teens.

13 Reasons Why sent a hard message that people needed to hear. But a second season could be almost dangerous. I'm a recovering cutter and this show was a big trigger for me and I'm sure countless others. The suicide scene was so graphic, I couldn't watch. While I think the message overall was good, I also think that people are too focused on the entertainment and revenge fantasy that they don't see the big picture: suicide is ugly and never justified. Let the show remain as a harsh warning and not just another piece of entertainment. It is degrading.

…

This definitely was one of the darkest shows I've ever seen.

I hope it opens kids' eyes up about bullying and social media and how one screenshot of photos can ruin a person's life.

…

I just finished the series and found it disturbingly emotional, raw and realistic. I'm at a loss for words.

Bullying can break someone's heart, destroy someone's reputation, break their spirit, and break their soul!

***13 Reasons Why** is an amazing show with a great message! The show inspired me to do public speaking at my school about the consequences of bullying. Because I've been bullied for 7 years at previous schools, and it sent me down a depression that lasted about 6 years and almost ended in suicide. After therapy I've come out stronger than ever, but sadly not everyone has that so I try to change that with telling people about my personal experiences and how we can work together and stop bullying!*

Reactions to *13 Reasons Why* from parents, teachers, and counselors have also been mixed. Some organizations, concerned about the effect the show can have on teens, have published guides for parents to use when they watch the program with their kids. Many counselors are upset about the way the school counselor is portrayed. Many therapists are afraid that, for kids who are in crisis, *13 Reasons Why* could push them into the abyss. On the other hand, some posts by adults online strike a more favorable opinion.

So while I wouldn't recommend this series, I do think it's important for parents to honestly and openly discuss the troubling challenges it portrays. More importantly, our teens need to know that there is always hope and help.

The Netflix show has sparked a lot of conversations about bullying and abuse, but we also need to improve communication between teens and the adults who can actually help them.

…

I just can't bring myself to watch it. I already see kids in my elementary school every day who I worry about. I hear horror stories of the bullying going on in middle school. I'm sure HS is just as bad. Couple the bullying with mental illness & it's scary to see where it leads.

…

If any of you have Netflix and preteens or high schoolers, I highly recommend the series: **13 Reasons Why.** *It absolutely depicts the everyday bullying, drama and aftermath that some of our kids go though.*

…

Whether you or someone you know "loves" the series and the potential lessons about how bullying can cut deeply, bullying is never the sole reason why Hannah or anyone else ends her life. Just as important, no one gets to seek revenge by "returning" from the grave. The tapes are a convenient vehicle for a fictional TV show (and the book by the same name on which the show was based) but not realistic. The graphic portrayal of the suicide itself, along with the rape scenes, have prompted many to forcefully object— better to tell, not show.

Witnessing Bullying

There are many studies that show students who witness bullying could become as distressed, if not more so, than the victims themselves. Sounds crazy, right? If you've ever watched someone being bullied, you probably have felt fear that you might be next, anger that the abuse is happening, helplessness, or guilt because you could or would not do anything to stop it. The end result: witnesses of bullying are more prone to anxiety, depression, and/or helplessness.

(To be accurate, there are researchers who do not believe that those who witness bullying are just as likely to have long-lasting consequences. Brain imaging shows a stress response to witnessing bullying, but that stress response goes away quickly.)

So, why not stand up and be counted? Why not do what you can to stop the bullying? You probably have or have heard some answers.

- "I feel more comfortable being a member of a crowd. You know, 'Go along to get along.'"
- "Ah, the whole thing is just a joke. It's not that serious."
- "You know what? He/she had it coming."
- "If I snitch, everyone will start bullying me."
- "And what if I don't join in? Or actually try to break things up? I might be pushed together with the victims—the nerds, the disabled, the LGBTQ crowd."

BETHANNE'S STORY

BETHANNE: So I was homeschooled from kindergarten to third grade, and then in fourth grade, I started public school. And I mean it was fine for the first few months like no one really knew me. No one really bullied me. And I was definitely the tomboy. I wore like sneakers and jeans and a T-shirt every day and didn't wear makeup and didn't follow the crowd.

INTERVIEWER: How did the bullying start?

BETHANNE: This girl started calling me a tomboy and telling me that no one liked me. She said I was a fake, not a real person, who wanted to be like all the boys.

INTERVIEWER: This was before social media, right?

BETHANNE: Right. It was all verbal and in school and behind my back. But this girl turned my friends against me. I felt really unsafe in school. I grew up with two older brothers. We were always playing outside.

INTERVIEWER: So, do you think the bullying was some kind of gender thing?

BETHANNE: All I heard was the word *tomboy*.

INTERVIEWER: So how did you feel when this girl bullied you?

BETHANNE: I felt really alone . . . like I didn't have anyone except for one of my best guy friends who stuck with me through it all. But it was really rough because all these people that I thought were my friends . . . they took her side. I felt really insecure. This girl taunted me to my face during school and during recess. I think she did it a few times at lunch too.

INTERVIEWER: Would you describe her as popular, smart, someone with a lot of friends? You know, what some people call a "Queen Bee."

BETHANNE: No. She was just bigger than most girls in the class. I think she felt insecure and tried to make me feel the same way.

INTERVIEWER: How did things end?

BETHANNE: I moved. My parents got a divorce, and I went with my mother and one of my siblings to another state. I never saw the girl who bullied me again!

Even though Bethanne was in fourth grade and will be a junior in high school, the bullying is still fresh. She's forgotten some of the details but not many. Whether or not she'll carry this experience with her into adulthood remains to be seen. If the studies are accurate, she will.

CALLAN'S STORY

Callan's story took a different turn. The perpetrator was a boy in her eighth-grade class.

Callan had a "pretty laid back" middle school until more than midway through eighth grade when a boy she knew sent a "really long" text in which he professed his love. He followed her everywhere, he wrote, and knew everything about her. Callan didn't want to be mean so, with her mother's help, she crafted and texted a "gentle, kind" note that said she wasn't interested in anything more than a friendship. That didn't go as planned. The boy started a torrent of texts in which he called Callan all kinds of nasty things.

One day during lunch when Callan's cousin must have said something to the "stalker," he jumped over a table, grabbed her by the throat, and tried to strangle her. Callan sprang to her cousin's defense and, once adults in the lunchroom saw the ruckus, they sent all three to the principal's office. After Callan and her cousin told the story, the principal looked at Callan and told her to "keep control of her womanly wiles." And be careful, he said, of the boys in this school because you can't control yourself.

Callan was horrified. Neither she nor her cousin said a word to anyone after that. Still the bullying/abuse continued. The bully would come up behind Callan in the hallways and pinch her side or her thighs and then run away. He pulled her hair and pushed her into lockers. Friends saw all of this but laughed it off. They told Callan she was "too sensitive" and just needed to deal with the situation. Things came to a head when Callan's mom started noticing some bruises on her daughter and insisted that Callan spill the beans. Callan refused. But after a lot

> **. . . THE PRINCIPAL LOOKED AT CALLAN AND TOLD HER TO 'KEEP CONTROL OF HER WOMANLY WILES.'**

of pressure, Callan told her mother everything. Her mother called a cop. His response: "Oh, this is just another girl having issues, causing herself problems."

With a push from her mother, Callan didn't hold back: she finally explained the whole story from beginning to end. This time, a liaison officer set up what was, in fact, a restraining order that forbid the boy from coming within ten feet of Callan. The last she heard, the guy had moved to another state.

Surprisingly, Callan never saw the experience as bullying. She didn't put all the facts together: the constant, repeated taunting, her friends' unwillingness to step up and help put a stop to the harassment, Callan's hesitation to tell her mother, school officials, and her feelings as a victim. "I never thought of it that way," she told me.

When I asked her if there were any long-term effects of the experience, she was clear: "It's made me more cautious around boys. And it destroyed my faith in the belief that everybody wants to be friends—wants the best for you."

What Callan didn't articulate but that is clear in her story is the sexist comments made to her by the school principal ("Keep control of your womanly wiles" and "Be careful of the boys in this school because you can't control yourself"). In the principal's mind, the fact that she was bullied took a back seat. She was blamed as the problem and the instigator. Except for her mother, none of the men took her seriously. She was, after all, a girl who must have egged the boy on—an all-too-familiar stance taken against girls and women.

Cyber Bullying: Nowhere to Run, Nowhere to Hide

Back in the day, lots of kids were bullied—at school, on the school bus, in the neighborhood. But when you were in your front door, you were "safe." You couldn't be hounded in texts or on social media or on your cell phone. Landlines were all there were and, if you didn't want to answer the phone when it rang, you didn't have to.

My, how things have changed! Today, almost all communication is done electronically. It makes staying in touch as easy as a click. But there are downsides, certainly when it involves bullying. If you're the victim, there is no escape. Like everyone else, you're attached. It's a form of addiction. You have to read texts, log on to Facebook or Instagram or any of the other social media sites. For victims of bullying, there's no way to escape. (Well, you could close your social media accounts, stop looking at your phone . . . but the chances of that are mighty slim.) So, you continue to get slammed. Rumors spread like a raging river overflowing its banks. Supposed friends turn on you and join the "fun." Next day, you go back to school and get bullied all over again. It's almost impossible to see your life outside of social media as any different from your life inside social media. It's all of a piece.

> **TODAY, ALMOST ALL COMMUNICATION IS DONE ELECTRONICALLY . . . IF YOU'RE THE VICTIM, THERE IS NO ESCAPE.**

Why would you want to go to school and have to face the music every day? You wouldn't. How can you concentrate in class when you're always looking over your shoulder or listening to people laughing at you? You can't. If you're predisposed to anxiety, you'll probably be even more anxious. Same goes for depression. And suicide? Bullying along with other factors can increase your risk.

What's the Solution?

"You never really understand another person until you consider things from his point of view—until you climb inside of his skin and walk around in it." —*To Kill a Mockingbird,* Harper Lee

There are a wealth of anti-bullying campaigns, programs, and organizations out there. Some of these programs are geared toward teens, others toward adults, and still others toward teachers and school officials. Before I run down a few of them, why don't you make a mental or written list of reasons why kids bully other kids? You may have personal experience, on one end of bullying or the other. So, give it a shot. The following is a list from CRC Health.*

- Being gay, lesbian, bisexual or transgender
- Being shy or socially awkward
- Having a learning or behavioral disability
- Having low self-esteem (someone perceived as weak who won't put up a fight)
- Posing a threat to someone's confidence, power, popularity

So, how does your list stack up? Are there other reasons why kids bully?

Okay, here's another challenge: What suggestions might you give to bullies and witnesses to bullying? Earlier, I went over some of the excuses teens choose not to get involved. Let's flip the scenario and brainstorm strategies witnesses and bullies *can* do to help curb a problem that is only getting worse. For example, how important is it for student leaders/mentors to be the first line of defense? What about reporting your concerns to a "trusted" adult? Now, it's your turn.

Strategies:
Ways to Stop/React to Bullying

Nancy Willard is the director of Embrace Civility in the Digital Age. Her program is targeted to/for adults, but her strategies are ones you and your friends can use to help stop bullying.

---

* www.crchealth.com/youth-programs/5-reasons-teens-bullied/

- **Fact:** Teens who are bullied but who have supportive friends are less distressed than kids without support. Being connected is key.

- **Positive psychology:** We don't always have control over what happens to us, but we can control what we think of ourselves and how we respond. Translation: If you are bullied, you can take revenge, curl up in a ball, or live by the old adage: "Sticks and stones will break my bones, but words will never hurt me." You can feel empathy for the bully and try to understand what's going on in his life that makes him want to take out his anger/frustration/abuse on someone else. I get it: this is a lot easier than it sounds, right? But it is possible. It takes practice, a kind of reverse kindness, and, again, those supportive friends.

- **Respond to hurtful situations.** This is another tactic that dovetails into positive psychology. If you can do it, calmly tell the bully to stop. And if you think that's a waste of your time and won't work, then hold your head high and walk away.

- **Kindness:** When it comes down to it, the most successful anti-bullying programs focus on that old adage "treat others how you would like to be treated." Sure. Sure. It sounds kinda obvious. But to tell the truth, given all the reasons you and your peers want to climb up or stay at the top of the social ladder—the lure of social media and the anonymity it affords—it's not as easy as it sounds. What does kindness really mean? Civility? Speaking up? Taking action? Putting yourself in the other guy's shoes?

- **In their book** *Words Wound: Delete Cyberbullying and Make Kindness Go Viral,* authors Justin Patching and Sameer Hinduja suggest a host of strategies for "deleting" cyberbullying—strategies that apply to face-to-face bullying too. It's important, they write, to realize that cyberbullying (bullying) affects everyone, no matter who's being targeted. The authors suggest that you may want to be a mentor and to relay to another student who's being bullied, among other messages, that he is not alone in feeling the pain and loneliness it can cause. Check out *Words Wound* online or in your local library or bookstore. It's a good read with lots of good suggestions.

Other resources you may want to check out: Steps to Respect (www.cfchildren.org/bullying-prevention); and Olweus Bullying Prevention Program (www.violencepreventionworks.org/public/olweus_scope.page).

CHAPTER EIGHT | # LGBTQ TEENS: OVERCOMING THE STIGMA WITH RESILIENCY AND PRIDE

Oh, no, not I!

I will survive.

Oh, as long as I know how to love
I know I'll stay alive.

I've got all my life to live.

I've got all my love to give.

And I'll survive,

I will survive, hey, hey.

"I Will Survive" — *Gloria Gaynor*

An Abridged Glossary of Terms

If you're what Ashley Mardell calls an "LGBTQIA+ novice" in her book *The ABC's of LGBT+*, you might want to have a look at the following glossary of terms. And, if you are an "LGBTQIA+ expert," you might still find a word or two you don't know. This is an abridged glossary from Mardell's book because, to tell the truth, it takes more than a quick read to understand the subtle and not-so-subtle differences between terms. (BTW, in this book, I'm using LGBTQ. Why? Because those are the groups about which there has been a good deal of research—the results of which will be presented in this chapter. And when I use the Q, I am using the definition of queer, not questioning.)

Agender/genderless: Someone who is without gender, gender neutral, and/or rejects the concept of gender for themselves.

Androgyne: A person is both a man and woman, neither a man nor woman, and/or somewhere in between man and woman.

Androgynous: Possessing qualities which are traditionally associated as both masculine and feminine, neither masculine nor feminine, and/or in between masculine and feminine.

Asexual: Someone who experiences little or no sexual attraction toward individuals of any gender.

Bicurious: Someone curious about having sexual/romantic attractions and/or experiences with more than one gender.

Binary: The rigid way society divides sex and gender into only two categories: 1) male/men and 2) female/women.

Bisexual: Being attracted to two or more genders.

Cisgender/Cis: A person whose gender identity is the same as their sex and/or gender assigned at birth.

Female to Female/FTF: Someone whose sex and/or gender was assigned male at birth and who rejects that their gender was ever male.

Fluid: Not fixed, able to change.

FTM: Acronym for "female to male."

Gay: (the G in LGBTQ) This label can refer to men who are attracted to men; it can refer to people who are primarily attracted to the same or similar gender as their own; or it can be an umbrella term for anyone who is not **straight.**

Gender dysphoria: Distress or unhappiness experienced because one's gender does not match their sex and/or gender assigned at birth.

Gender euphoria: Extreme happiness, or comfort ability, experienced because a person's gender is being affirmed.

Gender identity: The identifier (or lack of identifier) someone uses to communicate how they understand their personal gender, navigate within or outside our societal gender systems, and/or desire to be perceived by others.

Gender neutral: Having a gender that is neutral.

Gender roles: Societal roles, positions, behaviors, and/or responsibilities allowed or expected from men and women based on societal norms.

Genderqueer: Someone whose gender exists outside of or beyond society's concept of gender.

Heterosexual/Straight: Being attracted to the other binary gender.

Lesbian: (the L in LGBTQ) Women (as well as non-binary and genderqueer people who feel a connection to womanhood) who are attracted to other women.

Male to Male/MTM: Someone whose sex and/or gender was assigned female at birth and who rejects that their gender was ever female.

Non-binary/nb: Existing or identifying outside the sex/gender binary, being neither a man nor woman, or being only partially or a combination of these things.

Polyamory: The practice or desire of relationships involving more than two people.

Pronouns: Words used to refer to specific people when their proper names are not being used (e.g., he, she, they, ze, e, etc.).

Queer: (The Q in LGBTQ) Describes a sexual and/or gender identity that falls outside societal norms. This term has a history of being used as a slur. Although it has been reclaimed by many LGBTQ people, not everyone is comfortable using it.

Questioning: (the other definition of Q in LGBTQ) Being unsure of one's sexual/romantic orientation or gender identity. *Note: In this book, Q stands for Queer.

Romantic attraction: Attraction that is romantic, not sexual.

Sex/gender assignment: Society's propensity to label an infant as male or female, man or woman, at birth, usually based on the appearance of their genitals.

What is the difference between gender and sex?

In general terms, "sex" refers to the biological differences between males and females, such as the genitalia and genetic differences. "Gender" is more difficult to define but can refer to the role of a male or female in society (gender role), or an individual's concept of themselves (gender identity).

Trans man: (the T in LGBTQ) Someone who was assigned female at birth and is a man.

Trans woman: (the T in LGBTQ) Someone who was assigned male at birth and is a woman.

Transgender: (the T in LGBTQ) An umbrella term for anyone whose gender identity does not match their sex and/or gender assigned at birth.

Transition: The process of accepting oneself and/or pursuing changes in order to affirm one's gender.

Transsexual: A person whose gender is different from their sex/gender assigned at birth. This is an older term that has fallen out of popular usage in favor of the word "transgender."

Whew! That's a lot to take in. Thanks to author Ashley Mardell for all her hard work.

Because *Dead Serious* is a book about teen suicide and not a book about the spectrum of gender and sex, the glossary is meant to help clarify some of the terms we hear more and more these days and to understand ways in which the interviewees for this chapter self-identify.

It is exciting to see several new/expanded reports and surveys of LGBT youth, most between ages thirteen and seventeen. I'm hesitant to fill your brains with figures and statistics and have grappled with how much to include. In some cases, I'll provide summaries with links to the full reports; in others, I'll do my best to highlight the most important findings.

Doing Just Fine, Thank You

To use Mardell's terminology, if you're a "LGBTQIA+ novice," a lot of the stories and strategies in this chapter might be ones you've not heard about before. And if you're an "LGBTQUIA+ expert" (i.e., this is your life), you will, hopefully, recognize parts of yourself.

It's true that LGBTQ youth deal with issues that "straight" youth do not. And I'll talk about some of those shortly. But it's important to stress that the majority of LGBTQ teens, particularly those who are out to family and friends, are happy and optimistic and envision a fulfilled life ahead of them.

MILENKA'S STORY

Milenka, seventeen, identifies as an asexual homo/romantic. She doesn't experience sexual attraction but feels romantic attraction toward females. "A lot of people," says Milenka, "experience romantic and sexual attraction simultaneously. For me, it's romantic like holding hands, feeling emotionally close to somebody." Has she ever had sex? No. "It seems foreign and unnecessary to me." Milenka has a girlfriend who is also asexual. They knew each other for a year before the relationship became romantic. "Our relationship looks like any other lesbian relationship, but we don't have sex." Does she feel that there is anything in her past that helped form her gender identity? No. "I was never sexually abused and have good relationships with my parents."

Milenka has been out to her parents since she started dating her girlfriend. "I think they knew because I was never interested in guys. But when I told them, they didn't really have a reaction. They just said, 'Okay.' And I knew they'd be accepting because we grew up around a lot of homosexual and lesbian couples in our building. I didn't have worries about coming out." Since then, her parents have been curious about the differences between romantic and sexual attraction but have had many more questions about Milanka's friends who are transgender.

Milenka attends a public college-prep school in Chicago where, she says, students and teachers are very accepting of the LGBTQ community. "I'm really lucky. If I didn't go to this school, I probably wouldn't have known about my sexual identity. The subject is talked about a lot." The majority of LGBTQ students are out at Milenka's school but many are not out to their families. There are a lot of families, she says, that are very conservative, and kids are afraid of being kicked out or not having family financial support to attend college.

Milenka is very aware of the ways in which our society is geared toward heterosexuals and the assumption that, if a girl is attracted to a guy, it must be sexual when, in truth, it can be admiration or respect or some other feeling. "This can be very confusing because that's the way society is set up. For me, figuring out that I was gay has made my relationships with men a lot easier and more comfortable. Before, I used to feel that, if I ever got close to a guy, I'd have to date him. Now, I understand that that doesn't have to happen."

While Milenka has never been threatened or assaulted, she knows that life can be very different for LGBTQ youth and that living in a small town or conservative enclave can make big problems for other gay youth. She spent some time during a summer in a small Minnesota town, where she felt a "negative vibe" and could imagine how isolated gay teens could feel.

Milenka is confident and articulate with a deep understanding of herself and her gender identity. She is a thinker whose perceptions are much more mature than her seventeen years.

"Gender-expansive" Children and Young Adults

In June 2017, *The New York Times* ran a photo essay by Annie Tritt. Tritt began photographing "gender-expansive" children and young adults. "In the younger participants," Tritt wrote, "I have found self-assuredness and confidence; they are clear about who they are. In the older youths—especially the nonbinary ones who identify as both genders, or neither—I see a willingness to break free from boxes society puts us into. In all of them, there is creativity and compassion for peers and strangers alike."

Alas, I can't include photos. It's too expensive. But I can relate snippets—brief thoughts in some of the participants' own words. Here's the link to the article: *www.nytimes.com/2017/01/23/health/trans-gender-children-youth.html*

...

MAX, 13, NONBINARY

"I texted my mom that I am attracted to boys and that I feel more girl than boy. Later that year, I found the term nonbinary. It just felt right. I still am often scared of the reactions of people when I tell them."

CHOLE, 20, TRANSGENDER WOMAN

"I understand that my gender does not define me or who I am. I refuse to let gender roles and female-male privilege control me. 'I am perfectly imperfect. And proud.'"

ZAK, 13, TRANSGENDER BOY

"When I was twelve, I realized that transgender was a thing. It made sense. I'm straight—I'm a straight guy in a girl's body . . . I hate looking like this, I hate the body that I have. I want it to transform, and it is wrong that I have to wait until I'm an adult."

LILY, 12, TRANSGENDER GIRL

". . . At the end of the day, people can say what they want about you, but the only voice that matters to you is yours. They just don't struggle with the things we struggle with."

...

Kids are coming out earlier and earlier. While studies in the 1970s documented LGBT young adults coming out, on average, in their early twenties, the latest research demonstrates that the average age has dropped to anywhere between fourteen and sixteen. Caitlin Ryan, a PhD at San Francisco State University's Family Acceptance Project who has been researching LGBT adolescents for more than twenty-five years, began extensive outreach and in-depth interviews with "queer youth" in the early 2000s. "We found the average age of coming out was a little over thirteen. And it's dropping down even more."

Not a Level Playing Field

All teens, regardless of their gender/sex identity, worry about the same things: grades, making friends, dating, getting into college. But LGBTQ teens face an extra set of stressors that most straight teens do not.

- **Being outed** – Having someone identify your sex/gender identity before you're ready.

  "I first came out to my dad, sister, and two really close friends. One of those friends decided to tell pretty much everyone on our baseball team because, in his words, he wanted to warn them.

  "I was really mad at him. My teammates started acting kind of weird around me, they stopped inviting me places, and things like that. It was my senior year of high school so I decided to just stick with it. I stopped being friends with the guy who outed me after that."

  It is NEVER okay to out someone without his/her permission.

- **Rejection by family and friends**
  You may not cop to it, but every teen needs a supportive family— for advice, perspective, and love. It may be a stretch to admit the importance of being accepted by your family, but somewhere in

that gut of yours, you know it's the truth. This is particularly true for LGBT teens who face a host of challenges growing up and sure don't need family rejection to be one of them.

In *Growing Up LGBT in America*—a 2012 survey among more than ten thousand LGBT youth ages thirteen to seventeen—the teens were asked to describe the most important problem facing their lives. "Non-accepting families" ranked number one, with 26 percent of the respondents. When they were asked to describe one thing in their lives they would like to change, 15 percent said "my parent/family situation." For those teens—particularly those who are not out to their family—they often fear how their family will react, knowing they are homo-/bi-/transphobic or swayed by their religion that condemns homosexuality. Still, given the fear of rejection and the disappointment they may well cause their family, more than half of the teens surveyed said they are out to their immediate family, about half said they have an adult in the family they could turn to for help, but less than a third chose their family among a list of places where they most often hear positive messages about being LGBT.

Why does family support matter? Caitlin Ryan has plenty to say about that. "It's a child's birthright that we really support all of their gifts and abilities," Ryan says. Her research shows that the way parents, foster parents, caregivers, and families react to their LGBT children has a "powerful relationship to their children's health, mental health, and well-being as a young adult."

When families reject their LGBT children (even if unintended), they may try to change their child's sexual orientation or gender identity, assume it's just a "phase," or prevent them from having LGBT friends. The results? Suicide attempts. High levels of depression. Using illegal drugs. High risk for HIV and sexually transmitted diseases

On the positive side, the Family Acceptance Project has developed research-based intervention models for educating and counseling families with LGBT children and has found that, once parents understand the physical and mental effects of their words and actions, they *can* change. They can help protect their children against the stresses they face and act as a buffer against the stigma, victimization, and health risks.

> **"My parents were generally accepting when I came out to them. They are both artists and have been around queer people most of their lives. My mother was scared because so many of her gay friends died from AIDS. Still, my parents gave me a lot of freedom."**
> — *Sky, 25*

- **Physical Safety at School and Beyond**
  LGBT youth are twice as likely as their peers to say they have been physically assaulted, kicked, or shoved at school. More than one third say they don't come out at school because they will be treated differently or judged.

  Growing Up LGBT in America supported the fact that growing up lesbian, gay, bisexual, or transgender can be a rough ride with all kinds of challenges. When asked what the most difficult problem they were facing in their lives "these days," 21 percent said "trouble at school/bullying." (Interestingly, 22 percent of non-LGBT youth listed "trouble with classes/exams/grades.") The report found that 51 percent of LGBT youth have been verbally harassed and called names at school. That number compares to 25 percent of non-LGBT students.

  LGBT YOUTH ARE TWICE AS LIKELY AS THEIR PEERS TO SAY THEY HAVE BEEN PHYSICALLY ASSAULTED, KICKED, OR SHOVED AT SCHOOL.

  Despite these statistics, a healthy 75 percent of LGBT teens say that most of their peers don't have a problem with their gender identity.

AUGUST'S STORY

Nineteen-year-old August, who identifies as a non-binary transgender, was sexually abused at school from the time she was ten until age twelve. She doesn't remember much from that time: "Probably a survival mechanism. I felt like a robot. I figured my abuser would either leave or that I'd go to another school." Understandably, August hated to go to school but because she wasn't being bullied in the "traditional" sense, her parents didn't get it. "I couldn't tell them. They would never understand."

August didn't know the word *rape,* didn't even hear the word until a year after the abuse began. To this day, she is deeply upset that the school withheld information because the teachers and administrators didn't want to upset the students or add to their own discomfort. August tried her best to put up a good front. She didn't want anyone to find out about the sexual abuse. "I showed just enough emotion so people didn't think something was going on. Any time I thought I might share the secret, I shut down. I didn't tell anyone until this year."

To make things even more confusing, she began having feelings for girls, not boys. "I had never heard the word *gay* or seen any evidence of gay people. In fact, I thought I was an alien and meditated a few times to see if I could unlock my memories of having lived on another planet." Things just didn't add up.

In eighth grade, August had a boyfriend, went to church every day, and tried to "pray the gay away," as people say. "I deeply hated myself and prayed to have the strength to fix myself." In her freshman year, a friend who decided she didn't want to be friends outed August and called her a *dyke.* "It was bad back then but, as I look back, I see it as positive. I didn't know how much longer I could stay in the 'closet.'"

August developed an eating disorder (ED) when she couldn't put the sexual assault behind her. "Subconsciously, I hoped I'd get sick and die." In high school, she attempted suicide a "couple" of times.

"I had other brushes with sexual assault that brought up everything from the past. I felt trapped, hopeless." She overdosed. Took pills at night and was in bed the entire night before her parents found her. She spent a week in the hospital.

"I've been on my death bed more times than I can recommend." Each time after recovering, "I would chuckle a bit and ask my parents how many times had they been sitting with me next to my hospital bed. They probably thought I was mentally ill. I did see a therapist but was misdiagnosed with depression and PTSD. Eventually, I was told I was bipolar. I was on medication for a while but didn't think it was helping. I'm off it now and have learned to live with my mood swings."

And she's "found community."

"I'm involved in a youth program for LBGTQ teens. It's the first time I've been around queers my age and heard them talking about abuse, self-abuse, gender . . . It's really validating, comforting. It has affected my mental health in a very positive way. I am not alone."

- **Homelessness**

  It's easy to jump to the conclusion that because somewhere between 20 and 40 percent of homeless youth are LGBT, they must be delinquents who cause tremendous discord at home or who are running from the law or unable to abide by rules set by their parents. Not true. The majority of homeless LGBT youth are what David Bond, vice president of Programs, The Trevor Project, labeled "refugees or asylum seekers" who are escaping really bad conditions at home or have been rejected, often kicked out. According to one study, 26 percent of gay teens were kicked out of their homes when they came out to their parents.

  Parents who are unwilling to accept their children's gender identity are seen as adversaries instead of allies. They may have physically abused their children and, worse yet, a relative or close friend to the family may have sexually abused them. For many homeless LGBT youth living on the street (or in shelters or foster care), their only way to "survive" has been to choose the worst of two evils: fend for themselves or stay in a toxic, often dangerous situation.

"I spoke to my momma's boyfriend's uncle, and he was like, 'What? You talking to me? I don't speak to faggies. I shoot faggies.' It's messed up." — *an 18-year-old homeless African American gay male from Detroit, Michigan.*

"My auntie caught me and my ex-girlfriend . . . we were just in bed together, and she told the whole church. She told the whole church!" — *homeless 19-year-old lesbian from Ann Arbor, Michigan*

"An Epidemic of Homelessness" (a comprehensive report about *LGBT* youth and homelessness) begins with the tragic story of Ali Forney, a homeless transgender youth in New York City. The following is an edited version of that story from the report.

ALI'S STORY ("AN EPIDEMIC OF HOMELESSNESS")

Ali grew up with his single mother in a housing project in a violent area of Brooklyn, "a world of poverty-blighted high-rises, beat-up cars, stark store fronts and warehouses." He began working as a prostitute when he was thirteen to help him survive—to pay for a meal and shelter. As the authors of the report discovered, Ali got in trouble in school and was eventually sent to a group home for troubled youth. He ran away and then spent years "bouncing around the foster care system." Eventually, Ali lived at StreetWork in New York, a drop-in center and live-in facility for homeless youth up to age twenty-four.

After living at StreetWork for a year, he, like many other displaced youth, tried to reunite with his family. Ali's effort lasted no more than a few days and he landed back at the agency. The fact that he identified as transgender and gay was just one of the issues that made reunification harder. Ali was murdered by a still-unidentified assailant at four a.m. on a cold winter night.

"Ali's life and death is a tragic example of what can happen when LGBT youth are forced onto the streets as their home, shelter or foster care environment is untenable."

In its executive summary, "An Epidemic of Homelessness" details situations and risks homeless LGBT youth face:*

- Mental health issues like depression
- Substance abuse
- Risky sexual behavior
- Victimization
- Harassment and Violence
- The report notes that transgender youth (possibly as many as one in five) are homeless and often ostracized from shelters
- While all homeless youth face a ton of problems, LGBT youth's problems are more pronounced and require federal and state and local money, programs and housing.

- **Substance Abuse**
  National research has shown that substance abuse among LGBT youth is more than two times compared with their peers. It's not a stretch to understand why vulnerable kids who don't cope well with stress can turn to drugs and alcohol as a way to numb their pain. It's a way to survive.

---

* www.thetaskforce.org/static_html/downloads/HomelessYouth.pdf

Percentage of youth in different housing situations and the substances they use

Substance	Homeless youth on the street	Homeless youth in shelters	Non-homeless youth
Tobacco	81%	71%	49%
Alcohol	81%	67%	57%
Marijuana	75%	52%	23%
Crack cocaine	26%	8%	1.4%
Intravenous drugs	17%	4%	1%
Other drugs stimulants, hallucinogens, inhalants	55%	34%	16%

Adapted from Greene, J. M., Ennet, S. T. & Ringwalt, C. L. (1997). Substance use among runaway and homeless youth in three national samples. American Journal of Public Health, 87(2).

The chart above paints a clear and alarming picture of how being homeless affects the amount and kind of substances youth use. (The numbers do not differentiate between LGBT and non-LGBT teens.)

So, what makes one kid resilient and another at risk for substance abuse and other bad choices? David Bond of The Trevor Foundation has some ideas:

- Poor self-esteem
- Poor physical and/or mental wellness
- Little or no satisfaction with life
- Trouble making friends/feeling connected to other people

"We each have the ability to improve, even strengthen each of these protective factors," writes Bond in an op-ed for *The Advocate*. "It's when these base elements, the things that make each of us who we are, come under chronic attack and are threatened that we become vulnerable."*

*https://www.thetrevorproject.org/trvr_press/
the-complicated-relationship-between-bullying-and-suicide/

- **Suicide**

  So, now we come to the ultimate end game. It's not a pretty picture. It is dead serious. Suicide is the second leading cause of death for all young Americans ages ten to twenty-four. But the rate of suicide **attempts** is four times greater for LGB youth and two times greater for "questioning" youth.

  (Okay, let's catch our collective breath. Where did the word *questioning* come into all of this? Well, it's what some folks associate with the "Q" in LGBTQ. Others use the "Q" for queer. Still others use both. You might remember that, for purposes of this book, I said that I would use the "Q" for queer. That's because there's limited data on "questioning" or "unsure" youth. And, yep, one of those happens to be the most recent (2016) report by the CDC about sexual identity and risky behaviors, of which suicide attempts is the riskiest of all. So, for this one time, I'll break my stance and use the Q for questioning.)

  Back to the stark facts and stories about suicide and LGBTQ young people.

SKY'S STORY

Sky, now twenty-five, is a Chicago clothing designer who specializes in clothes for "queer, gender non conforming identities, and visible and invisible disabilities [and] disorders." She uses the term "gender fluid" to describe her changing interest in other women, both sexes, or "whatever"—and the way she presents to the world. She wears clothes that can be worn by "either gender."

Sky says she always felt gender fluid but didn't have the vocabulary to use. When she was younger, Sky presented as a girl. In grade school, her best friend was very "butch," and, in high school, Sky started "playing around" with more masculine clothing and binding her chest. But she didn't have access to comfortable lingerie at the time; thus, one of her goals when she started designing her own clothing line.

When Sky came out to her mother, her mother was generally accepting but scared. She'd been a professional dancer when she was younger and had lost a lot of male friends to AIDS. She was most concerned about Sky's health. "Actually," says Sky, "I had to come out a couple of times"; first, as a lesbian, then as a straight female who dated boys ("because I wanted to have sex"), then lesbian again. Now I just like the word *queer* because it's the most open—an umbrella term that inside of it I can change."

Ever since she can remember, Sky has suffered anxiety, panic attacks, and depression, "Even with all of the support from my parents, it didn't feel like it was enough. There were no resources. I never saw an older version of myself. That was very damaging. And there was no discussion in school about gender identity. No resources for queer kids. (Sky does feel that things have changed since she was in high school. The media is much more inclusive. Gay marriage is now the law of the land. [Sky was actually going to marry her last girlfriend, but then they broke up.] Kids, she says, are out much earlier, and they know a lot more.)

> **"EVEN WITH ALL OF THE SUPPORT FROM MY PARENTS, IT DIDN'T FEEL LIKE ENOUGH."**

Sky's panic attacks began earlier, but the one she remembers first occurred when she transferred schools in second grade. She started hyperventilating, crying uncontrollably, and getting confused. "I've had them so, so much in my life—mostly, during times of change and stress." She thought about suicide a lot. By high school, her suicidal ideation (thinking about suicide) was so frequent that she was put on medication. But the meds made her ill, and she went off the drugs "cold turkey"—something patients are warned not to do. The effects were devastating: Sky took a bunch of pills and was hospitalized. "My desire to die was very strong;

strangely, my time in the hospital was so bad that I decided it had to be worse than death. But once I was released, I still had a rough time. I felt terrible and took a semester off." Does she think being gender fluid impacted her mental health? Definitely.

Toward the end of her semester off, she met an "amazing" artist who had also struggled with mental health issues. "Talking to her helped me so much. She'd always been told she was 'crazy,' which sounded so familiar. I decided that I'd had enough of panic attacks and thoughts about suicide." So, Sky had what she calls a rebirthing ceremony. She describes it as a "goofy art ceremony," during which she pledged to becoming a new person with strong mental health. And it worked! She didn't have a panic attack for six months and has, she says, transformed her life.

Sky is one of the lucky ones whose suicide attempt did not lead to her death. But her history reflects many of the facts about LGBTQ youth and their suicidal behavior—facts documented in the 2016 *Sexual Identity, Sex of Sexual Contacts, and Health-Risk Behaviors Among Students in Grades 9-12 (CDC).*

- Most LGB youth who attempt suicide have underlying medical health issues, such as depression, anxiety, and panic disorders. (The same goes for heterosexual youth.)

- Lesbian and gay youth are three times likelier than their heterosexual peers to report thoughts of suicide. Bisexual youth are five times more likely than their heterosexual peers.

- Suicide attempts by LGB youth and questioning youth are four to six times more likely to result in injury, poisoning, or overdose that requires treatment from a doctor or nurse, compared to their straight peers.

- During the twelve months before the CDC survey, gay, lesbian, and bisexual youth were three times more likely than heterosexual students to have made a plan about how they would attempt suicide.

- In a national study, 40 percent of transgender adults reported having made a suicide attempt. 92 percent of these individuals reported having attempted suicide before the age of twenty-five.

We don't know how many LGBTQ youth complete suicides every year. Autopsies don't reveal whether a person is straight or gay. What we DO know is that legalizing same-sex marriage was a step in the right direction for reducing the stigma associated with LGBTQ identities, improving psychological outcomes for youth, and reducing suicide attempts among all teens and particularly LGBTQ teens.

On Being Transgender: It's Not a Disorder

Wayne and Kelly Maines are parents of adopted identical twin boys, Jonas and Wyatt. As the twins grew older, Wyatt started insisting that he was a girl. Over the course of many years, Wyatt's parents had Wyatt's name changed to Nicole.

Pulitzer Prize-winning journalist Amy Ellis Nutt interviewed the Maines. What follows is an edited version of their interview, which aired on National Public Radio's (NPR) program "Fresh Air." You can listen to the entire program at www.npr.org/sections/health-shots/2015/10/19/449937765/becoming-nicole-recounts-one-familys-acceptance-of-their-transgender-child

WAYNE MAINES: . . . If I would say to her, "You don't want to be a girl," she'd say, "Yes I do." I'm a forty-year-old guy having this debate with this little kid and I'm losing, you know? It was hard. . . . You have this vision of what you think the American dream is and your family, and it's not what it is. I've learned more from my two children and Kelly than I ever thought possible. I learned that everybody needs to be who they need to be, and I learned that people, little children, know who they are at that age.

KELLY MAINES: Back then . . . the popular way of proceeding was gender neutral, try to keep her gender neutral. But Nicole did not like that at all. It took a while. I think it was about when she was seven . . . we had a birthday party for her and Jonas and we gave her all the boys' toys . . . and she was very unhappy and I looked at Wayne and I said, "That's it. I'm not doing this anymore. It's not working. She's angry. She's doubting herself. This is not healthy. She has to have a safe place here."

AMY ELLIS NUTT: It's not a disorder. The problem for kids, for transgender people, isn't *within,* it's without. In other words, their trouble with their gender identity comes essentially because others view them one way when they view themselves another. . . . Nicole was a child who was never unsure of who she was, but she knew there was a problem with how other people and the rest of the world viewed her. And *that's* where the dysphoria comes in—when there's a mismatch between what we expect and what, perhaps, the sexual anatomy says, and what the brain is telling us. . . . Essentially we all begin in life asexual and then certain genes and hormones kick in, and our sexual anatomy is determined to either have male genitalia and male reproductive organs, or female. However, scientists are learning that while that happens at six weeks, it's not until six *months* that the brain masculinizes or feminizes. That is, that the hormones in the brain determine if this is the brain of a girl or is this the brain of a boy? . . . Identical twins obviously have the exact same DNA. What they don't have is the exact same epigenome, which means not all of the genetic switches are turned off and on in identical ways. . . . There are very few people that are one hundred percent totally masculine or one hundred percent totally feminine. We have traits of both, and so, ordinarily, it's

"THE PROBLEM FOR KIDS, FOR TRANSGENDER PEOPLE, ISN'T WITHIN, IT'S WITHOUT."

something in between. I think people are feeling more comfortable now saying, "Yeah, I've never felt one hundred percent masculine, but I'm mostly masculine." And, I think, it has become a more comfortable society to say that in. But I think it's also because the science is now supporting that.

...

Up until 2015, trans people had largely been excluded from LGB studies and research. That changed with the *U.S. Transgender Survey (USTS)* that provides a detailed look at the experiences of transgender people.

Experiences of people who were out as transgender in K–12 or believed classmates, teachers, or school staff thought they were transgender	
Verbally harassed because people thought they were transgender:	**54%**
Not allowed to dress in a way that fit their gender identity or expression:	**52%**
Disciplined for fighting back against bullies:	**36%**
Physically attacked because people thought they were transgender:	**24%**
Believe they were disciplined more harshly because teachers or staff thought they were transgender:	**20%**
Left a school because the mistreatment was so bad:	**17%**
Sexually assaulted because people thought they were transgender:	**13%**
Expelled from school:	**6%**
One or more experiences listed:	**77%**
Source: *USTS* Report	

It's not pretty. Transgender people are twice as likely to be living in poverty compared to the general population and three times more likely to be unemployed. Respondents reported higher than average rates of harassment, violence, and psychological distress. One-third reported issues in seeking healthcare, while 30 percent said they had at some time been homeless.

Hope

Despite all the challenges transgender kids and adults face, there is hope. More trans people are out and proud. Their voices have been lifted. The media have begun to tell the trans story in TV programs like *Transparent*, *Orange Is the New Black*, and *Faking It*, and in movies such as *Dallas Buyers Club* and *The Danish Girl*, based on a book by the same name. For young people and adults to see a version of themselves makes them feel less isolated, more accepted.

What holds true for LGB youth and young adults holds true for the transgender community. Family support and peer support can make a big difference in confidence, happiness, and optimism.

Amazon's award-winning TV show *Transparent* features the story of Mort Pfefferman, the father of three, who is transitioning from male to female, with a new name of Maura. She and Shea, a transgender female (in life as well as an actress), yoga teacher, and a friend, are role playing as Maura prepares for her new volunteer position as a suicide hotline "counselor." Shea plays the role of the "suicidal teen."

SHEA: I just feel like no one understands me.
MAURA: I've felt like that. I know what you're saying. You know, 'There's always darkness before the storm? Dawn?

SHEA: And I'm dead.
MAURA: This is hard . . . really hard.

SHEA: I know it's okay. You just have to get in there and intercept what they're feeling. They're about to harm themselves. You have to keep them from harming themselves. Okay?

MAURA: Yeah . . . okay. This is harder than I thought.

SHEA: I've had those thoughts.

MAURA: This is you?

SHEA nods.

MAURA: Oh, my God.

SHEA: Suicide . . . and sometimes I feel like it would be easier if I wasn't here.

MAURA: When was this?

SHEA: Freshman year of high school. Sophomore year. All of high school . . . and into college. . . . Pretty much until about three years ago and, um . . . I don't know . . . I guess I still have my days.

MAURA: Still?

SHEA nods.

MAURA: Now, you listen to me. When you have these thoughts, you'll call me, right? I mean the slightest thought like that. I mean, really, you call me.

Because I'll come over and tell you how fantastic and wonderful and unique and what a gorgeous soul you are and what a crappy, fucked-up world this would be without you. Do you understand me?

SHEA nods.

MAURA wraps her arms around SHEA and they hold each other.

SHEA: You're such a good mom.

Strategies:

Valuable Resources

Although Shea still has moments when she thinks about suicide, she is strong and resilient. She surrounds herself with friends like Maura and a wider community that affirms who she is and the life choices she's made. For Shea and all transgender people—for the LGBTQ community as a whole—the overarching message seems to be: focus on resilience, not risk; make decisions that feel right for YOU; develop ways to talk to yourself and identify your strengths and never be afraid to ask for help.

For a complete list:
www.youthallies.com/lgbt-youth-resources/national/

Faith in America
www.faithinamerica.org
Faith In America's mission is to educate the public about the harm caused when misguided religious teaching is used to place a religious and moral stamp of disapproval and inequality on the lives of gay and lesbian Americans, with emphasis on its horrific impact on youth and families.

Family Acceptance Project
http://familyproject.sfsu.edu
The Family Acceptance Project of the University of San Francisco has conducted invaluable research on the ways in which parental acceptance of LGBT youth impacts the health and safety of LGBT youth.

GayFamilySupport.com
www.gayfamilysupport.com
Gayfamilysupport.com is a website with an abundance of information and resources dedicated to assisting families support their LGBT children.

Gay, Lesbian & Straight Education Network (GLSEN)
www.glsen.org
GLSEN seeks to develop school climates where difference is valued for the positive contribution it makes to creating a more vibrant and diverse community.

GSA Network
www.gsanetwork.org
"Gay-Straight Alliance Network is a youth leadership organization that connects school-based Gay-Straight Alliances (GSAs) to each other and community resources through peer support, leadership development, and training."

It Gets Better Project
www.itgetsbetter.org
The It Gets Better Project was created to show young LGBT people the levels of happiness, potential, and positivity their lives will reach—if they can just get through their teen years. The It Gets Better Project wants to remind teenagers in the LGBT community that they are not alone—and it WILL get better.

PFLAG
www.pflag.org
PFLAG is the largest organization in the nation offering support to parents, families and friends of LGBT persons. They have numerous local chapters around the country where parents can find information and the support of other parents of LGBT children.

Trans Student Equality Resources
www.transstudent.org
"Trans Student Equality Resources is a youth-led organization dedicated to improving the educational environment for trans and gender nonconforming students through advocacy and empowerment. We believe that trans and gender nonconforming youth should be allowed the same opportunities and respect enjoyed by their peers and that education is a matter of civil rights."

TransYouth Family Allies

www.imatyfa.org

"TYFA empowers children and families by partnering with educators, service providers and communities to develop supportive environments in which gender may be expressed and respected." The organization envisions "a society free of suicide and violence in which ALL children are respected and celebrated."

The Trevor Project

www.thetrevorproject.org

The Trevor Project is a national organization providing crisis intervention and suicide prevention services to lesbian, gay, bisexual, transgender and questioning young people ages 13-24.

CHAPTER NINE | **CONNECTIONS**

If you ever find yourself stuck in the middle of the sea,

I'll sail the world to find you

If you ever find yourself lost in the dark and you can't see,

I'll be the light to guide you

Find out what we're made of

When we are called to help our friends in need

"Count On Me" — *Bruno Mars*

As Bruno wrote, a friend will sail around the world to find you, guide you when you can't see, and help find what you and he are "made of." And he's right: most good friends will do whatever it takes to be there for each other. There's a hitch, though. It's not always so easy to deal with heavy feelings like depression—even suicide. What are the "right" things to say?

What if you mess up? What if you make things worse?

Here's the deal: some of you are born with the "listening" gene and know exactly what to say, when and how. But if you're like most of us, when it comes to dealing with complex problems, you feel like you did on the first day of high school (or middle school)—lost, nervous, confused.

So, stick around. The stories and strategies coming your way will help you know what to say and do when a friend needs your help.

JOSH'S STORY

Josh started giving things away—his books, his calculators, his good pens. He wouldn't need them anymore. Josh had had enough. He couldn't stand the pressure: all the pushing to stay at the top of his class, to get all A's, to get into the best college. He was tired. The pain was too much.

Josh had decided to take his own life.

He walked home from school alone, working out the details of his suicide.

"Hey, Josh," his friend, Dylan, yelled, interrupting his thoughts.

Why did Dylan have to bother him now? Josh kept walking.

"Wait up!" Dylan said again, as he ran to catch up with Josh.

Josh didn't stop.

"What's wrong with you?" Dylan asked, out of breath, once he'd caught up.

"Nothing."

"Why didn't you wait?"

"Didn't feel like it."

"Didn't feel like it? Well, screw you!"

"Yeah, screw me. That's what I'm about to do."

Dylan was surprised. Why was Josh acting so hostile? "Something bothering you?" he asked.

"Yeah . . . lots of things."

"Like what?"

"Like I've had it up to here," he said, pointing to his neck.

"What could possibly be wrong with you?" Dylan asked. "Your life is all set."

"That's what you think," Josh mumbled.

"That's what I know. You've got it all together. Valedictorian of the senior class . . . Harvard freshman. What more could you ask for?"

"Plenty."

"Come on, Josh, you're acting crazy."

"I feel crazy. I'm all messed up inside." He paused. Should he even bother?

"You? Messed up? Come on, you've got to be joking."

Fine. He'd tell him. "I'm going to kill myself."

Dylan looked at his friend. He couldn't be serious. Not Josh.

"I mean it. I want to die," Josh said, as if reading Dylan's thoughts.

"That's the dumbest thing I've ever heard."

"Dumb to you, maybe . . ."

Dylan started to laugh. "Here's Mr. Together telling me he wants to die. Give me a break."

Josh was angry. "I'll give you a break," he said as he walked away. "You'll never have to deal with me again!"

Dylan stood and watched his best friend practically trip over his own feet in his hurry to get away. Josh was upset. He'd cool off. Everything would be fine.

Everything was not fine. Dylan followed his plan and took his own life.

...

Josh had taken a big risk by letting Dylan in on his problems and his plan. But Dylan hadn't taken him seriously. Dylan couldn't believe that someone who apparently had everything going for him would want to kill himself. He was sure Josh was joking. And when Josh told Dylan he was dead serious, Dylan kicked him to the curb. He told him it was the dumbest thing he'd ever heard. Dylan's inability to listen to Josh without criticizing— without judging—made Josh angry. Here he had opened up and tried to talk about his suicidal feelings, and all he'd gotten was a supposed friend who thought it was all one big joke.

Here's Take Two of the same story. Only this time, I've changed the dialogue to give you some ideas how Dylan could have reacted and said things differently.

DYLAN'S STORY TAKE 2

When Dylan saw Josh giving things away, he thought it was a bit strange. What was Josh doing? Didn't he need his books, calculators, and pens?

Dylan pulled Josh aside after lunch. "Why are you giving all your stuff away?" he asked.

"Don't need it," Josh mumbled. "Don't need anything."

Dylan was confused. Josh wasn't making sense. "I don't get it," he said.

"Nobody gets it. That's the point."

Josh was talking in circles. "You sound unhappy," Dylan said.

"I'm not feeling too great. That's for sure."

"Interested in talking? If you are, I'm willing to listen."

Should he tell him? "The pressure is too much. My parents, school, myself . . ."

Dylan felt sorry for him. "It must be rough trying to get all A's."

Josh nodded.

"When I was up for Most Valuable Player of the baseball team, I was so nervous. I couldn't concentrate on hitting the ball."

"I know what you mean," Josh said sadly.

Dylan was afraid. "You're not thinking of doing anything crazy, are you?"

Josh stared down at his shoes.

"Come on, Josh, fill me in."

Okay. He'd tell him. "I'm going to kill myself."

"You're really down, aren't you?"

"Yeah." He started to cry. "I can't take it anymore."

Dylan bit the inside of his lip. He couldn't panic. Not now. He'd have to take charge. "I'm worried about you," he said sincerely.

"Thanks."

"I want to help."

"Nobody can help."

Dylan had to think fast. "How about talking to Ms. Dreiser?"

"She wouldn't understand."

"Why not try her? You might be surprised."

Josh was tired. "I can handle it. Really, I can."

"I won't leave you alone," Dylan said. "You're my best friend. I won't let you hurt yourself."

Josh was relieved. He slumped down on the floor in front of his locker, knowing that Dylan meant what he had said.

Strategies:

Listening

So, why do you think Dylan was more successful this time around in getting his friend to calm down and believe that Dylan really cared?

- He listened instead of interrupting

- He let Josh say what he had to say without judging him, putting him down, telling him what he should do

- He "mirrored" what Josh was saying. "You sound unhappy." "It must be tough having to get all A's." "I know what you mean."

- He vowed that he wouldn't leave Josh alone and told him how much he cared. "You're my best friend. I won't let you **hurt** yourself."

Your Friends Are the First to Know

When you have a problem, where do your turn? If you're like the majority of your fellow teens, you turn to a friend or to a trained peer leader.

Let's face it: us older folks (yep, me, too) have a harder time remembering what it's like to be a teen. We think back on *our* teenage years as the "best time of their lives." We can't remember how much pressure there was to get good grades. We've forgotten the pain of breaking up with a boyfriend or girlfriend. (Well, maybe.) We don't recall those

> **OLDER FOLKS HAVE A HARDER TIME REMEMBERING WHAT IT'S LIKE TO BE A TEEN.**

days when being like everyone else was more important than anything in the world. But your friends? That's totally different. They know what's up and are right there with you, trying to make some sense out of it all.

Strategies:

Mirroring ("Mirror On The Wall—")

The trick of good listening is getting people to talk about themselves and their feelings. One of the best ways to help someone better understand their feelings is to be a mirror, to reflect back the feelings you think you hear and see.

> **THE TRICK OF GOOD LISTENING IS GETTING PEOPLE TO TALK ABOUT THEMSELVES AND THEIR FEELINGS.**

(Okay. I didn't come up with the mirror image idea. That was someone a lot more adept at all this listening skill talk than I am. In fact, I first heard about this when I took a parent effectiveness training program because my then two-year-old son was out of control. But that's another story for another time.)

Here's how mirroring works: a good friend of yours wanted the nomination for class president but didn't get it. Looking defeated, he says: "I didn't get the nomination. There were too many people more qualified than me."

After giving yourself enough time to think about what your friend was feeling and what made him feel that way, you might say: "You're feeling that the other kids are better than you because you weren't nominated."

You reflected, or mirrored, your friend's hurt feelings ("You're feeling the other kids are better than you".) and you told him why you thought he was feeling hurt ("because you weren't nominated."). Feedback is what's going on here. Not repetition. If you simply repeated what was said, you'd get your friend angry in a hurry. He'd think you were nothing more than an annoying recording app on a cell phone.

Fine, you think. This mirroring business sounds like it may work, but is there a pattern you can follow until you get the hang of it? Some people like using this format: You feel _____because

_____. But don't think you're locked into this pattern. You can change *You feel* to *You're feeling, You sound, You seem,* or anything else that works. You can change *because* to *about, with, at,* or *by.* The important thing is that you catch the meaning behind the words and restate what you think you hear. Unless you have psychic powers, you can't read your friend's mind. So don't tell him what's going on. Mirror what you *think* he has said. If you're checking out a hunch—not playing a know-it-all—you'll have a much better chance of getting your friend to talk.

Here is an example of how mirroring works.

JASMINE: I don't see why my mother won't let me go to the party.
SUE: You're angry because your mom won't let you go.

JASMINE: I sure am! She's so unfair.
SUE: You think she's not treating you right.

JASMINE: I know she's not. She said I had to finish my homework, and I did. She doesn't believe me.
SUE: You're upset because she doesn't think you're telling the truth.

JASMINE: She never believes me.
SUE: Can you show her your assignment notebook and the completed homework?

JASMINE: Maybe.
SUE: You're not sure whether she'll change her mind.

JASMINE: My mother is very stubborn.
SUE: That frustrates you, because it's hard to get her to see things your way.

JASMINE: You said it! But maybe if I cool down and talk to her nicely, she'll let me go to the party.

Take it from me: mirroring requires practice. It's so easy to get caught up in the moment and burst right in with your own reactions or suggestions. "Your mother can't let go. She has to be in control." Oops. That's not going to cut it. You'll just get your friend more tied up than she already is. Nothing will be solved. Matters will probably be worse. So, take a deep breath, put yourself in your friend's shoes and give mirroring a shot. (BTW, this mirroring technique works in all kinds of situations: in "sparring" with a sibling or parent; working on an issue with your current partner (if there is one); dealing with a teacher whom you feel is asking too much of you or not acknowledging the time you're putting in to class.)

Strategies:

When a Friend Won't Talk

Even the best listeners (including trained professionals) run into people who won't talk. What's next? First, you might try making a guess about nonverbal messages . . . eye and facial expressions, gestures, and posture. If your friend is smiling, or gritting her teeth, or fidgeting, say something like: "You seem happy." "Looks like you're angry." "You seem really nervous." Your friend may tell you you're off base. Or your "guess" may open up a good conversation. "I'm nervous. You can say that again! My parents are going to kill me when they see these grades."

Another way to get a conversation going is to ask a question. "How's it going with you and Marc?" You may get a one-word answer: "Okay," "Great," "Fine"—all ways of saying "I don't feel like talking." Or your simple question could start an interesting talk.

"How's it going with Marc?"

"Not so hot. He's never interested in doing anything."

"You're bored because of it?"

"I'm losing interest fast!"

"Sounds like you're thinking of breaking up with him."

"Yeah, but if I do that, who is there left to go out with?"

Once the listener asked a direct question and got an answer, she used mirroring to reflect what she thought her friend was feeling and why. Mirroring encouraged her friend to talk more about her boyfriend and why she was unhappy with him. It showed her friend that she was listening carefully and that she cared.

Strategies:

Paying Attention to Nonverbal Clues

Believe it or not, you can say a lot without uttering a word. How? The way you look at a person, your posture, the way you move all give clear messages about how you're feeling. You're not convinced? Picture this: You finally get up the nerve to tell your best friend that you think you need psychiatric help. Your whole world is caving in. Nothing is going right.

Take One

"I've got to talk to you," you say. Your friend looks away.

"Come on, it's really important."

Your friend shuffles back and forth, flipping the pages of the book he's holding.

"I need to talk to you, and you couldn't care less."

"Who said I don't care? Did I say that?"

"No, you didn't say it . . . well, not exactly. But that's what you're telling me."

What went wrong? Why did you lose faith in your friend and his interest in what you had to say? Your friend didn't make eye contact with you; he looked away. He moved around while you were talking and fidgeted with his book. His actions told you he wasn't really interested in what you were saying, even though he denied not caring.

Take Two

"I've got to talk to you."

Your friend looks you straight in the eye.

"I think I need psychiatric help."

Your friend leans forward.

"Nothing is going right. Nothing."

Several people walk by the two of you in the school corridor. Your friend doesn't seem to notice.

"The minute I wake up, I feel sick to my stomach. The feeling never goes away."

Right off the bat, your friend showed you he was interested in what you had to say. He made eye contact but didn't stare. That made you want to keep talking. "I think I need psychiatric help." There. You said it. Would he laugh in your face? No. Instead, he leaned forward.

You kept talking. Other people walked by the two of you in the school corridor, but your friend still concentrated on you and what you were saying. His actions told you that he wanted to hear more and really cared.

Strategies:

How to Ask Good Questions

You've keyed in on a friend's nonverbal messages—her dejected look and lack of energy—and "guessed" that she is depressed. Almost inaudibly, she admits you're right and mumbles something about "hurting so much she wishes she could die." You give yourself enough time to word your response and then say, "You must be very unhappy if you're talking about death." Your friend doesn't answer. She probably knows that you're willing to listen, but doesn't have the strength to talk. You can wait her out or you can try asking some good questions. Asking questions is the key to finding out more information and to deciding where you might go for help.

Questions that can be answered with a "yes," "no," or defensive response won't get you anywhere.

"Are you still having trouble at home?"

"Yes."

"Why don't you talk to your parents?"

"I can't."

"Do you think you should talk to a counselor?"

"No."

Questions like these don't encourage a friend to share information. They may even cut off your attempt at conversation.

Questions that do encourage sharing often begin with *where, when, what, who, which,* or *how.*

"*What* is making you feel so down?"

"*When* did your parents separate?"

"*How* are you going to talk to them?"

These kinds of questions usually keep a conversation going. They ask for information that you need or for feelings that your friend can share. Yet asking a good question does not guarantee that your friend will open up. The way you ask the question—your tone of voice and the nonverbal messages you send—matter. No one who is challenged is likely to want to talk. But even so, the tone of your voice and your nonverbal messages can fail, even if your question is a good one and your heart is in the right place.

...

Whether or not you are a trained listener/peer leader or just someone who doesn't shy away from talking about tough subjects, the bottom line is this: you are **not responsible for solving anyone else's problems**—particularly when it comes to things as serious as suicide. It is not in your job description to prevent someone from taking her own life. **It *is* in that description to listen and then serve as a connection to a "trusted" adult—a teacher, counselor,**

coach, member of the clergy, a parent. This adult is probably well-liked and easy to talk to. But he is not the big boss in the chain of command. Let's say you talk to Mr. Lyons, the high school science teacher. He's a great guy, but his deal is science, not kids who are thinking about suicide. His job? He needs to go to *his* list of experienced professionals who *are* trained in working with troubled teens and connect that person with the teen considering suicide.

Suicide Prevention Programs That Make the Grade

So, what can be done to switch things up so that you or your peers who are having problems can find the support you need? Sadly, there are very few suicide prevention programs in middle schools because the majority of staff still operate on the misconception that talking about suicide (and other issues) encourages those at the top of the waterfall to take the plunge.

There are plenty of suicide prevention programs in high schools and beyond, some small in scope, some national and international. What makes the good programs work is that students are involved from the get go. They are the movers and shakers, the peer leaders, the ones upfront who go upstream. It's not a top down hierarchy where teachers are in charge and students follow their lead. It's just the opposite: students set the agenda, create the game plans; their opinions and ideas drive the program. "They create a recognition that it's okay to be helped and there are people who can be there," says Dorothy Espelage, professor of Psychology, University of Florida, an expert in bullying along with sexual and dating violence.

> **WHAT MAKES THE GOOD PROGRAMS WORK IS THAT STUDENTS ARE INVOLVED FROM THE GET GO.**

I was in the middle of my interview with Espelage when she said that I absolutely must get in touch with Scott LoMurray, executive director of a program called Sources of Strength. I made a note to check out their website and call LoMurray. (You might recall that I borrowed his parable about the man walking by a river who saw kids falling over a waterfall.) LoMurray was happy to talk and share what he and his staff have learned over the years about how to empower students and local communities to identify kids at risk long before they are considering taking their lives.

Before I tell you all about Sources of Strength, I want to survey a few other suicide prevention programs big and small. There is Buddies Helping Buddies, the brainchild of Gabby Frost who was in high school when she launched her program. "It's more like pen pals," she says, "where we match you with a buddy who shares the same interests and age. This is not an alternative for therapy or counseling. It is made to help buddies make a friend who can be there during good and rough times." Since its inception in 2013, more than 170,000 people have signed up. On the organization's website, (www.buddy-project.org) Gabby writes, "Having just one friend to support you through the hardships of your life can really make a difference. I created Buddy Project to show that to the world."

The website includes a valuable list of help lines. (Some of these numbers can be found earlier in this book.)

Strategies:

Suicide Hotlines:

Crisis Text Line (24/7 and confidential):
text START to 741-741

Trevor Project:
1-866-488-7386

Sexuality Support:
1-800-246-7743

Trans Lifeline:
877-565-8860

Rape and Sexual Assault:
1-800-656-4673

Runaway:
1-800-843-5200, 1-800-843-5678, 1-800-621-4000

After Abortion Hotline/Pro-Voice:
1-866-439-4253

Self Harm:
1-800-DONT CUT (1-800-366-8288)

Pregnancy Hotline :
1-800-4-OPTIONS (1-800-467-8466)

Gay, Lesbian, Bisexual, and Transgender (GLBT) Youth Support Line:
800-850-8078

National Association for Children of Alcoholics:
1-888-55-4COAS (1-888-554-2627)

National Child Abuse Hotline:
1-800-422-4453

National Drug Abuse Hotline:
1-800-662-HELP (1-800-662-4357)

Eating Disorders Awareness and Prevention:
1-800-931-2237 (Hours:8am-noon daily, PT)

Adolescent Suicide Helpline:
1-800-621-4000

Fire Within

Fire Within was developed under the tutelage of Sally Spencer Thomas, CEO and cofounder of the Carson J. Spencer Foundation. Carson was Sally's brother. He took his life in 2004. In the hopes of helping prevent more suicides, Thomas and friends came at

Fire Within from an entrepreneurial point of view. Her brother was an entrepreneur and business leader. "We wanted to honor the way he lived and address the way he died."

Thomas's beef with some other suicide prevention programs is that they either follow the "State Trooper Effect" or count on adults (teachers and counselors). Maybe your school has a program like this that is well-intentioned but not very successful. Why? Because adults are usually the last people to know if you or a friend is in crisis. Or maybe the school administration organizes an assembly with a speaker

ADULTS ARE USUALLY THE LAST PEOPLE TO KNOW IF YOU OR A FRIEND IS IN CRISIS.

who can talk about teen suicide. Or maybe students hang up anti-suicide and anti-bullying posters on the hallway walls or in the bathroom stalls. "The problem," says Thomas "is that you're paying attention but, once the speaker finishes or you've read the posters, everything is in the rearview mirror." (The "State Trooper Effect.") Once the speaker (substitute trooper) is gone, you revert to old behavior.

Fire Within differs from most, if not all, other suicide prevention programs with its emphasis on the "business" skills required to launch a successful prevention program: a business plan, market research, budget and financing. Then the students get an introduction to the public health approach to suicide prevention and how they can evaluate who is distressed, what's driving that distress and what resources are out there to assist in helping folks upstream (sound familiar?) before there's a crisis.

As of this writing, the Carson J. Spencer Foundation is ceasing operations at the end of June 2017. The Fire Within program will be continuing but not until the 2018/2019 school year. Suicide prevention will remain one of the social issues, as will mental health awareness, homelessness, domestic violence prevention and more.

The Trevor Project: "Saving Young Lives" in the LGBTQ Community

The Trevor Project itself was founded in 1998 and takes its name from an eighteen-minute movie that tells the story of a thirteen-year-old who ends up attempting suicide as he tries to make sense of being gay.

The organization's twenty-four-hour suicide hotline serves LGBTQ youth who are struggling with their gender identity and thoughts of harming themselves. Some are depressed, possibly contemplating suicide. Others have questions about coming out to family and friends, bullying, homelessness, and sexual and physical abuse.

Strategies:

Where to Get Help

Trevor Lifeline: 866-488-7386

The 24/7 lifeline is staffed by highly trained volunteers supported by a professional staff. The Lifeline handles forty-five thousand calls per year.

In an article published in *The Daily Beast**, an online news and entertainment site, Amet Paley, Trevor Project CEO, praised the volunteers and the crucial role they play in changing—sometimes, saving—the lives of an LGBTQ youth.

"The volunteers here change lives," Paley said. "Someone may be on the brink of killing themselves, and there is no higher calling than saving the lives of people in crisis. This type of work is always with you, but that's okay. It's such a privilege and blessing to be able to spend my professional life doing something like this."

---

* https://www.thedailybeast.com/the-trevor-project-hears-every-day-how-president-trump-is-putting-lgbt-teens-in-danger

You've heard the stories about bullying and how harmful it can be. And you're up on how bullying can be even worse for LGBTQ kids. To complicate matters, online emotional abuse can be done anonymously, and the victim has no way of escaping. He or she is not safe. The comments can be spread to a much wider audience. "The emotional impact can be much greater," says David Bond, VP of Programs, the Trevor Project. "Yet young people have a compulsive need to check social media. 'What are they saying now?' That's where TrevorSpace comes in. It is not open to the public. It's like Facebook for LGBTQ youth."

TrevorSpace: www.trevorspace.org
A social networking site for LGBTQ young people ages thirteen through twenty-four and their friends and allies.

LGBTQ youth can chat with a TrevorChat counselor seven days a week between 3 p.m. to 10 p.m. ET/12 p.m. to 7 p.m. PT. And there are other resources as well: 1-866-488-7386

TrevorText: 1-202-304-1200
A confidential, secure resource that provides live help for LGBTQ youth with a trained specialist, over text messages.

...

Whichever tool seems the most comfortable, they all share the same basic philosophy for those who call or chat or text:

- Your life is worth living.

- You are loved.

- You have dignity.

- Who you love and who you are does not lessen you as a person.

- There are people all around the world who not only think there is nothing wrong with being a LGBTQ youth but who celebrate their gender diversity.

- You are strong and courageous for picking up the phone, using Trevor Space, TrevorText, or TevorSpace and sharing your story and concerns.

Based on the premise that young people reveal more to friends than to their parents and other adults (ring a bell?), The Trevor Project also supports student awareness of the warning signs, risk factors, and ways to help a friend or peer under stress with what they call their Lifeguard Workshop, a free online program. You can check out the video and other resources at: www.thetrevorproject.org/pages/lifeguard

Sources of Strength – Peers Rule

What do you do if you are the civilian director of the Police Youth Bureau in Bismarck, North Dakota, and you attend thirty funerals in three years—many of them for teens who took their own lives? Well, you could be frustrated and upset and not know where to turn. You could continue with the same-old suicide prevention programs that were failing. Or you could create a new kind of program that puts kids and their ideas smack dab in the middle. That's what Mark LoMurray, the aforementioned civilian director, chose to do. His idea was to train peer leaders to listen, to help shift the culture in schools and to be the first line of defense for kids who were struggling **before** there was a crisis. LoMurray's idea ultimately morphed into Sources of Strength (SOS), a program now in thirty states with well over 10,000 trained high school students called peer leaders.

You and your friends have a lot more information at your fingertips than adults did at your age. You have the Internet, social media, 24/7 cable news (back in the day, there were only three news channels), images and shows/movies that would have been X-rated . . . You are exposed to a lot, and many of your ideas are more creative than any adult might imagine.

Example: SOS peer leaders in one school came up the brainy idea to dress up as bears and walk the school hallways, giving hugs all around. Other students thought it was weird, maybe crazy but, in the end, it was a fun experience that changed the culture in the school that day.

What sets SOS apart from other suicide prevention programs is that kids are involved from the beginning. Their ideas drive the program. They have a seat at the head of the table, not at the "kiddie" table in another room.

Now don't get me wrong: not everyone who is either nominated or signs up to become an SOS peer leader is gung ho about what they've gotten themselves into. Take Bethanne. "I was a bit skeptical at first. How is this program going to help kids who are suicidal? But the more I got into it, the more I realized that, as a peer leader, I could become someone who was a safe bet when someone just wanted to talk. And if they were in crisis, I knew right away how to go to a trusted adult who could get them the help they needed."

"When kids walk in the door for training, you can see the skepticism on their faces," says Jon Widmier, Director of Student Services in Golden, Colorado. "They're wondering whether signing up for a suicide peer program is a good idea. But then you see them despite themselves begin to warm up and to open up about what's going well in their lives."

Scott LoMurray is the elder LoMurray's son and manages the day-to-day operations at SOS. "Everyone gets knocked down in life," he says. "The challenge is to get back up in ways that are healthy."

SOS, says LoMurray, trains peer leaders to be the eyes and ears of their fellow students. They are the models of change. SOS, he stresses, is a wellness model that not only deals with suicide prevention but

"EVERYONE GETS KNOCKED DOWN IN LIFE. THE CHALLENGE IS TO GET BACK UP IN WAYS THAT ARE HEALTHY."

also with drug/alcohol abuse, unwanted pregnancy, and academic difficulties. "We are not merely trying to intervene but to prevent these problems from happening in the first place." SOS is not a one-shot deal. Kids are in the program for at least a year—usually, more.

When students sign up or are nominated to become an SOS peer leader, they are not faced with a lot of lecturing by adults. Instead, there are a whole host of materials, games, videos that empower them to have "skin in the game." It is their voice, supported by trained adults, that drives the program.

Peer leaders are **NOT** counselors. They are students who **do** break the code of silence that prevents some kids from "snitching" about a friend's problems. They never feel as if they are out there alone; they know they have competent backup to whom they can turn when a student swims into rough water without the tools to swim back to safety.

Another cool thing about SOS is that peer leaders are not just the all A students but students representing all kinds of groups: geeks; creative folks; athletes; punk rockers; LGBTQ teens; different ethnic groups . . . You name a group, and they have a voice. No one feels left out, excluded.

Check out an online SOS video at https://sourcesofstrength. org/. And hear what peer leaders are saying about SOS at https:// sourcesofstrength.org/

SOS Spinoffs: We Have Your Back

One of these programs, Cobbler2Cobbler, is a good example of a team that is doing a great job employing the principles of Sources of Strength and making it their own.

> **"We are knocking down the barriers between freshmen and the rest of the people in the school. We talk about suicide honestly. It's not like Romeo and Juliet. It's not romanticized at all."** — *Callan, 18*

"When kids aren't going to listen to their teachers, I can talk to them because we're around the same age. We hear things the adults don't." — *Tylor, 18*

This year, there are eighty juniors and seniors who've gone through a rigorous Cobbler2Cobbler training program before they can "get out there" as mentors. Like the more than ten thousand peer leaders that SOS has trained since it began, mentors in Cobbler2Cobbler key in on any student who may just want to talk or who is struggling with a serious problem.

There used to be a teen suicide every other month in Rapid City High School. Since the fall of 2011, there have been none.

Talk about success!

What Now?

Now that you have all the goods, what's your next move? Encourage your school to start a suicide prevention like Sources of Strength? Call any of the many hotlines when you need to talk to someone? Become a better listener? Do your part to stop bullying? Appreciate the extra stress many LGBTQ teens experience? Find a trusted adult to help you work through some rough patches? Focus on what's good about your life? Be a good friend who will "come running" wherever you are?

Suicide *is* preventable. No one has to die because they feel hopeless, helpless, disconnected. To use the upstream parable one last time, it's crucial to make it to calm waters, learn the ways you can navigate without going under—without falling over the waterfall. Give yourself kudos for a job well done. Understand that, when you need it, asking for help is a brave and healthy thing to do. And if you have a friend who is grappling with an issue big or small, help him by listening and then, if necessary, connecting him to an adult who will take it from there. You have all the tools to help break the cycle of teen suicide.

Hey, ain't it good to know that you've got a friend? People can be so cold.

They'll hurt you and desert you.

Well, they'll take your soul if you let them, oh yeah, but don't you let them.

You just call out my name, and you know where ever I am I'll come running to see you again.

Winter, spring, summer, or fall, all you have to do is call, Lord, I'll be there, yeah, yeah, you've got a friend. You've got a friend.

Ain't it good to know you've got a friend. Ain't it good to know you've got a friend.

Oh, yeah, yeah, you've got a friend.

"You've Got a Friend" – James Taylor

Other Books by Jane Leder

Dead Serious: A Book for Teenagers about Teenage Suicide (1st edition)

Brothers&Sisters: How They Shape Our Lives

The Sibling Connection: How Siblings Shape Our Lives

Thanks For The Memories: Love, Sex, and World War II

⊦RΛƆICΛL

WITH DAVID PLATT

Radical with David Platt, a half-hour national teaching program, airs daily on Moody Radio. Bestselling author, sought-after conference speaker, and pastor, David Platt brings to each program solid, passionate Bible teaching aimed at equipping and mobilizing Christians to make disciples among the nations so that the Lord receives the glory due His name.

www.radicalwithdavidplatt.org

MOODYRADIO

Where you turn. For life.

rightnow MEDIA

FREE ONLINE STREAMING OF THE
LIFE ON MISSION
YOUTH VIDEO BIBLE STUDY

FOR PURCHASING THE *LIFE ON MISSION*
BOOK, YOU GET FREE ACCESS TO THESE
BIBLE STUDY VIDEOS – PERFECT FOR
YOUTH MINISTRY OR PERSONAL DEVOTION.

TO ACCESS THESE VIDEOS FOR 90 DAYS,
VISIT RightNowMedia.org/LifeOnMission
AND USE PROMO CODE: **VFN8C3QN**

LIFE ON MISSION:
5-Session Bible Study

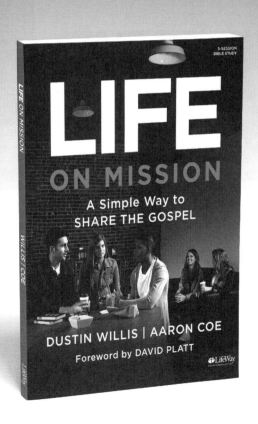

The good news of God's grace must be spoken. Other than one's own salvation, there may not be a greater joy than explaining the gospel and watching God do what only He can do: save people. We have developed a 5-week video-driven Bible study for groups. This study walks through God's heart for His mission and what it practically looks like to intentionally share the gospel.

LifeOnMissionbook.com
Releases November 1, 2014

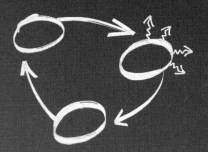

3 CIRCLES:
LIFE CONVERSATION GUIDE

Life change. It all begins with a conversation.

The gospel of Jesus Christ is the most profound reality of life. But sharing it with someone can be as simple as three circles. Discover how you can share the gospel with anyone using the Life Conversation Guide, a companion resource to the *Life On Mission* book.

sendnetwork.com/3Circles

Download the App

INTERESTED IN PARTNERING WITH SEND NORTH AMERICA?

MOBILIZE ME

namb.net/mobilizeme

Praise for *Li*

Willis and Coe give an inspiring and l........ .....o the world of everyday mission. They clearly lay out before us the challenge to reach North America and offer the gospel-centered, biblical approach to how God is going to build His church through the efforts of ordinary people.

MATT CARTER, pastor of preaching, Austin Stone Community Church and coauthor of *The Real Win*

Being on mission needs to be rerouted. It has been focused on methods and models more than shaped by the gospel, God's mission, and the person of Jesus. Read *Life on Mission* and find yourself being more driven to focus your life and mission on these.

ERIC M. MASON, pastor of Epiphany Fellowship and author of *Manhood Restored* and *Beat God to the Punch*

God calls and equips His people to serve in very specific contexts related to how He uniquely gifts them. Work is worship, and I realized that early in my NFL kicking career. Done in a God-honoring fashion, work screams to a dark, hurting world there is a Creator God who intends for His children to live a full, abundant life. This book challenges me to stay living "on mission" and to know that I am His handiwork created in Christ Jesus to do very specific great works He has prepared in advance for me to do. We are all "missionaries" and Aaron helps me remember God will accomplish immeasurably more in and through me than I could ever ask or imagine when I live "life on mission."

TODD PETERSON, NFL placekicker 1993–2006
Chairman, Pro Athletes Outreach

We must be intentional, passionate, and strategic in mobilizing the church on mission. I am convinced that *Life on Mission* can help us accomplish this, resulting in accelerating our commitment to reaching our region, North America, and the world.

RONNIE FLOYD, president of the Southern Baptist Convention and pastor of Cross Church, Northwest Arkansas

A compelling book that connects mission to worship and shows how one cannot really believe the gospel and not be moved into mission. This book does more than describe mission; it compels action.

J. D. GREEAR, pastor of The Summit Church and author of *Gospel: Recovering the Power That Made Christianity Revolutionary*

The Great Commission is not for a select, elite few. It is for the whole body of Christ. *Life on Mission* makes that argument and then shows us in practical, concrete ways how to join God in His mission to make His Name famous among all peoples near and far. We all have a choice, an opportunity, to be on mission no matter who we are, where we live, or what we do. So read this book with much profit. Read it and then get to work as God's missionary in the mission field He has placed you.

DANIEL L. AKIN, president, Southeastern Baptist Theological Seminary

We are all called as leaders to be on mission as agents of the gospel, not just those in full-time ministry. *Life on Mission* defines what this looks like, how you can get there, and the good news that we all need—our lives are meant to be on mission for God! Take your next step to being on mission wherever God has placed you. Read this book!

BRAD LOMENICK, author, *The Catalyst Leader* and former president and key visionary, Catalyst

Aaron Coe is one of the most dynamic leaders in contemporary evangelicalism. This book is a theologically rooted and practically applied primer on how to join Jesus in his mission. I can think of no one with more personal credibility to challenge us in this way. This book can change your perspective, and maybe even your life.

RUSSELL D. MOORE, president, Southern Baptist Ethics & Religious Liberty Commission

Dustin Willis hits a simple message that profoundly changed my life. Focus on God's agenda while you live life and you will begin to see that people all around you are lost and in need of a Savior. This book shows us the need to pray for people in our workplace, the grocery line, soccer fields, and even in our own family. Willis and Coe provide a simple framework to love these people in a natural and friendly way that brings glory to God. This book is must-read for those that want to have purpose in their work and play.

STEVE VON FANGE, vice president information systems, Blue Cross & Blue Shield of SC

The evangelical church in North America was not built on professional mission workers and physical church buildings. It was the Holy Spirit's use of everyday Christians living on mission, knowing their context, and seeing opportunities to start ministries and churches that fueled the spread of the gospel. This book goes a long way in helping equip God's people for the work of everyday mission and ministry.

TREVIN WAX, managing editor of The Gospel Project, author of *Gospel-Centered Teaching, Counterfeit Gospels,* and *Holy Subversion.*

LIFE
ON MISSION
Joining the Everyday Mission of God

DUSTIN WILLIS | AARON COE
WITH THE SEND NETWORK TEAM

MOODY PUBLISHERS
CHICAGO

Edited by Ginger Kolbaba
Interior design: Erik M. Peterson
Cover design: Faceout Studio and Marcus Williamson
Cover images: Shutterstock #94785715 / #160438778 / #150875567 / #39895024

Library of Congress Cataloging-in-Publication Data

Willis, Dustin.
   Life on mission : gospel, mission, ministry / Dustin Willis, Aaron Coe, with the Send Network Team.
      pages cm
   Includes bibliographical references.
   ISBN 978-0-8024-1221-8
   1. Missions—Textbooks. 2. Witness bearing (Christianity)—Textbooks.
3. Evangelistic work—Textbooks. I. Title.
   BV2090.W54 2014
   266--dc23
                                    2014008812

DEDICATION

To the thousands of missionaries who are working hard every day to make Jesus known in North America, many of whom are doing so without great fanfare and much financial reward.

One hundred percent of the royalties from this book will go directly toward supporting missionaries in North America through Send North America.

CONTENTS

FOREWORD BY DAVID PLATT   11

INTRODUCTION   17

THE BIG PICTURE

CHAPTER 1:   Everyday Missionary   25

CHAPTER 2:   The Current Reality   33

CHAPTER 3:   The Mission of God   39

CHAPTER 4:   Kingdom Realignment   45

GOSPEL FOUNDATIONS

CHAPTER 5:   The Gospel   59

CHAPTER 6:   Spiritual Maturity   75

CHAPTER 7:   Biblical Community   85

CHAPTER 8:   Intentional Discipleship   95

MISSION PRACTICES

CHAPTER 9:   Identify   107

CHAPTER 10:   Invest   119

CHAPTER 11:   Invite   129

CHAPTER 12:   Increase   141

MINISTRY STEPS

CHAPTER 13:   Pitfalls and Plans   151

APPENDIX: LEADER'S GUIDE: SIX-WEEK STUDY   161

NOTES   181

ACKNOWLEDGMENTS   184

"As the Father has sent Me, I also send you."
—JESUS (John 20:21)

FOREWORD

Ordinary people with extraordinary power preaching, praying, giving, and suffering for the spread of the gospel.

This is the picture of the early church that we see on the pages of the New Testament. A small band of twelve men responded to a life-changing invitation: "Follow me, and I will make you fishers of men" (Matthew 4:19). In the days to come, they watched Jesus, listened to Him, and learned from Him how to love, teach, and serve others the same way that He did. Then came the moment when they saw Him die on a cross for their sins, only to rise from the dead three days later. Soon thereafter, He gathered them on a mountainside and said to them, "All authority in heaven and on earth has been given to me. Therefore go and make disciples of all nations, baptizing them in the name of the Father and of the Son and of the Holy Spirit, and teaching them to obey everything I have commanded you. And surely I am with you always, to the very end of the age" (Matthew 28:18–20). Just like Jesus had said from the beginning, these followers would now become fishers of men. His authoritative commission would become their consuming ambition.

Not long thereafter, they gathered together with a small group of others, about 120 in all, and they waited. True to His promise, Jesus sent His Spirit to every one of them, and immediately they began proclaiming the gospel. In the days to come, they scattered from Jerusalem to Judea to Samaria to the ends of the earth, and within one generation, they grew to over four hundred times the size they were when they started.

How did this happen?

The spread of the gospel in the book of Acts took place primarily

because ordinary people empowered by an extraordinary presence were proclaiming the gospel everywhere they went. To be sure, God did appoint well-known apostles like Peter, John, and Paul for certain positions of leadership in the church. Yet it was anonymous Christians (i.e., not the apostles) who first took the gospel to Judea and Samaria, and it was unnamed believers who founded the church at Antioch, which became a base for mission to the Gentile world. It was un-identified followers of Jesus who spread the gospel throughout all of Asia. Disciples were made and churches were multiplied in places the apostles never went. The good news of Jesus spread not just through gifted preachers, but through everyday people whose lives had been transformed by the power of Christ. They were going from house to house and in marketplaces and shops along streets and travel routes, leading people to faith in Jesus on a daily basis.

This is how the gospel penetrated the world during the first cen-tury: through self-denying, Spirit-empowered disciples of Jesus who were making disciples of Jesus. Followers of Jesus were fishing for men. Disciples were making disciples. Christians were not known for casual association with Christ and His church; instead, they were known for complete abandonment to Christ and His cause. The great commis-sion was not a choice for them to consider but a command for them to obey. And though they faced untold trials and unthinkable perse-cution, they experienced unimaginable joy as they joined with Jesus in the advancement of His kingdom.

I want to be part of a movement like that. I want to be part of a people who really believe that we have the Spirit of God in each of us for the spread of the gospel through all of us. I want to be a part of a people who are gladly sacrificing the pleasures, pursuits, and posses-sions of this world because we are living for treasure in the world to come. I want to be part of a people who are forsaking every earthly ambition in favor of one eternal aspiration: to see disciples made and churches multiplied from our houses to our communities to our cities to the nations.

This kind of movement involves all of us. Every single follower of Christ fishing for men. Every single disciple making disciples. Ordinary people spreading the gospel in extraordinary ways all over the world. Men and women from diverse backgrounds with different gifts and distinct platforms making disciples and multiplying churches through every domain of society in every place on the planet. This is God's design for His church, and disciples of Jesus must not settle for anything less.

This kind of movement is what this book is all about. In the pages that lie ahead, Dustin Willis and Aaron Coe explain biblical foundations and explore practical implications for how God has designed your life to be a part of His purpose in the world. I encourage you not only to read this book but to apply it. And as you do, to join in what God is doing in your neighborhood, in North America and among the nations for the sake of His great name.

—David Platt

A weak gospel foundation leads to fragile mission practices.

INTRODUCTION

For almost nine years my wife and I (Aaron) served in New York City as church planters. I grew up in Kentucky in a little community outside of Louisville called Highview, which, at the time, was a three-stoplight town. Not an urban juggernaut by any stretch. My wife grew up in Oakway, South Carolina, which is home, even to this day, to one flashing stoplight. I was "uptown" and "citified" compared to her.

The New York metro area has about 22 million residents. This means approximately 27,000 people inhabit each square mile.[1] (For the sake of perspective, the state of Mississippi has about 63 people per square mile.)[2] So there were days when our "new" home city felt overwhelming. But we knew God had called us there for a purpose. A lot of New Yorkers don't know Jesus or attend church, and we were trying to start a church in a city that needed thousands more.

One day while walking through Manhattan, I prayed: "Lord, how are we going to reach all these people?" I felt so insignificant. I'll never forget God's answer: *Aaron, you are not going to reach New York City by yourself.* Then I felt God reveal that *He* would reach the city—by raising up hundreds of committed believers.

While lostness continues to pervade New York City and other global cities, God has chosen not to leave our communities in spiritual disrepair. He has made plans for ordinary men and women to make disciples and start churches in the unlikeliest and most unreached of places.

Maybe these churches won't be big by numerical standards or led by fully funded pastors with a paid church staff. But what I realized then and continue to see is the gospel moves forward on the shoulders of men and women willing to do the difficult work of making disciples.

By no means does Columbia, South Carolina, compare to the density and diversity of New York City, but seeing everyday, ordinary people live out God's mission is just as vital to that community. I (Dustin) will never forget examining a Columbia demographic study with the other pastors at my church. We could not shake the fact that 100,000 people within our city did not know Jesus. How could we display the gospel to every man, woman, and child? What event(s) would bring about transformation? What could we do?

Then one of the pastors laid out a map of Columbia and said, "Mark where you live." After seeing our names scattered across the map, we took this simple idea and produced an oversized map that displayed where every church member lived. We drew circles around sectors of the city where high concentrations of our members lived. We then marked dots for specific homes that could carry great influence within those neighborhoods, and then highlighted specific city blocks where we wanted to concentrate the most effort and support. While we knew that the idea of 100,000 people was not intimidating to God, seeing on a map where our members lived began to help us understand that exposing our city to the gospel was possible.

Strategically informing our people about those far from God who lived on their street or in their neighborhood and then empowering them to work together to live out the gospel with their neighbors moved us from an overwhelmed and paralyzed state to an encouraged place of movement. We realized that within our community a large event or new program wouldn't bring consistent transformation, but believers banding together to take responsibility for their dot on the map *would*.

YOUR LIFE MATTERS TO GOD'S MISSION

In the late 1930s my (Aaron) great-great-grandparents Lucinda and Samuel Clements moved from their home in Louisville, Kentucky, to an emerging suburban part of town. Upon their arrival, Grandma Lucy noticed that none of her new neighbors attended church.

Burdened by this reality she invited her neighbors to go to church with her. But when each Sunday rolled around, no one showed up. Being a feisty and persistent woman, she asked why they refused to go to church. She discovered that most of them didn't have a car or other means to travel to her church several miles away.

So Grandma Lucy determined that if her neighbors could not go to church, she would bring church to them. And in 1939, underneath a large tree in her front yard, Grandma Lucy started a Sunday school. At first, it was mostly made up of children, but over time adults began to attend too. After several years, enough people showed up that they turned that Sunday school into a church. Now, for almost nine decades, the ministry that Grandma Lucy started has been faithfully proclaiming the gospel.

It would have been easier for Lucinda Clements just to keep attending her home church, since she and my great-great-grandfather had a car. But she did not choose the easy path. As a result of her faithfulness and an understanding that her life on mission mattered, countless generations have been impacted for eternity.

The church in North America has been built by everyday missionaries such as Lucinda Clements. Throughout US history, as people settled new areas, they also started a church if one didn't exist. The Baptists had the "farmer/preacher" and the Methodists had the circuit riders. Believers understood that they were responsible to start a gospel work if none existed. As a result, in the early 1800s there was one Protestant church in the United States for every 875 people. By the beginning of World War I that ratio was one Christian church for every 430 people.[3] During that one-hundred-year span, church planting efforts significantly outpaced the population growth.

But after World War I something happened: church planting slowed

significantly. The population began to outpace new church planting and growth. Today, in places such as Alabama and Mississippi, there's one evangelical church for about every 750 people.[4] In states such as Indiana, Iowa, and Kansas, there is one evangelical church for every 1,500–1,800 people.[5] In states such as New Jersey and New York, there is one evangelical church for every 6,000–7,500 people.[6] The Northeast Corridor and Utah have the same lack of evangelical engagement as unreached people groups, with less than 2 percent claiming to be "born again" Christians.[7] In Canada the evangelical presence is as low as 0.5 percent in cities such as Montreal, and Canada as a whole is only about 7 percent evangelical.[8]

As you can see, we have work to do. We have an opportunity to pick up where previous generations have left off, but in order to do that we need to adopt their mindset: that every believer is to live a life on mission. No Christ-follower is exempt from using the gifts God has given for building His kingdom.

A CHURCH ON EVERY CORNER (IS NOT ENOUGH)

Most experts say that in order to effectively impact an area with the gospel you need to have one church for every 1,000 people in urban areas and one church for every 500 people in rural areas.[9] If you choose to use those statistics as your guide, then many places in North America are experiencing a significant deficit. On the other hand, just because a church exists in that community doesn't mean it's alive and vibrant. In the United States about 4,000 evangelical churches close their doors every year. Of those that remain open, about 80 percent identify themselves as plateaued, meaning that they have not seen growth in many years.[10]

In his book *Good to Great*, author Jim Collins said that great companies are those that "confront the brutal facts."[11] Well, the brutal facts are that things are not as good for the North American church as some might think. However, there is no need for despair. We have the ability through the Holy Spirit's power to turn the tide—if everyone does his or her part.

As I (Aaron) mentioned earlier, my years in New York City were at times overwhelming. The city seemed so big and impenetrable. But I believed that God was going to raise up an army of people to carry out His mission. In 2007 a group of Christians commissioned a study to look at the growth of Christianity in New York over a period of time.[12] The researchers went block by block in Manhattan to uncover the state of the church in that borough, believing it would indicate what was happening across the city. What they found was encouraging: Since 1990, Manhattan's evangelical population had grown from less than 1 percent in that year to almost 4 percent by 2007. Even more encouraging was that 40 percent of the evangelical churches had been planted since September 11, 2001. Incredible!

Here is the deal. The same God who promised to build His church in Matthew 16[13] and the one who is answering my prayers for NYC today is the same God who wants to see His church move forward on mission in your city. But this movement will not happen unless you do your part. You may not be a pastor or a church planter, but you *are* called to be something. God has equipped you uniquely to use your gifts for His kingdom's sake. The question is, are you willing to live out your calling?

THE BIG PICTURE

There is nothing more freeing than abandoning your own mission and joining the everyday mission of God.

EVERYDAY MISSIONARY

n the beginning God . . . The first words of Scripture supply for us the ultimate foundation for missions. The heartbeat of God is that He would be worshiped among all people. The writer of the Psalms conveys this sentiment when he said of God, "I will be exalted among the nations, I will be exalted in the earth!"[1] From the beginning of time in the garden, God's desire was to have a relationship with creation and for creation to see God for who He is: their Creator. As a result of the fall and sin's entrance into the world, however, humankind was inclined toward self-worship and not God-centered exaltation. Because humans' self-inclination does not square with God's righteous jealousy for His name, God is on a mission for God.[2] According to one popular writer, "Missions exists because worship does not."[3] God desires that all people worship Him and give Him the glory that is due His name.

Therefore, the mission of God requires that believers leverage their lives for His glory. The Great Commission is not for a select few; it is for the entirety of the church. The movement of God's mission sweeps across everyday, ordinary lives to draw in businesspeople, soccer moms, grandmothers, neighbors, students, lawyers, teachers, baristas, contractors, white collar, blue collar, or no collar at all. Regular people like you and me united by the one who lifts the curse of the fall. Filled with His spirit, laying down our lives, denying

> Everyday missionaries are those who practice life on mission where God has placed them.

ourselves for the mission of God and the good of others. This is the invitation.

Welcome to the movement of life on mission. Through His church, this is God's plan to change the world.

Many people believe that mission and ministry are carried out by a select few professional clergy or an elite number of mission agencies and nonprofit organizations. But here's the reality: God's mission was given to every member of His church. We are called to be everyday missionaries. Everyday missionaries are those who practice life on mission where God has placed them, whether that be at an office complex, a developing country, or a college campus. It is incumbent on every believer to have an "all hands on deck" mentality in order for the mission to reach its fullest potential. Ephesians 4 tells us that God has given leaders to the church in order to build up His people until they "become mature, attaining to the whole measure of the fullness of Christ" (Eph. 4:13 NIV). Notice it does not say that our leaders were placed over us to do all the work. When we choose to join God on His mission through His church, we dare to be the everyday missionaries we are called to be.

> If you are a follower of Jesus, then He has a purpose and plan for you.

Your life has a mission. If you are a follower of Jesus, then He has a purpose and plan for you. But not only does God have a plan for you, Ephesians 3:20 tells us that God is able "to do far more abundantly beyond all that we ask or think, according to the power that works within us" (NASB). He wants to do more in and through you than you can imagine. Think about that: The God of the universe has a plan far beyond what your mind can conceive. What exactly does that look like? What does that mean? How will it all play out in the coming weeks and in the next five years?

MORE THAN "ME"

The purpose of God's mission isn't really about us. We live in a culture that is all about "me." Social media has allowed us to usher in the "selfie"

generation—a generation, if we aren't careful, that defines itself by self-promotion. As we begin to understand what our lives on mission are about, it is vital to understand our goals. The ultimate goal is not that we would do good things for others. It's not even to start churches or share our faith. Yes, those are good aspects of the mission, but they are not the ultimate aim. The ultimate aim of our lives is to bring glory to God.

> The ultimate aim of our lives is to bring glory to God.

If we look again at Ephesians 3:20, where we learn that God wants to do abundantly more through our lives than we can imagine, we must continue reading through verse 21, which explains the central purpose of any effort we give to God's mission. It says, "To him be glory in the church and in Christ Jesus throughout all generations, forever and ever" (ESV). One early church document tells us, "Man's chief and highest end is to glorify God, and fully to enjoy him forever."[4] The goal is glory!

The purpose of your parenting is to glorify God. The purpose of your job is to give God glory. And the purpose of your life's mission: you guessed it, to glorify God. In 1 Corinthians 10:31 it says, "Whether You eat or drink, or whatever you do, do everything for God's glory." You don't have to waste years wondering what your purpose is.

> Life on mission is about intersecting gospel intentionality into our everyday routines.

Maybe you think, *Okay, I get it. Living for God's glory is the aim, and joining God in His mission to reach my community and beyond is a means toward that great intention, but I have no idea how I'm going to add mission to the already-consistent chaos called my life.*

I (Dustin) recently participated in a conference in Austin, Texas, where I heard teacher after teacher expound on how we cannot just look at mission as something to add to our schedules but something to intersect with our current daily rhythms. Life on mission is about

A weak gospel foundation leads to very fragile mission practices.

intersecting gospel intentionality into our everyday routines.

Adding something to the calendar can seem like an overwhelming task. God may call you to add elements, and if so, be obedient and add away. However, this book's objective is not to get you involved in some new mission program or create another church event, but rather to walk alongside you in creating a gospel intentionality within your already-present everyday rhythms.

WHAT DRIVES THE MISSION?

Living life on mission should be driven not out of guilty obligation, but rather out of embracing the identity and purpose given to us in Christ. Often, though, we are confused about our ministry motive, as well as about how to actually act on the knowledge we have. When it comes to understanding God's Word and living out God's mission, many of us tend to fall into one of three camps.

1. The "I'm not a professional" camp

Sarah represents many of us in that she rarely—if ever—takes action. She thinks she can't be a part of God's mission to redeem the world because she's not a professional minister. She equates ministry with paid professionals. She doesn't realize that *every* Christian is called to make disciples—that a Christian is necessarily a missionary in everyday life—and that her life on mission matters more than she could ever dream.

2. The "I'm too busy pondering" camp

Chris is passionate about learning as much about God as he can. He feels that knowledge about God will be his secret to his future ministry success. He loves going to seminars, reading books, and studying theology. He loves to talk about spiritual things with other believers,

but his involvement in actual ministry is minimal. He goes to church, of course, but to say he is on mission with God would be a lie. He has no intentional relationships and hasn't had a conversation with a nonbeliever in months. Though he goes "deep" in theology, he has forgotten to apply any of it to his life.

3. The "Why are we doing this?" camp

Stan, however, is the opposite of Chris. Stan is eager and task oriented. He has gotten the idea from his church that he is supposed to be active in ministry, and he has become the epitome of active. He helps with every ministry his church does, and he dutifully has conversations about Jesus with whoever will listen. But the conversations are often awkward and forced because, in reality, Stan doesn't really know what to say—he just knows he's supposed to talk. None of his words come from a legitimate overflow of meditating on the gospel and applying it to his life. They are parroted lines that he's memorized over years of familiarity with all things "church."

Chris understood the biblical foundations for ministry, but they didn't make it to his life. Stan understood the process of being a missionary, but without the biblical foundations. Too often we see people either digging deep into doctrine but never applying it, or we see those who eagerly engage in missionary activity while never digging deep into why mission work even matters. A weak gospel foundation leads to very fragile mission practices.

You don't have to fall into any of these camps because there is an altogether different option. Understanding that your life on mission matters, along with both the biblical foundations and the missionary process, is necessary to becoming an empowered everyday missionary—and the goal for this book is to train you in all three areas. Sarah will learn that she doesn't have to be a "professional" for her life on mission to matter; Stan will develop biblical foundations; and Chris will learn the practical missionary process that results from a solid biblical foundation.

A SIMPLE PROCESS

Though the need is great, through the power of the Holy Spirit, we can join God in His mission and see real change take place across North America. While mission can work itself out in many different ways, we want to offer a simple, clear process laid out in Scripture that effectively multiplies disciples and sends out everyday missionaries.

We recognize that mission and discipleship have been overly programmed and made excessively complicated, and we have no desire to do either of those. In the Scriptures, we do not see a syllabus for a program, but rather a gospel-rich missionary process.

We believe that this simple, reproducible approach, which is rooted in Jesus' example and the early church's ministry, will prove extremely effective as you follow Jesus in making disciples. The content is adaptable to any context and can function well as an individual study, but we strongly encourage walking through it with a small group of people. It is essential to interact with the content, which is threaded with powerful questions, to help you take your next steps.

We want to answer the *why, what, how, who,* and *what next* questions as you spend time working through *Life on Mission.*

- **WHY** does mission work even matter?
- **WHAT** is foundational to my growth and development?
- **HOW** do I apply the mission God has given me?
- To **WHOM** is God calling me?
- **WHAT** do the **NEXT** steps look like for me?

Our mission is driven by the truth of the gospel and defined by the mission of God. God's mission is to take what is broken and redeem it—not simply to make it better but to make it new. And the exciting part is that God Himself invites us to follow Him into a broken world as we live LIFE ON MISSION!

When things seem bleak, God shows up and shines His light into the situation.

THE CURRENT REALITY

I magine a movement of God across North America that changes the culture and attitudes of people. Imagine friends and family, once hopeless, understanding for the first time they have been given an eternal purpose that is bigger than them. Communities that are desperate being filled with courage that comes only by way of the gospel. Cities of great brokenness experiencing the newness that comes through Jesus alone.

Can you picture it?

Our role as everyday missionaries is to introduce people to Jesus, actively be part of their journey to become like Christ, and teach them to repeat the process with others. This is the desired reality, but before we move forward we must honestly examine the current reality of the mission field known as North America.

The gospel of Jesus has indeed taken root on this continent. We have historically been a land that sends missionaries to the nations who haven't heard the gospel. However, today the North American church is in decline. In his book *The Great Evangelical Recession*, John Dickerson shows that:

- Of America's 316 million people, evangelicals account for about 22 to 28 million, that means a staggering 93 percent or so are non-evangelicals.
- America's evangelical population loses 2.6 million people per decade.[1]

Denominations—from mainline to evangelical—are struggling. Consider these estimates:

- Southern Baptists report 16 million members, but only 6.1 million attend a worship service on any given Sunday.[2]
- The Presbyterian Church in America (PCA) averages one church for every 176,000 people.[3]
- The Evangelical Free Church has one congregation for every 209,333 people.[4]
- In Canada, there's one Christian Missionary Alliance church for every 81,206 people.[5]

And the list goes on.

While some evangelical denominations are on the rise, catching up with the population growth and cultural changes is another matter entirely. Here are some more statistics to consider.

- While some individual churches are growing, the evangelical numbers as a whole are shrinking, while the population is growing faster now than during the Baby Boom.[6]
- Researchers suggest that in thirty years, if the trends continue, the numbers of US evangelicals will have dropped to about 16 million, while the population will have jumped to more than 400 million.[7]

According to Outreach Canada and professor and researcher Reginald Bibby, the realities in Canada are not much better:

- Since 1980, almost three Canadian churches have closed their doors every week.
- While evangelicalism is rising above other denominations, only three in ten Canadians see religion as significant to their lives.
- The percentage of Canadian teens claiming no religion has climbed to more than 30 percent since 1980. But, Bibby says,

a majority are still keeping the door open toward spiritual things.[8]

In 2010, I (Dustin) joined some college students from the church I pastored in South Carolina and we spent a week in downtown Boston as a mission trip. One morning as I sat in a coffee shop in Boston's financial district, I pulled out my Bible to do some work on a research paper for a seminary class I was taking. A man at an adjacent table suddenly took an interest in what I was doing and the Bible that was sitting next to my computer.

"Is that a Bible?" the man asked.

"Yes," I answered. That seemed to open the door, and we began a bit of small talk about our backgrounds, family, sports, and jobs. That led to my explaining why I was in Boston.

"Wow," he said. "I've lived in Boston my entire life and I've never met a Christian out in public other than the eighteen people in my church. I've certainly never seen anyone reading a Bible at a coffee shop."

> Entire cities that were once vibrant, gospel-transformed places are now spiritually boarded-up wastelands that are far from Jesus.

The reality is, New England is now one of the most under-evangelized regions in the United States. In fact, less than 3.3 percent of this great city's population is involved in an evangelical church.[9] It's not just Boston. Entire cities that were once vibrant, gospel-transformed places are now spiritually boarded-up wastelands that are far from Jesus.

Travel five hours northeast up Highway 89 and you will find yourself in Montreal, a city that is only 0.7 percent evangelical.[10] In his article, "Overview of Montreal," Adam Miller, a writer for a major missions agency, describes Montreal as "a city with streets named after saints, with church buildings around almost every corner, but [where] things are not what they seem."[11] Montreal native and church planter François Verschelden says of his city, "Even if it seems like Jesus' presence is

here, it's not. There is a religious presence here. But His work is not known. His sacrifice is not known. Nobody can explain why Jesus died on the cross."[12]

Church buildings that once held thousands of worshipers every Sunday now serve as museums that people visit simply to observe great architecture and read placards that speak of church history. More and more church buildings are becoming new plots of real estate, lofts, and trendy concert venues. The brick and mortar of these buildings do not hold true gospel value, but the mission of the people who once populated the hallways and pews does.

On a positive side note, however, during a recent trip to Montreal, I (Dustin) learned that there are glimmers of hope. According to Jeff Christopherson, a native of Canada and mission strategist, for the last thirty years most Montreal church plants struggled to gather more than twenty-five people. But in 2013 more than six new churches were planted and each one had more than one hundred people. In fact, one church has grown to more than seven hundred people and baptized seventy new believers all in one year.

North America may have once been the center of evangelical Christianity, but that seems to be shifting to Asia, Africa, and Central America. In fact, many countries now send missionaries to North America. We praise God for the transformation taking place all over the planet, and we pray for more of it, but we must experience a resurgence of the Great Commission *here*. If the North American church grows in its gospel understanding and mission focus, the potential for what could take place all over the world grows only stronger and stronger as we send out gospel-centered missionaries, not only to our cities but also to the ends of the earth.

Can these depressed numerical trends be reversed? Is transformation possible? Is resurgence on the horizon?

How would you describe the church in North America?

CAN THESE BONES LIVE?

Declining numbers and evangelical regression can lead to frustration and mission paralysis for the church. We must remember that our God is still God and His desire for movement through His church can trump any current realities. Not sure that's true? Just look at the Old Testament prophet Ezekiel's story of how God brings life into a situation where death seems prominent.

> The hand of the LORD was on me, and He brought me out by His Spirit and set me down in the middle of the valley; it was full of bones. He led me all around them. There were a great many of them on the surface of the valley, and they were very dry. Then He said to me, "Son of man, can these bones live?" (Ezek. 37:1–3)

God showed Ezekiel a vision: a valley of dry bones—bones that were once full of life and vitality, but now lay dormant and dusty. In this vision, God breathed life into the bones and they stood as a living, breathing, and vast army.

When things seem bleak and hopeless, God shows up and breathes life into our situation. While this passage was not originally written about the North American church, the message certainly applies: Though we are a church in decline with some great needs, God can still breathe life into His church.

> When things seem bleak and hopeless, God shows up and breathes life into our situation.

How would you describe the church in your community/city?

How would you describe your church?

God has always been about forming a gospel people for a gospel mission.

THE MISSION OF GOD

I (Aaron) tend to be a take-action type of person. Actually, most personality profiles I take say, in effect, I would run over my own grandmother in a parking lot to reach a goal. When I was in college I was like most college students—broke. I remember one particular weekend I didn't have any money and it was going to be another week before I got paid from my job.

Desperate, I foraged through my house on a mission to find anything I could sell. Once I located the few items of any worth, I proceeded to move them onto the front lawn, along with a "yard sale" sign. Fortunately, I lived on a busy street and the people in my town liked to buy junk. After three hours, my take-action approach yielded me about forty dollars!

I'm not afraid to take action and neither is our culture as a whole. Too often we want to jump to the details answering the "what" and "how" questions: *What action steps must I take now? How do I do this?* But when it comes to the mission for which God has designed us, it can be dangerous to move to the "what" without asking the "why." As we push into the depths of what joining God in His mission looks like practically, we should take caution not to skip the "why," since answering that question is foundational both to our longevity and humility.

GOD'S MISSION

We read in the first chapter of Genesis that God created the world and called it good. He breathed life into humanity, the pinnacle of

creation—the very image-bearers of God.[1] Though designed to reflect Him, Adam and Eve chose self-interest over relationship with God. Genesis 3 tells the story of how they bit on the enemy's temptation and revolted against God, desiring to usurp His rule in an attempt to become gods themselves. They traded God's kingdom for their own kingdom, and it quickly crumbled.

The fabric of all creation was ripped as sin and self-immersion spread like poison to our souls. The next seven chapters of Genesis move from one devastation to the next, clearly displaying the effects of sin: deception, disobedience, and murder. The message is clear: Sin wreaks havoc.

Into this broken, bloody mess of a world, where people were reeling with pain they brought on themselves through sin, God stepped in. He chose Abram (Abraham) to become a part of His redeeming mission.

The LORD said to Abram: "Go out from your land, your relatives, and your father's house to the land that I will show you. I will make you into a great nation, I will bless you, I will make your name great, and you will be a blessing. I will bless those who bless you, I will curse those who treat you with contempt, and all the peoples on earth will be blessed through you." (Gen. 12:1–3)

God chose to use an ordinary man like Abram (whom he renamed Abraham) to bring about change. And throughout the Old Testament God continued from Abraham to gather a people for Himself and His mission. In Exodus 19:5–6, God said that His people were a "treasured possession" and a "kingdom of priests" (ESV). A priest's job was to represent God to the people—thus making Israel a group of people who would put God on display to the nations around them. God would use them to reveal Himself to the world and press forward in the promise He made to Abraham to bless the world through his descendants.

Since the start, God's plan to bless the world was to use everyday,

ordinary people who had been reconciled to Him. This is a theme we observe not only with Abram, but with others throughout Scripture: God took men and women like Moses, Joshua, Rahab, Nehemiah, Ruth, Peter, John, and many others. And He continues that same process today. In short, God has always been about forming a gospel people for a gospel mission.

THE ULTIMATE FULFILLMENT

As we move into the New Testament, we see that not only did God choose to use an ordinary man like Abraham to bring about change, but also Abraham's bloodline eventually led to the ultimate change-agent: God in the flesh, Jesus. He is the one true priest, the one true king, and the one true prophet.

God's plan culminated in Jesus—God in human flesh, sent on a rescue mission to reconcile the world to God through the cross and resurrection. Jesus is the ultimate missionary, on task to make a people for Himself who will be a blessing, or good news, to those who are without Him. With Jesus comes the tantalizing hope of redemption—the shocking idea that maybe all is not lost and the destruction caused by sin will not have the final word.

> God has always been about forming a gospel people for a gospel mission.

After His ascension, God sent the Holy Spirit, and the church began to spread the good news of reconciliation with God through Jesus. Second Corinthians 5:18–20 tells us that as the church we have been given the ministry of reconciliation. Those of us who have been reconciled to God through Jesus now form the group of everyday people whom God uses to bless the world.

Our missionary God is not waiting for you or me—He is already at work. And the exciting news is that He invites us to join in His mission of reconciliation. The current reality of our world is certainly a motivation for what we do as everyday missionaries, but the ultimate motivator is God Himself. As we are changed and freed, we are compelled

to be where He is—right in the middle of the greatest rescue mission ever given.

How crazy is it that we are invited into this mission? Not only are we reconciled to God, but we are also drafted to be missionaries along-side Him, spreading the same good news that rescued us from our self-made destruction. We, who were convicted of treason against the King of the universe, are by grace not only forgiven but also invited into His family, adopted as His sons and daughters, and bid to spread the message of hope to other traitors.

> With Jesus comes the tantalizing hope of redemption —the shocking idea that maybe all is not lost and the destruction caused by sin will not have the final word.

What an awesome invitation that is. The fact that many Christians do not respond to the invitation reveals that many do not comprehend how good the good news of Jesus really is.

Do you believe God is calling **YOU** to be on mission with Him? If so, in what ways? If not, why not? What do you sense He is saying to you about your role?

LIFE
ON MISSION

The irony of God's kingdom is this: True fulfillment is found in sacrifice; true identity is found as we lose ourselves in Christ; and our deepest questions are answered outside of ourselves.

KINGDOM REALIGNMENT

So God is on a mission to redeem and reconcile people to Himself. This mission sweeps both history and the globe, and it encompasses regular, ordinary people like you and me. Not just the ones who give sermons, but the ones who listen. Not just paid professionals, but average Joes and Josephinas working a nine-to-five job. Not just pastors and mission agency leaders, but businessmen and soccer moms.

However, if you're honest, you may say that you don't feel much like you are part of God's grand mission. After all, it's Wednesday. Everyone despises Wednesdays. Not only do you have to get the kids ready for school, you just realized you forgot to make their lunches last night. Now you're going to be late to your meeting, and you have to figure out what you're going to tell your boss. After a crazy day at work you somehow have to figure out how to get the kids to practice on time, and you still don't know what you'll make for dinner. At this point you are just hoping to get the day wrapped up in time to kick back and watch a little television later tonight.

A missionary bearing the hope of the world is not exactly how you would describe yourself. Maybe in theory, but in practice on a random Wednesday? Your mind is far from it.

Why don't we embrace God's mission? Because, frankly, we have our own mission. We have our own way of calling the shots. We decide what's meaningful or worthwhile and order our lives accordingly. Some people's life mission is to pursue entertainment and comfort. For others it's security or wealth. For others it may be rising up the corporate

ladder or being the most respected mom in the neighborhood. We like to be the boss of our own lives.

This goes back to the sin of our first parents in the garden of Eden. As we mentioned earlier, Adam and Eve chose to be king and queen of their own kingdom rather than joyfully submitting to the authority of God as King. We may read their story in Genesis 3 and shake our heads, but the fact is that we have all done the exact same thing in one way or another. In light of this, it's not surprising that some of Jesus' first words in His earthly ministry were: "Repent, because the kingdom of heaven has come near!" (Matt. 4:17).

Repent. That word stings our pride, but once we get past that, we realize it oozes with grace because it invites us into something better. Repent, because the kingdom already has a King, and you and I are not it.

If we are ever going to get swept up into God's kingdom, we will have to let go of our own. Our own ways of seeing and approaching our lives will have to be radically reoriented.

THE GOOD NEWS OF THE KINGDOM

In twenty-first-century United States, we don't exactly have the perfect context for *king* and *kingdom* language. In large part we are more familiar with democracy, in which every voice counts equally. For the vast majority of people throughout history, however, the language of monarchy would ring with weight, because it's exactly what they lived in. In their world if a king decreed something, it happened. No questions asked. If the king wanted something to become a law, it became a law. There was no system of checks and balances to make sure the king didn't become a tyrant.

The idea of living under a monarchy might seem unappealing because you know plenty of stories where power and authority corrupt and cause unthinkable damage. But the hesitation that arises when thinking about living under a solitary king or queen's rule lessens when you realize that the goodness (or badness) of living under such authority depends entirely, and we mean 100 percent, on the goodness (or badness) of the said king or queen. What would you think of

living under a perfectly good, perfectly wise King whose every decision was for your benefit and eternal good? That may in fact not be so unappealing.

Throughout His ministry, Jesus' message resounded with the truth that His kingdom had come, and that it was a kingdom of good news—not a kingdom of oppression and corruption. Who wouldn't want to live in that kingdom? Matthew 4:23 states that Jesus went all over Galilee "preaching the good news of the kingdom." Truly understanding this idea of good news begs some context.

Historically, during a time of war, kings would set off to battle for their people against the given enemy. If the king was defeated, his people would either become slaves to the enemy or be killed. Messengers would run back to the city yelling, "Run for your lives!"

However, when the king and his soldiers triumphed, he would send back a messenger to let the people know that the enemy had been defeated. The messenger would yell, "Good news! Good news!" This could have literally meant freedom from impending slavery or death. This news from the messenger is the same word we now use as the word *gospel*, which in its simplest form means, "good news."

The message of King Jesus is the gospel. Our King has gone before us and defeated the enemy, therefore imparting to us victory over the slavery of sin and death. This is no everyday good news—this is life-altering good news, and we who have been reconciled to God have now been given the privilege of spreading this good news to a world that is in desperate need of it. The good news of the kingdom is that God doesn't leave us in a state of sinful devastation, but calls us to turn from our sin and to look to Him for hope and restoration.

For the remainder of this chapter, let's look at why it is good news that Jesus is the King of His kingdom.

GOOD NEWS: JESUS IS ON THE THRONE

Several years ago I (Aaron) traveled to England for a conference. While there I took a day to see London. The last stop on my tour was at Buckingham Palace, home to Queen Elizabeth. The tour guide

> The King is on His throne reigning over His kingdom.

explained the tradition behind the changing of the guard and many of the other historic symbols. One especially memorable remark was about the significance of the flag on top of the palace. The guide explained that when the queen is not in residence, the flag does not fly. Though the Queen of England does not have the official power over the people that she once held, there is still a strong sense of national pride and security in knowing that she is there. For the people of England, when the flag is flying, the people can be assured that the queen is on her throne!

When looking at the decline and challenge facing the North American church (as we discussed in chapter 2), the task of the mission can seem daunting. However, we cannot allow any amount of hopelessness or despair to gain control over us. Why? Because the King is on His throne reigning over His kingdom.

From the beginning, God has reigned over the universe. Regardless of what the world tells us, that hasn't changed. He has always been the sovereign King of the cosmos, with ultimate rule and reign, and He will continue to be nothing less. He is the King of kings on a mission. He reminds us that whenever we read Matthew 16:18: "I . . . say to you that you are Peter, and on this rock I will build My church, and the forces of Hades will not overpower it."

The fact that God is on His throne and that Jesus is building His church should bring us great relief. We can release any unnecessary pressure or worry that ministry may tempt us to carry and trust that God *will* accomplish what He has set out to do.

GOOD NEWS: JESUS IS A DIFFERENT KIND OF KING

When you think about earthly kings and queens, odds are you may think about some faraway, inaccessible royalty who is unable (or simply uninterested) to relate to his subjects. You may think of an aloof and uncaring ruler who has only his own best interests in mind.

But Jesus is an altogether different kind of king. He took on the

very plight of His subjects to provide a way out of the mess they had made for themselves. He is far from aloof, uncaring, or inaccessible, someone who does not meddle in the affairs of His people. Jesus is a King who got down into the mess of humanity, who went to ultimate lengths to seek and save the lost and restore people back into His kingdom. Jesus is the

> Jesus is a King who got down into the mess of humanity, who went to ultimate lengths to seek and save the lost and restore people back into His kingdom.

best King imaginable, because He is that perfectly wise and good King who always works everything for the best for those who love Him and are called according to his purpose.[1]

Since Jesus is a different kind of king, we serve in a different kind of kingdom. The kingdom of God takes what culture tells us and turns it upside down. The more we grow in knowing this good King, the more the truths of an upside-down kingdom become real. Take a look at these cultural "norms" and how they compare to God's kingdom.

WHAT CULTURE SAYS: Be first.

WHAT GOD SAYS: The last will be first and the first will be last (see Matt. 20:16).

WHAT CULTURE SAYS: Step over others to exalt yourself.

WHAT GOD SAYS: Humble yourself to be exalted (see Matt. 23:12, James 4:10, 1 Peter 5:6).

WHAT CULTURE SAYS: Do whatever makes you look best.

WHAT GOD SAYS: Take the worst seat at the table instead of the best (see Luke 14:8–10).

WHAT CULTURE SAYS: Your life is what's most important.

WHAT GOD SAYS: Consider others better than yourself (see Phil. 2:3–4).

WHAT CULTURE SAYS: Always get/do what you want.

WHAT GOD SAYS: Die to your own desires (see Luke 9:23).

WHAT CULTURE SAYS: Take care of yourself first and foremost.

WHAT GOD SAYS: Whoever loses his life will find it (see Matt. 16:25).

WHAT CULTURE SAYS: Maybe forgive, but don't forget.

WHAT GOD SAYS: Love and pray for your enemies (see Matt. 5:44).

WHAT CULTURE SAYS: Have nothing to do with those who are against you.

WHAT GOD SAYS: Bless those who persecute you (see Rom. 12:14).

WHAT CULTURE SAYS: No one tells you what to do.

WHAT GOD SAYS: Go further than what you are asked (see Matt. 5:41).

> It is truly a good kingdom, with a good King, with good news for a hurting world.

The irony of the kingdom is that: (1) True fulfillment is found in sacrifice; (2) True identity is found as we lose ourselves in Christ; (3) Our deepest questions are answered outside of ourselves. It is truly a good kingdom, with a good King, with good news for a hurting world.

GOOD NEWS: THE KINGDOM IS ALL ABOUT JESUS

The reason our personal kingdoms feel so small is because . . . well, they are. No part of who we are is big enough to merit the weight and grandeur of a king because only one life is. The writer of Hebrews put it this way:

> Long ago God spoke to the fathers by the prophets at different times and in different ways. In these last days, He has spoken to us by His Son. God has appointed Him heir of all things and made the universe through Him. The Son is the radiance of God's glory and the exact expression of His nature, sustaining all things by His powerful word. After making purification for sins, He sat down at the right hand of the Majesty on high. So

He became higher in rank than the angels, just as the name He inherited is superior to theirs. (Heb. 1:1–4)

Here's an exercise for you. Answer the following questions based on the above passage:

1. By whom has God spoken to us?
2. Who is the heir of all things?
3. Through whom did God make the universe?
4. Who is the radiance of God's glory?
5. Who is the exact expression of God's nature?
6. Who sustains all things by His powerful Word?
7. Who purifies us from all sin?
8. Who is seated at the right hand of the Majesty?
9. Who is ranked higher than the angels?

If you grew up in and around the church, you know that the answers to the above questions are all the same and typically viewed as "Sunday school answers." In other words, if you don't know the answer while sitting in a building with stained glass windows, then simply say, "Jesus," and there is a good chance you'll answer the typical "Sunday school question" correctly. The answer really is that simple, though—Jesus. The kingdom really is all about Jesus—about who He is, what He has done, and what He continues to do as King.

Jesus is the one through whom God has spoken to all of humanity. *Jesus* is the King and heir with God the Father of all things. *Jesus* is the one through whom God the Father made the universe. *Jesus* is the exact expression of God's nature. *Jesus* is the radiance of God's glory. *Jesus* sustains all things by His powerful Word. *Jesus* purifies us from all our sin. *Jesus* is seated on the throne at the right hand of the Majesty.

Jesus is not only the King, creator, sustainer, and brilliance of God's glory, but also the means by which sinful man can be made clean again. It's good news that the kingdom is all about Jesus, because

worshiping Him is what all of creation was designed for. Reflecting God's glory is the only thing that will ever truly satisfy and enliven not only us as humans, but the very grass, oceans, rocks, and trees that cover the earth.

GOOD NEWS: JESUS IS A SERVANT KING

Throughout the New Testament we see over and over how Jesus served others. One poignant scene, in particular, is when He washed His disciples' feet (see John 13:1–17). But the apostle Paul shows a more profound portrait of Jesus as a servant King:

> Christ Jesus, who, existing in the form of God, did not consider equality with God as something to be used for His own advantage. Instead He emptied Himself by assuming the form of a slave, taking on the likeness of men. And when He had come as a man in His external form, He humbled Himself by becoming obedient to the point of death—even to death on a cross. For this reason God highly exalted Him and gave Him the name that is above every name, so that at the name of Jesus every knee will bow—of those who are in heaven and on earth and under the earth—and every tongue should confess that Jesus Christ is Lord, to the glory of God the Father. (Phil. 2:5–11)

Jesus completely turns our natural ideas about power, authority, and privilege upside down. The world values ascending whatever success or popularity ladder there happens to be nearby, while Jesus values descending to serve the least of those among us. His descent from heaven to save and serve us is our great motivation and example to humble ourselves and serve those around us. In the standard economy of a kingdom,

> Jesus is not only the King, creator, sustainer, and brilliance of God's glory, but also the means by which sinful man can be made clean again.

kings are not servants and servants are not kings, yet King Jesus is both. We have an all-powerful and mighty God who purifies us from our sin not by sitting idly by, but rather by exalting Himself through becoming the Servant King.

GOOD NEWS: WE GET TO REPENT

Jesus calls us to repent of building our own kingdoms, which is good news because kingdom realignment is the best thing that could ever happen to us. Before moving to the practical nature of living on mission we must first examine our hearts. Instead of living to pursue our own pleasure and attain our own glory—which is always fleeting—we get to be swept up in the greatest story that's ever been told and glorify the true and rightful King Jesus with our lives. He gives us a new and better purpose—one that will never fade or fail us—even in eternity and even on a Wednesday. Chasing after His fame and glory instead of our own is the best trade we could ever make.

> In the standard economy of a kingdom, kings are not servants and servants are not kings, yet King Jesus is both.

The kingdom of God is a real kingdom—not a sand castle like our meager attempts. We are not only invited into God's kingdom, we are also invited to be part of spreading the good news. We get to "plead on Christ's behalf, 'Be reconciled to God' " (2 Cor. 5:20).

The wayward are not lost forever. *King Jesus seeks and finds them.*

The traitors who chose treason over relationship are not hopeless after all. *King Jesus reconciles them to the Father.*

The prisoners and mourners are not left in their despair. *King Jesus breaks the chains of sin and grants freedom while giving comfort to the hurting.*

The poor and brokenhearted are not left by the wayside. *King Jesus restores us through kindness and transforms us to be spiritually rich.*

Indeed, it is a kingdom of good news. But we only have the opportunity to spread this news and plead on His behalf when we practice

kingdom realignment—when we leave behind our own kingdoms and pursue His. And this kingdom realignment leads us to a kingdom mentality, where, as everyday missionaries, we are more concerned with the bigger picture of God's kingdom than we are with ourselves.

In times past, how have you seen your life realign with God's kingdom purposes?

In what ways do you still need to surrender your kingdoms to Him?

GOSPEL FOUNDATIONS

The gospel is not something you simply "get." It is something you grow deeper in throughout your life.

THE GOSPEL

A life on mission is a calling of abandonment. It is the confession of our willingness to set aside—to abandon—our preferences to follow God's mission. Like a bungee jumper diving off a platform, we must relinquish our selfish hopes with total abandon to spread the true hope we have found in Jesus.

And like the bungee jumper, we soon discover that what once may have seemed dangerous or unappealing becomes the thrill of a lifetime once we let go. Living out a gospel mission is not a guilt- or fear-driven task—it is the good life. Author Tim Chester says, "The secret of gospel change is being convinced that Jesus is the good life and the fountain of joy. Any alternative would be the letdown."[1] We realize the good life as we see Jesus for all He is and follow Him without hesitation.

From birth we hold firmly on to things. Once a baby learns to hold a bottle, there is no going back to Momma and Daddy holding it. This pattern continues throughout life. A number of months ago my wife and I (Dustin) taught our two-year-old daughter, Piper, to use a spoon to feed herself. Now, if I even hint like I'm going in the direction of her spoon, she acts as if I have deeply offended her and attempts to send me to "time out." I think, *You're two. You get lost in your own room. Chill out.*

A teenager begins driving and it's as if he's cursed if he has to submit to riding with his parents ever again. And as adults we hold firmly to what we achieve—great job, financial success, beautiful house—as if that's all we have. It becomes the singular banner over our lives.

However, when we take on the mind of Jesus, we hold on to our plans and ideals loosely. We become more willing to follow His plans and ideals, even if on the surface they don't make sense and may not seem successful. The point is that we become willing to hold our plans in an open hand rather than a closed fist.

Several years ago my wife, Carmen, and I (Aaron) felt God calling us to adopt a child. After several attempts and upon discovering that more than fifteen thousand NYC foster children needed homes, we enlisted a social-worker friend to help us navigate the bureaucratic system and lead us to become "foster parents with the intention to adopt." We knew that fostering to adopt domestically would be a complicated endeavor. We had heard horror stories of those who had done it only to have a child taken away abruptly.

A few weeks after completing our foster care training, Joshua came to live with us. Joshua was six weeks premature. He spent his first twenty-two days in the hospital (most of that time in the Pediatric Intensive Care Unit). On the day Joshua came into our home he weighed just a little more than four pounds. The social workers brought him in a carrier and set him on our living room floor. They took a box of diapers and formula and set them on the kitchen counter. No instruction manual. No time to warm up to him. In a period of about eight minutes we became parents of a little boy.

As the social workers were leaving, one of them stopped and said, "By the way, Joshua has a sister in foster care. She's about eighteen months old. Would you take her too?"

Our child, plus Joshua, and now a third one? All under the age of four. Were we crazy? In that moment, my wife and I should have said no. Everything within us—our own desires and realities—wanted to say, *This one is* more *than plenty*. But through the power that can come only from the Holy Spirit, we looked at each other and said yes. And a few months later, Ella joined our family.

When Carmen and I entered the adoption process, we'd visualized how it would go. We thought we would get one child through a closed, foreign adoption. Instead we've ended up with two children

through domestic foster care. And though we've had our fair share of complications (as of this writing we're still waiting on the official adoption paperwork, four years into the process), we're thankful for the process God has taken us through, as He has used it to shape our attitudes and plans to align more with Christ's. God has proved that His plans are higher and greater than anything we can conjure up on our own. We just have to trust Him.

FIRST IMPORTANCE

Our ability to trust Jesus and hold our plans loosely is not built on our own merits. Being an everyday missionary is impossible without a solid foundation. The gospel is like that bungee cord that keeps the jumper connected to life, and our missions efforts are in vain if we are without our "gospel" cord. We must not jump off the platform without being securely fastened to the gospel of Jesus, because there is no other hope for us or for our aching world. An everyday missionary who is not grounded in the gospel is no missionary at all because he or she does not have good news to proclaim. Every other religious idea in the world primarily gives advice for one's life, whereas the gospel is an announcement of good news that *transforms* a life.

> The gospel is not something you simply "get." It is something you grow deeper in throughout your life.

Over the last decade, the word *missional* has grown in popularity. For the most part, this has been a great thing for the church, but there is potential danger if we don't have a clear understanding of what should always determine and drive the mission set forth for us. If we don't grow in the gospel, we will not get the mission.

Before you think, *I get the gospel, I know the gospel, I know why I'm on mission,* remember: The gospel is not something you simply "get." It is something you grow deeper in throughout your life.

This chapter lays the groundwork for the rest of the content you will read. You should consider jumping back to this chapter from time

to time as a reminder of what our mission is built upon. Theologian Charles Hodge said, "The gospel is so simple that small children can understand it, and it is so profound that studies by the wisest theologians will never exhaust its riches."[2] The more we dig into its depths, the richer this transforming news becomes.

If the gospel is not genuinely the foundation and motivation of our mission, we will likely falter and lead others astray. The more we grasp what Jesus has done for us and in us, the more we will be compelled by grace to clearly communicate Jesus to those around us.

Aaron and I (Dustin) have served as student/college pastors during our time as ministers, and, without fail, we've noticed a perpetual cycle of students who participate in mission work because it makes them feel good about themselves. These same students then head to college or into the workforce and leave the idea of a relationship with Christ back at their summer mission trip. Unfortunately, for many the motive for missions isn't the gospel—it is a guilt- or works-based mentality, built on the idea that we can somehow erase our sin or earn favor with God by doing the "right" things. To believe that our mission efforts in some way eradicate sin isn't much different from an Eastern-based karma belief with a splash of Jesus.

This reality is true not only for students, but also for many others in our churches, whether they wear a three-piece suit or a V-neck and skinny jeans. It is often that folks in the pews or chairs will "do" the periodic mission service project but leave the "real" mission work Monday through Friday to the hired "professional." Our mission efforts are vital and must increase as we move toward a more progressively post-Christian era, in which our values and worldviews are no longer based in the Christian faith. Our motivation for mission has to be that Jesus is already our great reward. When taking the risk of living selflessly on mission, we must be grounded and affixed

> The gospel is the starting point, the sustaining point, and the finishing point of all missions—to all of life.

to that gospel understanding. So the gospel is the starting point, the sustaining point, and the finishing point of all mission—to all of life. In 1 Corinthians 15:1–4 Paul wrote:

I want to clarify for you the gospel I proclaimed to you; you received it and have taken your stand on it. You are also saved by it, if you hold to the message I proclaimed to you—unless you believed for no purpose. For I passed on to you as most important what I also received: that Christ died for our sins according to the Scriptures, that He was buried, that He was raised on the third day according to the Scriptures.

The gospel of Jesus is of greatest importance. It applies to and affects everything (work, school, leadership, friendships, marriage, family). It is the ultimate game-changer.

Think about why you participate in mission work. What are some things that motivate you (e.g., compassion for the poor, experiencing new cultures, sharing the gospel)?

How do you consider yourself "sent" from God? Is there room for growth in your view on missions? How? Why?

How do you define the gospel?

List ways the gospel affects every area of your life (work, relationships, school, etc.) and your mission work.

Life: _____

Mission: _____

GOD'S HOLINESS AND GREATNESS

As created beings, we are measured and defined by comparison to our Creator. We cannot truly understand ourselves without first looking

at the awe-inspiring holiness and majesty of God.

In Isaiah 6, the prophet found himself standing in heaven. He saw the Lord sitting high on a throne, His robe filling the temple. Angels surrounded Him, singing, "Holy, holy, holy is the LORD of hosts; His glory fills the whole earth." While they sang, the foundations of the doorways shook and the temple filled with smoke.

This passage, among many others, describes the overwhelming "otherness" of God. He is completely holy; set apart, transcendent, all knowing, all powerful. He is the one and only true God, the creator and sustainer of all things, the one in whom all things "live and move and exist" (Acts 17:28). Being altogether righteous and holy, God cannot look upon or tolerate sin (see Hab. 1:13). It is an affront to His majesty, His character, and His design for life. Grasping and digesting the character of who God is will help us better understand the depths of the grace He has for us.

Spend a few minutes now to describe your understanding of the nature and character of God.

OUR SINFULNESS

As Isaiah saw God sitting on His throne, angels worshiping Him, while the foundations shook because of the weight of His glory, Isaiah had an immediate and gripping response: "Woe is me for I am ruined because I am a man of unclean lips and live among a people of unclean lips, and because my eyes have seen the King, the LORD of Hosts" (Isa. 6:5).

This was not a religious spectacle or some rote spiel spouted from memory. In this moment, in the presence of an all-holy God, Isaiah was overwhelmed by his own sinfulness. That reality is not the most exciting to own up to, but it's true to its core and necessary in order to grasp the full depth of the gospel. Every facet of our existence—even our so-called "good" works—is shot through with sin. Because of this, we are separated from God and rightfully under condemnation.

This is the reality of our human character:

- Even what we view as "good" works is viewed as polluted garments compared to God's goodness (see Isa. 64:6).
- We suppress the truth when we exchange the creator God for the created things of this world (see Rom. 1:18–25).
- By nature and choice, we are not good. Only God is good and we choose in and of ourselves not to fear or pursue Him (see Rom. 3:9–20).
- Our hostility leads toward evil deeds and further separation from God (see Col. 1:21).

Describe your understanding of the nature and character of humanity.

How is our nature and character different from God's?

What do you sacrifice for the most? What do you daydream about? ("If I just had more _____, I'd be happy.")

Where do you spend your time and money most frequently? In what do you tend to seek significance, worth, value, and acceptance?

The only way to truly evaluate ourselves is through an honest view of God's holiness and our own sinfulness. Like Isaiah, we have to look first at God to see ourselves clearly. How would you answer these statements?

God is holy, and I am _____.

God is forgiving, and I am _____.

God is generous, and I am _____.

God is caring, and I am _____.

God is alive, and I am _____.

If you wonder what should be written in the blanks above—the word *not* will suffice, when we are absent the grace of God. Sin is not just a setback or obstacle to overcome, it is a self-inflicted curse—a cancer we can do nothing in and of ourselves to remedy. As Louie Giglio stated, "Sin doesn't make us bad, sin makes us dead. The gospel doesn't make us better, the gospel makes us alive."[3]

As you know, our hearts are more than surface deep. Often deeper, underlying motivations are really driving our behaviors. If we are ever going to achieve true freedom from sin, we have to let God dig down to the roots of it.

For example, Gary was struggling with severe alcohol addiction and began attending a recovery ministry at my (Dustin's) church. Gary explained that he had a serious problem with alcohol for almost a decade, but he always thought he had it under control—until the previous weekend. He had taken friends to party at a strip club, only to wake up the next morning hung over and $6,000 poorer. This was a wake-up call for Gary and he finally realized he needed help. Interestingly before they even talked about idolatry in the recovery ministry, Gary explained it well: "You know, it's not even about the alcohol, or about lust. I'm a really nice drunk. People like me when I'm drunk. I'm generous. So when I go out with my friends and tell them to do whatever they want and the tab is on me, it makes me feel powerful and liked. That's the real issue. That's really why I do it."

Without realizing it, Gary had explained that his surface sin of alcohol and lust were really the deeper issues of approval and power. Isn't that fascinating? Our sin is deep and multifaceted, and it requires a deep and multifaceted cure.

Consider some of the sins you struggle with, and ask yourself why. What is the deeper reason you turn to these things? Ask the Holy Spirit to help you understand your true motivation.

But we don't stop at our sin. There is great news for those who recognize the hopelessness of their state, those who with Isaiah cry, "Woe is me!" That news is the boundless hope of grace.

"BUT GOD"

What happened to Isaiah is gratefully a foreshadowing of the gospel.

> Then one of the seraphim flew to me, and in his hand was a glowing coal that he had taken from the altar with tongs. He touched my mouth with it and said: "Now that this has touched your lips, your wickedness is removed and your sin is atoned for." Then I heard the voice of the Lord saying: "Who should I send? Who will go for Us?" I said: "Here I am. Send me." (Isa. 6:6–8)

After Isaiah was stunned by God's holiness, then overwhelmed by his own sinfulness, God stepped in to intervene in what felt like a hopeless situation. The burning coal from the altar symbolizes the cleansing, atoning work of Jesus applied to us by grace through faith.

It has been said that the two best words in the Bible are found in Ephesians 2:4: *But God*. In verses 1–3 of that chapter, we see the overwhelming weight we all feel, just as Isaiah did, when we are separated from God. These two words, *But God*, form the transition from the bad news of sin and condemnation to the unbelievable good news of forgiveness through Jesus: "*But God*, who is rich in mercy, because of His great love that He had for us, made us alive with the Messiah even though we were dead in trespasses. You are saved by grace!" (Eph. 2:4–5, emphasis added).

The reason we have hope is because God is rich in mercy. Mercy is simply God's compassion for the undeserving. The word *rich* in the above passage is the same word used to describe a wealthy king who has more money than he knows what to do with. That is how much mercy God has for us. His grace and mercy abound, proving to be more than sufficient for our many shortcomings. As Lamentations 3:22–23 says, His mercies "are new every morning." Pastor and author Tim Keller states, "The gospel is that Jesus lived the life you should have lived and died the death you should have died, in your place, so God can receive you not for your record and sake but for His record and sake."[4]

Throughout Scripture God is described as loving and compassionate, and this Ephesians passage grounds the saving work of Christ in the "great love that He had for us." Though we are more sinful than we'll ever truly know, we are *still* loved by God more than we could ever imagine.

"But God" is truly incredible news!

THE PRESSURE IS OFF

When I (Dustin) was pastoring in Columbia, South Carolina, one of our pastors, Brandon, met regularly with a young man named Jason. Jason struggled with a severe addiction to pornography that had plagued him for years. Over several months as they talked, Brandon realized there was more going on than sexual sin.

Jason kept expressing that he had a lot of anxiety over his obedience to God, or lack thereof. He said it was difficult for him even to hear grace-based sermons because he was consumed by feelings of failure.

"No matter what I do, I can't seem to be good enough," he would say. "I can't hit the proverbial ball right—even in the little things, like reading my Bible and praying. I constantly feel anxious and helpless."

Brandon noticed that Jason completely missed the gospel because he was so focused on his own performance, so he started to remind Jason of one of the gospel's basic tenets: We are affirmed and approved by God based on Jesus' performance, not our own.

"I have a new mantra for you, Jason," Brandon told him during one of their sessions. "*The pressure is off.* If Jesus is your Savior, the pressure is off. There is no need to perform. You are already forgiven, approved, and affirmed based solely on Jesus' righteousness. And there is *nothing* you can do to add or take away from Jesus' righteousness." Slowly but surely, that simple truth started to work freedom into Jason's soul.

The gospel is not based on what you do for God, but what God has done for you. It is not "you do" but "Jesus did." Sadly, this works-based righteousness is second nature to us, simply because of pride. We want to be good enough. We want to measure up on our own. Even mission and ministry can be turned into a performance for God—an act to

try to win His favor or affirmation. This is a dangerous subconscious ideology that leads to destruction, and we must be freed from it by continually going back to the gospel and reaffirming that we are already approved in Jesus, so there's no need to earn it.

How do you struggle with turning mission into a performance for God?

GROWING IN THE GOSPEL

The gospel is not only the *starting* point, it is also the point in *every* step of our journey. The gospel is how we become Christians, but it is also how we grow as believers—through meditating on it and applying it to every fabric of our lives.

When my (Dustin's) son, Jack, was three years old, he and I found ourselves making a pizza run in the ever-hospitable traffic that is Atlanta. It was around 5:30 p.m., and if I'm being completely vulnerable, I'm not sure whether Atlanta's rush-hour traffic was leading toward my sanctification or my madness. In an attempt to distract myself from the bumper-to-bumper surroundings, I asked my son a simple question.

"Jack, what is the gospel?"

From his car seat he looked directly into the mirror where he could see the reflection of my face and said, "The gospel is good news. Right, Daddy?"

"Yeah, son, that's right. But what is the good news?"

"The good news is that we get grace."

I pressed further. "Okay, but what is grace?"

He rolled his eyes as if to say, *Seriously, Dad, everybody knows that.* Then he said, "Grace is getting what we don't deserve."

As those words came out of his mouth, I thought, *I've got a little theologian on my hands. This is incredible.*

He went on to say, "You know, Daddy, when I deserve a time-out and you don't give me one? That's grace."

My son recently pushed his little sister down, quickly looked at

> The gospel is not based on what you do for God, but what God has done for you. It is not "you do" but "Jesus did."

me, and said, "Grace, Daddy, grace." To which I replied, "It's time to learn about justice. Justice, son, justice."

Nonetheless my son impressed me on this drive to grab a pizza. I wanted to dig a bit more so I asked him, "Okay, so we get what we don't deserve, but how do we get that? What had to take place?"

Quickly and emphatically he said, "Jesus died on the cross." There was an aggressive growl to his voice when he said "cross."

"That's right. But what did Jesus die for?" Finally, he seemed stumped as I continued to weave my way through the crazy traffic, all the while commenting on how people need to learn to drive: "Get out of the left lane. Move over!"

He thought long and hard, and said, "Hmmm, Daddy. Jesus died for your bad attitude."

I wish I could have taken a snapshot of the grin he wore that moment. His statement was not only hilarious, but the Holy Spirit used it to communicate and affirm in me a life-changing truth.

The gospel is not exclusively about salvation, but also about our sanctification, our becoming more and more like Jesus. The transforming nature of the gospel is that God, through the power of His grace, continually changes us to be like Jesus, even in our bad attitudes while driving to pick up a pizza.

If the gospel truly applies to every area, and our calling is to live life on mission, then we must examine, marinate, and apply the full truth of this great news.

You might think that the good news of Jesus grows less meaningful and prevalent as in time you move away from the point of your conversion, but the opposite is actually true. If you walk in honesty and confession, allowing the Holy Spirit to search your heart deeper and deeper, you realize quickly that your heart gets uglier the deeper you delve.

Not only do we struggle with wrong actions and behaviors, but with wrong thoughts, motivations, and desires. This causes us to grow more aware of our need for grace, and the work of Jesus becomes

bigger in scope and importance as we see the growing necessity for it.

EVERY FABRIC

I (Dustin) like using a red pen to go back through my journal and mark the places where I've seen circumstances change or where I have seen God move. This is a great practice, but leaving that red pen in your jeans pocket and then tossing the jeans into the washing machine is a terrible mistake—unless you hope for new red-themed attire.

I have learned firsthand, and to my wife's great disappointment, that if a person releases a single drop of potent red dye into a load of laundry, that dye will run its course until every stitch of fabric is red. Terrible news for clothes, but great illustration for how the good news of Jesus affects our lives in an all-encompassing way.

Author Dave Harvey stated, "The gospel is the heart of the Bible. Everything in Scripture is either preparation for the gospel, presentation of the gospel, or participation in the gospel."[5] The summation of the Scriptures is the message of the gospel; therefore, the gospel should transform every fabric of our lives. It reaches every facet of our being and leaves nothing untouched. Jesus doesn't make us halfway new, He makes us fully new.

Grasping the colossal contrast between God's holiness and our sinfulness leads us to a clearer view of what truly is so amazing about grace. And that will lead us down a path of reflecting His compassion to others as we mature and grow in the gospel.

So let's look back at the statements from page 65 and replace the word *not* with a new phrase.

Our reality absent of God's grace says: God is holy, and I am **NOT**. But a grace-filled reality says: God transforms me to be **HOLY** (see 1 Peter 2:9).

Our reality absent of God's grace says: God is forgiving, and I am **NOT**. But a grace-filled reality says: God transforms me to be **FORGIVING** (see Col. 3:13).

Our reality absent of God's grace says: God is generous, and I am **NOT**. But a grace-filled reality says: God transforms me to be **GENEROUS** (see 2 Cor. 8:8–15).

Our reality absent of God's grace says: God is caring, and I am **NOT**. But a grace-filled reality says: God transforms me to be **CARING** (see 1 Peter 5:1–7).

Our reality absent of God's grace says: God is alive, and I am **NOT**. But a grace-filled reality says: God transforms me to be **ALIVE** (see Col. 2:13).

HUMBLE CONFIDENCE

Understanding God's grace leads us more and more to a place of humble confidence—humbled by the weight of our sin and need for salvation, yet confident that in Jesus we have all the grace, mercy, approval, and affirmation we will ever need. His work really is sufficient. God does not love us any more or less based on our performance or lack thereof, so we can humbly bring every fabric of our lives out into the light.

Hebrews reminds us: "For we do not have a high priest who is unable to sympathize with our weaknesses, but One who has been tested in every way as we are, yet without sin. Therefore let us approach the throne of grace with boldness, so that we may receive mercy and find grace to help us at the proper time" (Heb. 4:15–16).

What implication does Hebrews 4:15–16 have for your life?

Your community and the people God puts in your path need to be exposed to people who are holy, forgiving, generous, caring, and alive. This type of person isn't self-made, but transformed. The gospel of Jesus is the only means by which this type of person is possible. It's through grace and *grace alone*.

Where does the gospel need to be applied to your life in this moment?

THE GOSPEL FUELS THE MISSION

Take a look back at Isaiah 6 from earlier in this chapter. The timeline of events is insightful. Isaiah didn't run off to the mission field after realizing his own sin, hoping that working for God would somehow make up for his wickedness, and thus earn God's approval.

However, as Isaiah encountered a powerful foreshadowing of the gospel—being cleansed and having his sin atoned for—he became a changed man. He also became a compelled man. When God called out, "Who should I send? Who will go for Us?" Isaiah, compelled by grace, quickly volunteered himself by saying, "Here I am. Send me." The grace of God had humbled him, changed him, given him hope, and moved him. It then became a compelling force, calling him outward toward God's mission. And God can do the same for you.

How does God's grace fuel your mission?

Our world does not simply need people who know more facts about God, but rather people who are falling deeper in love with who God is.

SPIRITUAL MATURITY

There are two things they put in the hands of Kentucky boys when they are born: a bottle and a basketball. Basketball is a year-round obsession for the state. When I moved to Tennessee for college, I (Aaron) was astonished that people actually cared about football. In Kentucky we used football to get us in shape for basketball season.

From the time I was small, I played basketball. By my sophomore year of high school I was on the varsity team. Though I was becoming a good individual player, our team wasn't very good. During my sophomore and junior years we won just fourteen out of sixty games.

My senior year we got a new coach, and everything changed. This coach had been an assistant at the University of Kentucky under Rick Pitino and chose to start his coaching career at our high school (his alma mater).

I'll never forget our first practice. He told us the reason we'd been so bad was that we had a bunch of head knowledge about basketball but didn't execute on that knowledge. For the first hour or so of practice he repeated to us the fundamentals of basketball, and he told us that we would concentrate on getting those right before we moved to more complicated aspects of the game.

For the first time in a long while, our team gained both knowledge about the game and how to practically execute that knowledge. That combination led to a massive change that season. We won twenty games and made it to the district finals for the first time in our school's history.

In a similar manner, long-term success in our given life mission is dependent upon our spiritual growth and maturity. Having a knowledge of theology is great if we are taking a test, but that amounts to zero if we don't apply it. Theology applied to everyday life through the Spirit of God at work in us, however, results in spiritual maturity. This Spirit-led growth is essential in order to live a successful, enduring life on mission.

THE MATURITY GAP

In Hebrews 5:11–14, the author told the recipients that although they should be teachers by now, they still needed someone to teach them the basics about God. Instead of being able to eat solid food, the author said that the people still needed milk as would infants who cannot feed themselves. The image is an alarming one, prompting us to picture an older child or even adult who still drinks formula from a bottle.

One truth that the author related in Hebrews 5 is that although there should be a correlation between the amount of time a person has known Jesus and their spiritual maturity, it doesn't always work that way. There are many believers whose maturity falls way behind their spiritual age. At times there is a gap of jarring proportions.

So what can we do for those who fall behind in spiritual maturity? The image from Hebrews 5 again rings true—we have to start where that person is spiritually. Milk has to come before solid food, and if their lives do not show that they have grasped the basics of Christianity (the "milk"), then we go back to the basics.

BASIC #1: THE SUPREMACY OF GOD

One of the marks of a person who is spiritually maturing is that they have a big view of God. They have come to trust that He is King and able to do what He says He will do.

It is important to understand that God is at the center of His mission and that, by default, as we discussed in chapter 4, we are not. If we believe that God is supreme, then we are in a good position to

mature spiritually. Our desires and decisions will be in submission to Him, fostering a lifetime of repentance and realigning our hearts toward His heart and kingdom.

A big view of God is the starting point for mission. Paul understood this when he prayed his desire for the church at Ephesus, that they be able to understand the "breadth and length and height and depth" of the love of God.[1] He knew that a deep understanding of God would result in a deeper faith. Throughout Scripture the people who were used in the greatest capacities were the ones who had a high view of God.

Nehemiah had a big view of God. Upon hearing of Jerusalem's destruction, he appealed to his "great and awesome" God prior to approaching the Persian king to ask permission to go rebuild the city walls—knowing full well that such an approach would mean risking his life.[2]

Similarly, Queen Esther knew that her life could be ended if she approached the Persian king about aiding in the plight of the Jews, her people. However, after prayer and fasting, her view of God emboldened her toward her calling to a royal position "for such a time as this." If it cost her life, she believed, so be it.[3]

And we can't overlook the apostle Paul's view of God. In Acts 9, Paul encountered the risen Jesus, which radically altered his life's trajectory. He moved from persecuting the church to being persecuted for the church.

What would cause a person to risk his or her life for the sake of the mission? It is an unwavering belief in the God of the mission. Missional "pep talks" or guilt sessions will not ultimately make you satisfied in your life on mission; only a robust picture of God will enable this type of action. Theology professor Keith Whitfield supports this idea: "We will not be able to recover a vision and passion for missions until we recover the grandeur that God made us to know and worship Him and make Him known throughout the whole earth."[4]

As we seek to mature, we must consider the supremacy of God and be drawn to reflect upon the attributes that make Him supreme. As we

consider and personalize those attributes, a maturity of faith in who God is becomes more pronounced.

BASIC #2: THE SOVEREIGNTY OF GOD

God is sovereign. God is involved in every aspect of His creation from providing food for us (see Matt. 6:11) to knowing the number of days we will live (see Ps. 139). All of our talents are a result of God's goodness to us (see 1 Cor. 4:7). Author Wayne Grudem says that David understood that his military skill came from God when he wrote in Psalm 18 that "he trains my hands for war so that my arms can bend a bow of bronze."[5] An everyday missionary must understand that God is at work in the world and is asking His children to respond in obedience to that work. It is not up to us to determine the focus of our mission; it is up to us to follow God. This should come as a huge relief since God has not left us alone in the missionary enterprise.

The fact that God is sovereign should give us hope that as long as we follow in obedience, we are in the center of God's will. There will be many days on our journey when things will not seem to go right. Walking through personal kingdom realignment and joining the everyday mission of God is not a simple and clean process. Everyday mission is messy. It will not always go as planned. People will reject us. We will say the wrong thing at the wrong time and often conversations will become more difficult before they become easy. Walking through the messiness of mission with the right perspective can act as a breeding ground for spiritual maturity. We may be tempted to think that somehow we have missed God's plan. But it is in those moments, if we are faithful, that we can trust we are right where we are supposed to be.

James 1:2 (esv) says that we are to "count it all joy . . . when [we] meet trials of various kinds." Experiencing joy in the midst of trials is a sign of spiritual maturity, and the only way a person can have joy in the midst of hardship is to know that the sovereign one who commands joy will be faithful to deliver on His promises.

Many of us live under the weight of failure because our success metrics are derived from the wrong source. Understanding God is in

control of all things will work as a great starting point toward freedom from those metrics and, ultimately, grow us toward maturity. And a sign of that maturity is accepting that God is sovereign over your mission. There is not one ounce of it that He has not orchestrated.

BASIC # 3: THE LOVE OF GOD

God is loving. From third-grade Sunday school onward, you probably understood that "God so loved the world."[6] Why does God love and why should that love help develop maturity and propel us toward mission?

In God's act of creation recorded in Genesis, we see that when God created people, He created them in His "image," and He referred to His creation as "very good." So from the beginning a distinctive relationship existed between the Creator and His creation. As we have already highlighted in chapter 3, by Genesis 3, people had rebelled against the Creator and ushered sin into the world.

Because of His holiness, God had every right to banish humanity from the face of the earth (as we discussed in chapter 5). But He chose not to do that. In a mysterious act of grace, He chose to have mercy on His people and pursue a relationship with them. In the Old Testament this relationship manifested itself in God's covenant with Israel. In the New Testament, God's covenantal relationship with Israel came to completion through Christ's work on the cross—and not only for Israel, but for *all* people. In that one act, Christ, who knew no sin, became sin for the people. He took upon Himself God's wrath, which was intended for the people. This was His greatest act of love toward His creation. That understanding allows us to clearly see that His mission—and ours—is not the result of duty, but the result of his great love for us (see Eph. 2).

Any time we consider God's wonders, it further deepens our faith in who He is. We increasingly recognize our need for Jesus and the cross (see John 3:30). That lends itself to more maturity, which in turn makes us more and more passionate about the things of Christ, such as consistently reading and meditating on the Scriptures (see

Rom. 10:17 and Ps. 119:11), regularly spending time with God in prayer (see Luke 11:5–9), and serving the poor, the marginalized, the despised, and the imprisoned (see Matt. 25:35–36).

As we continue to comprehend more and more who God is and who we are in Christ, and as a result we apply that understanding to every aspect of our lives, then we reach the very essence of what it means to grow in spiritual maturity. As Jesus continues to transform our hearts and as we submit our sinful nature to the Holy Spirit's work, spiritual maturity will be consistently present. While this does not mean we will be perfect or even near perfect, we will see evidence of heart change and a more Christlike attitude.

MATURITY AND CHANGE

The gospel doesn't just free you, it changes you. In Galatians 5, Paul gave us a picture of what the change in our lives will look like when we are being molded by the Holy Spirit.

The fruit of the Spirit is love, joy, peace, patience, kindness, goodness, faith, gentleness, self-control. Against such things there is no law. Now those who belong to Christ Jesus have crucified the flesh with its passions and desires. Since we live by the Spirit, we must also follow the Spirit. (Gal. 5:22–25)

When we walk with Jesus, we consistently develop more and more of these characteristics (or fruit). As we spend time with Him, confess our sin to Him, and surrender our wills to Him, our hearts will actually change. It won't simply be white-knuckled behavior modification— no, it will be deep-down, soul-level change. When circumstances heat up and the "real" you comes out, there will be a marked difference from the way you would have reacted in the past to that situation. Fruit is what comes off of a tree and it can't be faked. The same is true with spiritual fruit—it is only the result of Holy Spirit–led maturity and heart change.

Take Jared and Tammy, for example. They are active in their church

and have been Christians for about ten years. For many years, their marriage was a wreck. They would have knock-down, drag-out fights that would often end with one of them leaving. But since becoming believers and seeing how the gospel applies to their marriage, Jared and Tammy are slowly but surely seeing their marriage transformed. They still argue, but where unbridled pride and self-interest had been present, there is now humility. Where defensiveness, anger, and harsh words were once rampant, there is a spirit of gentleness and understanding. Where the works of the flesh once took control, now the fruit of the Spirit (see Gal. 5:22–25) is growing and evident.

Both of them are fighting for the humility to see themselves as the "worst of sinners"[7] in their marriage (see 1 Tim. 1:15). They realize that through the gospel, they have been forgiven so much, and that realization fuels them to forgive each other. They look first to the log in their own eyes before pointing out the speck in the eye of the other (see Matt. 7:1–5). Their kids no longer run for cover when they hear the first hint of disagreement.

As Jared and Tammy seek Jesus through prayer and Scripture, their lives are changing. Their marriage is a testament to God's grace instead of a monument to sin's destruction. They realize that if God is supreme, His design for life and marriage is trustworthy. They understand that in God's sovereignty they were led to each other for both their sanctification (growth in the gospel) and God's glory. They are "the one" for each other not because the other is perfect, but because they are married to each other. They have also come to understand that all of this—their marriage, their faith, and their entire lives—is nothing but evidence of God's great love for them.

KNOWING VERSUS APPLYING

Who would you say is more mature: the person who knows a hundred things about God and applies one of them, or the person who knows two things about God and applies both? In reality, the person who knows only two things but applies both things would be more mature, right?

Many of us tend to define spiritual maturity by how much knowledge a person seems to have. If someone owns big books by dead guys, quotes Scripture in every conversation, and throws around Greek or Hebrew every now and then, they certainly give off an air of maturity, don't they? But unfortunately, knowledge does not equal maturity.

Humility, obedience, and mercy are far more closely tied to maturity. Holding our lives up as clay to be molded and shaped by God and His truth is the real mark of maturity. One of my (Dustin's) mentors in college, Dwight Robertson, consistently told me, "The greatest gift we can give the world around us is our closeness with God." Our world does not simply need people who know more facts about God, but rather people who are falling deeper in love with who God is and applying His truth to everyday life.

How would your life be different if you were to begin applying the basic truths about God to your life? How would the lives of those around you be different?

What does spiritual maturity look like to you?

Reread Galatians 5 (found on page 80 in this chapter). Write a short three- to four-word description of each of the fruit of the Spirit. Which ones do you see strongly in your life? Which ones do you still need work on?

Pray for growth in each of these areas as they are a picture of spiritual maturity.

LIFE
ON MISSION

We need one another to carry out the mission of God.

BIBLICAL COMMUNITY

L iving in a city (Columbia, South Carolina) that is in a humid subtropical climate does not lend itself to a plethora of winter storms, but on the rare occasion that it snows, the place shuts down. On one of those infrequent occasions the snow and ice rolled into our unprepared southern city, and the heating system failed for one of my (Dustin's) neighbors.

Addie was a college-age girl who had been attending our church gatherings and lived a couple streets over from me. When her rental house's heat broke down, she and her roommates crashed at our house. My wife is gifted in hospitality so having them stay with us was a treat: a lot of sledding, hot chocolate, soup, and conversations.

They stayed with us three days, and during that snow-venture Addie began to open up to my wife and me about her past and the deep pain and veiled scars she had carried around. Addie had been sexually abused by a family member for most of her young life. Through her tears she described how her view of what a father should be and how a family should love had been shattered. My wife and I were heartbroken for her and could see that this was one of the first times this guarded girl had told of her agonizing past. As she continued to make herself vulnerable, we experienced the beginnings of an arduous healing process.

In the months and years to come, our church family loved her and cared for her as our sister. Not only did we get to experience the different stages of healing with her, but we had the blessing of watching God

use her story and the power of biblical community to bring restoration and redemption for others.

Years after our snow-mageddon (I'm pretty sure it was little more than a dusting) had long melted away and right before God called my wife and me to move to Atlanta, we received a handwritten letter from Addie. It was meek and poetic, and even now as I reflect on it my eyes are filled with tears.

Addie explained how her fragmented portrait of family became redeemed through the simple but effective mission that comes by means of biblical community. She wrote simply how she knew now what family was and how, through the community of her new brothers and sisters, she had learned she has a heavenly Father who can be trusted and who loves her deeply.

She said that though the wounds of her past still carried a sting, God was slowly but surely making her new and that all had started through the redemption of understanding what community could and should be. She closed the letter with the simple phrase, "Thank you for being my family. We have a good Dad, don't we?"

This is a picture of biblical community: being part of the family of God and working together so that people see a clear portrait of who God can be as their Father. As believers we may not be in the same family bloodline, but Ephesians 2 explains how we all share in the uniting truth that we have been blood-bought and adopted into a family with God Himself as our Father. Biblical community is woven into the fabric of living as an everyday missionary.

At that time you were without the Messiah, excluded from the citizenship of Israel, and foreigners to the covenants of the promise, without hope and without God in the world. But now in Christ Jesus, you who were far away have been brought near by the blood of the Messiah. For He is our peace, who made both groups one and tore down the dividing wall of hostility. In His flesh, He made of no effect the law consisting of commands and expressed in regulations, so that He might create in Himself one

new man from the two, resulting in peace. He did this so that He might reconcile both to God in one body through the cross and put the hostility to death by it. When the Messiah came, He proclaimed the good news of peace to you who were far away and peace to those who were near. For through Him we both have access by one Spirit to the Father. So then you are no longer foreigners and strangers, but fellow citizens with the saints, and members of God's household, built on the foundation of the apostles and prophets, with Christ Jesus Himself as the cornerstone. The whole building, being put together by Him, grows into a holy sanctuary in the Lord. You also are being built together for God's dwelling in the Spirit. (Eph. 2:12–22)

God has reconciled believers to Himself and adopted them as sons and daughters into His family. As God's children, the church is designed to function as a family, united in heart and purpose. Biblical community is built upon committed, authentic, and caring relationships that urge one another toward Jesus and His mission. God never intended for us to live out the Christian life alone.

> God never intended for us to live out the Christian life alone.

Together as believers we make up the body of Christ and operate as a picture of gospel transformation to the world in which we exist. Foundationally, everyday missionaries understand their biblical calling to be anchored to a group of believers, to whom they confess, with whom they repent, celebrate, live in faith, and are daily sent out on mission.

Here are some characteristics of people who are connected to biblical community:

- They have people with whom they are honest and transparent about their struggles with sin (see James 5:16).
- They gracefully confront sin in other believers and humbly accept correction brought by others (see Gal. 6:1–2).

- They willingly sacrifice in order to help others carry their burdens (see Gal. 6:2).
- They celebrate and see the value of God's unique giftedness and life experiences within each individual (see Rom. 12:6–8).
- They practice hospitality that helps nurture relationships (see Heb. 13:2).

COMMUNITY: NON-NEGOTIABLE

A solitary faith is not a Christian faith.

Our North American culture places high value on independence and individualism, so it can be difficult for us to understand the necessity of community. *Why can't it just be me and Jesus?* we think, toting our Bibles off in some lone-ranger mission to save the world.

The problem is, you can't choose Jesus and not choose the church. They are a package deal. And by church we don't mean a group of people you sing songs and listen to a sermon with once a week. That is certainly one of the valid expressions of church and one we should be consistently involved in, but going to a service once a week is not walking in biblical community. Biblical community is the group of believers with whom we walk through the good, the bad, and the ugly of life while digging deeper into the gospel.

We are given many commands in the New Testament about living out our faith. Sometimes these are referred to as the "one another" commands. And they all deal with the idea of living a life on mission through community. Here are a few of them:

- Love one another (see John 13:34).
- Show family affection to one another (see Rom. 12:10).
- Outdo one another in showing honor (see Rom. 12:10).
- Accept one another (see Rom. 15:7).
- Serve one another through love (see Gal. 5:13).
- Carry one another's burdens (see Gal. 6:2).
- Be kind and compassionate to one another, forgiving one another (see Eph. 4:32).

- Encourage one another (see 1 Thess. 4:18).
- Confess your sins to one another and pray for one another (see James 5:16).
- Be hospitable to one another (see 1 Peter 4:9).
- Clothe yourselves with humility toward one another (see 1 Peter 5:5).

God is not simply putting more to-dos on our list to make the Christian life more difficult, but rather He is using these foundational tools to grow us toward our own spiritual maturity and to further His mission in the world. The beautiful thing is that as we obediently pursue these commands, Christ is put on display to those around us. We actually become the body of Christ, as we are called in the New Testament.

Recently a popular Christian writer wrote a blog post on why he rarely attends church anymore. His rationale was that he had "graduated" from church and had found other ways to connect with God. Specifically, he said that it was through his work that he found his deepest God-connection.

Though we understand the sentiment, it is not remotely close to being biblical. Throughout the New Testament, particularly in Romans 12 and 1 Corinthians 12 and 14, we see that Christ-followers are all given different gifts (serving, teaching, exhortation, etc.) to exercise *within* biblical community. Every place in Scripture where we observe a spiritual gift, we always find it in a collective list with other spiritual gifts that other individuals may possess. Spiritual gifts are not about individuals but purposed to build and edify the church and its mission. This means that the church is designed to be interdependent, working together toward one uniting mission. If one rogue member "graduates" from the body, then the body will not function with one another as it should—and the rogue member won't either.

THE MESSINESS OF "ONE ANOTHER"

So how can you practice these "one another" commands by yourself on your lone-ranger mission? You're right, you can't. And you're not

meant to. Community is your support system, your sustaining grace when you need encouragement, prayer, rebuke, or help with a struggle. To be sure, while biblical community is an essential part of Christian living, it can be extremely arduous. Real relationships are messy and you can get hurt. Listen, I (Dustin) received my undergrad degree in marketing, so I realize the above statement is not the most attractive to tell people when you want them to become an involved Christian.

The church is a bunch of sinful people getting together with a bunch of sinful people working out sinful lives and believing that God will somehow use it all to grow the group toward maturity. Sounds like a crazy idea, but that is the mystery of how the Holy Spirit works—through imperfect people. I'm sure nine out of ten people reading this book have been hurt by someone in the church, and the tenth person is simply in denial. But as we embrace the messy tension that is community, with its call for patience, grace, and perseverance, God will build His kingdom. Just because community is difficult doesn't give you an "out" option.

Just like soldiers in the army, biblical community is the people you walk into battle with—the people who will get in your face when you need it. It is the circle of brothers and sisters with whom you do life, reminding one another consistently of the grace we so desperately need.

So why are we so often resistant to walking in the light of community? Jesus answers this question in John 3:19–21.

This, then, is the judgment: The light has come into the world, and people loved darkness rather than the light because their deeds were evil. For everyone who practices wicked things hates the light and avoids it, so that his deeds may not be exposed. But anyone who lives by the truth comes to the light, so that his works may be shown to be accomplished by God. (John 3:19–21)

In short, we are prideful people. We don't like to expose our failures and weaknesses, and we like to pretend we have our acts together. But

as Hebrews 4:13 reminds us: "No creature is hidden from Him, but all things are naked and exposed to the eyes of Him to whom we must give an account.".

> How have you seen the "one another" commands lived out in your community? How did they put the body of Christ on display for you and others around you?

NO MORE HIDING OR PRETENDING

Isn't trying to hide from God and others exhausting? The good news of the gospel is that God fully knows us—down to our darkest moments; yet He loves us more than we could ever imagine. So we don't have to put on a façade; we are free to walk out into the light of reality.

If we are truly accepted in Jesus, then we can be honest with others and not put on a show to try to win their approval. If we have been forgiven by Jesus, we can forgive others. If we understand that our righteousness has been accomplished by Jesus, we are free to stop trying to earn it on our own abilities.

Community is essential because it is one of the primary ways we grow in the gospel. If we don't practice the "one anothers" and live honestly and openly, we simply don't have the opportunities to apply the gospel. We fake it, and our growth is phony.

Yes, community can be tough, but what are you waiting for? Your righteousness has been accomplished in God. Step out of the obscurity of delusion and into the freedom of honesty. The more we lean into that honesty, the more we start to see how numerous our imperfections really are—which is a sign of maturity. As we observe our sin, it can lead us to confession.

When you hear the word *confession* what comes to your mind? First John 1:5–10 explains how walking in the light allows us fellowship with others and that God has forgiveness waiting on us. We simply need to confess our sin. How good is *that* good news? God has forgiveness ready for us. All we have to do is honestly say, "I'm wrong." Confession can be one of the most freeing practices. James 5:16 tells

us there is healing when we confess and allow others to pray for us. We can all think of a time where we worked hard to conceal a sin, until finally we reached the breaking point and confessed it. Remember how freeing that felt? That relief is the truth of James 5:16 directly touching us. And that's part of biblical community: applying God's love and forgiveness to our relationships.

What and how does that challenge your view of confession?

FRONT YARDS, BREAKING CARS, AND LIVING ON MISSION

When my wife and I (Dustin) moved to Atlanta, God blessed us with an incredible avenue for mission, also known as our neighborhood. We regularly invite our neighbors plus families in our church community group to cookouts in our front yard. We are intentional about inviting our community group because (1) we want to encourage other Christians to engage with their neighbors; (2) we know that some people may have greater connection with our neighbors than we do; (3) we desire to display Jesus through our group to our neighbors.

That plan has been a blessing. For instance, my neighbor Andrew is a car maniac. He's the kind of guy that if nothing is wrong with his car, he will break something simply to have something to work on.

I know nothing about cars. When I take my car to a mechanic, I'm the guy who makes sounds to describe what's wrong with it. I am every mechanic's dream client. However, Clay from my community group knows cars, and through one of the neighborhood cookouts, Clay and Andrew struck up a conversation. They now hang out on a regular basis, talking cars and on occasion talking gospel. Andrew said recently, "You and your friends really care about one another. You guys are like family. It's just different."

Andrew's not a Christian yet, but he is seeing Jesus through biblical community. Jesus said in John 13:35, "By this all people will know that you are My disciples, if you have love for one another." The way we relate to one another can put the gospel on display in much the

same way as a service project does in a city. Our intentionality in loving one another plays a foundationally vital part in living out our everyday mission.

Who are you wrestling alongside through the truths of the gospel? Who's confronting you in your sin? Who are you confronting? Who are you confessing to? Who are you walking in repentance with? Who are you learning the idea of forgiveness from? Who are you partnering with to live out mission?

Take a few minutes and list the people you are or should be living out the gospel with. Spend some time praying about what next steps you could and should take to strengthen your commitment to biblical community.

As you walk in community with the names listed above and you begin to confront, confess, repent, and forgive, together you will grow in your understanding of the cross of Christ. You see, the cross confronts our sin, causes confession, and delivers forgiveness. The cross is where unity is made possible and where biblical community can truly grow. Mission is but an overflow of living a cross-centered life, and living in biblical community is foundational to growing in the gospel.

An everyday missionary is committed to making disciples who make disciples.

INTENTIONAL
DISCIPLESHIP

Our role as everyday missionaries is to introduce people to Christ, actively be part of their journey to become like Christ, and teach them to repeat the process with others. The simple calling is to make disciples. A disciple is one who continually seeks to follow Jesus through the power of the Holy Spirit and in biblical community.

When I (Dustin) was a college freshman, I debated whether to go full force into the party scene or maybe take my walk with Jesus more seriously. I spent my first week on an A/B schedule—and I'm not talking about my academic schedule. On Thursday I spent my evening at a campus ministry singing songs to Jesus, while on Friday I was at a rush party trying to flee from temptation with five hundred of my new closest friends. It was a legitimate debate and I wasn't sure what I wanted to do, but it was my first year of "freedom" and the choice was all mine.

One Friday night one of the ministries was having a free cookout. Free food . . . I was there. While there I met Matt New, who was a year ahead of me in school. Matt and eight other guys and I hit it off and began hanging out: we ate wings, played ultimate Frisbee, went to football games, and read the Bible. That last part was a big deal, because the extent of my Bible reading had been on game days in high school, hoping that would get me on God's good side and clinch a football victory out of it. But with Matt and the crew, I found myself enthralled with what the Scriptures said. I wasn't just reading it as a

good luck charm; I was reading it because I wanted clarity and reason. Also, Matt walked me through the confusing passages and helped me find the answers in God's Word to my problems. I still remember Matt saying, "How do we interpret Scripture? With Scripture."

We'd get together to talk about what we read that week and then Matt would ask me great questions and then listen well. There wasn't a set time that we would we meet and there wasn't a set of ten questions he asked me every time. It was natural and just happened, as we would hang out here and there. For the first time I was growing in my relationship with Jesus. As I read the book of John, I discovered that the idea of discipleship was not a class or program I attended on a Sunday night, but rather a relationship with regular intentionality focused on the gospel and my spiritual growth. After hanging out with Matt for about two years, it finally hit me: I was being discipled.

I told Matt, "Hey, man, you're discipling me."

"Yeah, I know."

I acted as if I were offended. "But you didn't tell me."

His response was priceless and forever changed me. In his matter-of-fact manner, he said, "Well, now you know, and you should probably go do the same thing with some other guys."

I've been doing that ever since. And it all started with a guy who was just a year older than me, being willing to be an active part of my journey to become like Christ.

We are to make disciples who multiply themselves: disciples who make disciples.

JESUS' PROMISE AND INSTRUCTION

While on earth, Jesus offered some clear explanation about His role and ours in His kingdom. One was through a promise, and the other was through an instruction.

Earlier we talked about Jesus' promise in Matthew 16:18: "I also say to you that you are Peter, and on this rock I will build My church, and the forces of Hades will not overpower it." This is an incredible promise: Jesus will build the church. Often as Christians we take on

the responsibility that Jesus said He would deliver on. Are we called to edify the church? Absolutely. But too often we try to build what *we* have defined the church to be: a narrowed view that includes the building we gather in on Sundays and the programs that exist within the brick and mortar of that building. Our time quickly becomes wrapped up in the next, greatest, and latest program, which makes us feel we are building the church. But that is God's role. We can bring people into a building, but we can't bring them into the family. Only the Holy Spirit does that.

Instead we need to focus on the instruction Jesus gave His disciples—and, ultimately, us. After His resurrection, Jesus told His disciples: "Go . . . and make disciples of all nations, baptizing them in the name of the Father and of the Son and of the Holy Spirit, teaching them to observe everything I have commanded you" (Matt. 28:19–20).

We aren't suggesting that programs are wrong or that we shouldn't have church buildings, but when our structures and programs short-circuit the simple, sometimes messy, command to make disciples, then we need to revisit the Bible and, perhaps, rethink what our churches are doing. Because as we understand both Jesus' promise and His instruction, we must conclude that *Jesus builds His church and we make disciples.*

What practical implication does Matthew 28:16–20 have in your life right now?

YOUR MISSION: MAKE DISCIPLES

The life of the church and the mission of the church are inexorably bound within the all-encompassing reality of discipleship. Growth and discipleship cannot happen apart from Christian community, and your church's mission to make disciples can only be truly accomplished in the context of a community centered on the gospel. There are no "professional Christians" or "disciple-making specialists" who do all the work.

Anyone in need of sanctification (everyone) must submit to

discipleship under Christ within the context of biblical community, and anyone submitted to discipleship under Christ will obediently apply their gifts and personality to make disciples of friends, family, neighbors, and coworkers. No exceptions.

As we've mentioned before, too often church members forfeit their given mission and leave the work to pastors and missions agencies. But that's really not their role. One of a pastor's primary responsibilities is to equip *God's people to do the work* of ministry (see Eph. 4:12). Maybe you question your talents and abilities to serve or speak. But when you offer them to God, He uses them through you. God is in the habit of taking the ordinary person and using him or her for His glory. God could use any means to communicate the hope that is offered through Jesus, yet He chooses to use ordinary people like you and me (see Acts 4:13). No degree, no specialized class, no certain church status are required to make disciples where God has placed you.

As followers of Jesus, we are everyday missionaries who understand we are sent, just as Jesus was sent. Being entrusted with the ministry of reconciliation, everyday missionaries see God's heart for those who do not know Him, and they realize that they were once in a place without hope.

The apostle Paul reminded Christ-followers of that truth when he wrote:

If anyone is in Christ, he is a new creation; old things have passed away, and look, new things have come. Everything is from God, who reconciled us to Himself through Christ and gave us the ministry of reconciliation: That is, in Christ, God was reconciling the world to Himself, not counting their trespasses against them, and He has committed the message of reconciliation to us. Therefore, we are ambassadors for Christ, certain that God is appealing through us. We plead on Christ's behalf, "Be reconciled to God." He made the One who did not know sin to be sin for us, so that we might become the righteousness of God in Him. (2 Cor. 5:17–21)

Take note of the order in which the above passage was written.

- In Christ we are a new creation.
- Through Christ alone, we are made right before a Holy God.
- As new creations who are made right before God we now represent Christ to the world around us.

The above pattern of events is displayed similarly throughout Scripture. Earlier in chapter 6 of this book we worked through Isaiah 6 and we asked you to pay particular attention to the order of the events:

- Isaiah recognized God's holiness.
- Isaiah saw his need to be made right after realizing his sinfulness.
- God alone cleansed him of his sin and changed him.
- After being transformed, Isaiah committed to joining God in His mission.

And just as we are continually transformed by Christ's shaping us in biblical community, we continually seek for others to be reconciled to God and transformed just as we are—this is disciple-making. The church's mission is, in many ways, an expression of gratitude, and it's certainly (according to 2 Corinthians 5) a sign that we have life.

As we grow in our understanding that "He made the One who did not know sin to be sin for us, so that we might become the righteousness of God in Him," our hearts become compelled toward making disciples. We need to hear the simple truth of that Scripture often. That this glorious reality never becomes less true is enough to wreck us every day for the rest of our lives. That's what Jesus does: He comes in and wrecks our lives, in the best way possible. And when we are truly moved by something—when we genuinely love something—we can't help but talk about it.

This is why we cannot simply hope disciple-making into existence. We cannot put a sign on our church property that says, "Now Making

Disciples! Join Us." It takes time and effort and sacrifice. It's messy. Author Walter A. Henrichsen wrote, "Disciples are made, not born."[1] In other words, it's not easy. But it is doable.

Jesus was a great model for disciple-making. His ministry strategy was to pick twelve people and spend a ton of time with them. He didn't give them a manual or send them to a conference; He just did life with them. For three years they traveled, ate meals, and did ministry together. And then after the crucifixion and resurrection, Jesus stood before them and told them to keep doing what He taught them, and that He would be with them (see Matt. 28).

And they did. Empowered by the Holy Spirit, the gospel spread from twelve men to millions upon millions of people for the next two thousand years. What started as an intense three-year flame of life-on-life discipleship turned into a forest fire of epic proportions.

YOU REPRODUCE WHO YOU ARE

My (Dustin's) father was a carpenter. As early as I can remember, if I saw him driving a nail, I found some crew member's hammer and did my best to mimic him. From childhood on, we replicate what we see our parents do. This carries forward into school age as we are influenced by friends and peer pressure. We are continually shaped one way or another by our environments, especially the people around us. We are a fiercely relational people.

Think about it: Odds are at some point you've heard a parent, teacher, or coach say, "Do as I say, not as I do!" And when you hear that statement, you naturally push back because you realize that isn't how things work.

Wayne Cordeiro, pastor of New Hope Community Church in Oahu, Hawaii, told a group of pastors, "You teach people what you know, but you reproduce who you are."

I (Dustin) sought to make this statement a personal mantra as I led my church. For instance, one of my greatest joys as a pastor was doing "Family Vacation" with our church. Once a year we would take a retreat with all of our members and reflect on God's work, study the

Scriptures together, talk about where God was taking us, and do whatever we could to have fun. In the effort to have "fun" on one particular trip, we decided to organize a dodge ball tournament. We broke into teams in an elimination-style tournament, which we played in a parking garage. The theory being, if you can dodge a parking garage pillar, you can dodge a ball! (Did I mention I was a very young pastor?) My team was eliminated early, so I watched our church family compete against one another. There was so much pride-filled smack talk, it was crazy. One girl threw the ball while she simultaneously hit her hand on a pillar (there was blood) and then proceeded to tell the college guy across the way to get his tail out of the game.

Scenes like this continued throughout the tournament and toward the end I leaned over to my wife and said, "What is wrong with these people? They want to win way more than they care for the people they're playing the game with."

In only a way my wife can, she replied, "Hmmm, you teach people what you know, but you reproduce who you are." If you can't say amen, say ouch, right?

My wife was right. I'd taught our church what it meant to love one another, what it meant to put one another's needs above the other, and what it looked like to fight against pride. And yet our church took a lot of their cues not from my teaching but from my life. I'm competitive to the point that I try to beat the driving destination time on my phone's GPS. That night turned into a time of personal confession and a move toward a repentant heart. I was teaching one thing but I was reproducing who I was.

If you want the people around you to live on mission, then you live on mission. If you want to see the people around you walk in humility, seek to walk in humility.

Discipleship is far more than just divulging information. Discipleship happens as we watch people and imitate them and as others watch us and imitate us. As the apostle Paul told believers: "Imitate me, as I also imitate Christ" (1 Cor. 11:1). Just as we have been served by following those who are more mature, we have the great task of

helping those behind us take the next steps toward a deeper relationship with Jesus.

Like a line of hikers ascending a mountain, we keep our eyes on those ahead of us to follow in their footsteps. We listen to the advice they throw back to avoid missing the next step. And as we do so, we also look over our shoulders to those behind us. We tell them what to watch out for, where the sure steps are. We reach back and pull them along when necessary, trying our best to make sure they reach the mountaintop.

As we pursue God's mission, we have to focus on following those ahead of us, while at the same time helping those behind us stay on track. That includes:

- investing in relationships with those around us;
- teaching people to study and be obedient to Scripture;
- using "teachable moments" and showing how the gospel impacts all areas;
- being honest about failures, which clearly displays living under grace;
- seeing ministry as a way to "get people done" rather than using people to get ministry done.

THE WRONG MAN

Toni was a college student in my (Dustin's) church when she became a disciple of Christ. God rescued her from a painful past, and she quickly got connected to my church where she continued to grow.

Amazed by Jesus' work in her life, Toni wanted to spread that good news to others and be a part of making disciples. God specifically gave her a heart for the homeless, so she and some friends started walking through a downtown park, handing out food, and starting conversations with the homeless people she encountered.

One afternoon she saw a small Hispanic man in his late thirties. He was passed out, drunk, lying in a ditch, adjacent to the park. Toni felt led to get his attention, so she said, "Hey, wake up!"

And he did. He woke up and began talking to Toni and the others. He introduced himself as "Alex" and told them about his past, which included why he was drinking *rubbing* alcohol.

The next Sunday, Alex came to church with Toni and her friends. His personality quickly began to show, as he would laugh and say things like, "You guys catch the wrong man."

What started as a gospel-fueled walk in the park for Toni led to incredible things for Alex. Soon Alex came to know Jesus. Alex was baptized in the midst of the roaring cheers of his new church family. Over time Alex got a job, moved off the streets, joined a small group, and started to minister to the homeless, bringing others around our church family.

When we join God in His mission, nothing is insignificant. A short conversation or even a walk in the park can lead to disciple-making opportunities when the God of the universe is involved.

Which is easier—to be disciples or to make disciples? How do the two work together?

What are some barriers that hinder you from being a disciple who makes disciples? What do you need to say no to so that you can say yes to disciple-making?

What is God preparing you for? How does that play into His mission of reconciliation?

The Bible is God's story of using people who overcome great obstacles to accomplish His mission. What are some of the obstacles in your life?

MISSION PRACTICES

*Identify people who
need the gospel.*

IDENTIFY

E veryday missionaries don't just study, learn, and sit around all day reflecting on the gospel in a quiet room. They have an urgency to act—living out their faith in real life. In this section we transition from solid gospel foundations to strong mission practices.

In studying Scripture—in particular the life of Jesus and the ministry of Paul—we have discerned four clear-cut practices to help as you live on mission:

Identify people who need the gospel.
Invest in others as you share the gospel.
Invite people into disciple-making relationships.
Increase disciple-making by sending people to make more disciples.

As you study these practices, ask the Holy Spirit for wisdom and insight into how you can pursue them.

People who live on mission are always on the move toward others. They don't wait for the world to come to them, they seek and find the people who have needs. Jesus was one of these movers. In Mark 5, Jesus encountered a man possessed by demons, who was an outcast in his community and forced to live in a graveyard among a herd of pigs. The graveyard was across the Sea of Galilee where Jesus had been

doing ministry. Jesus knew the man was there and decided to visit him. Jesus had nothing to gain by going to this man. After all, the great crowds who were following His ministry were on the opposite side of the lake. But Jesus went to that one man whom society had written off. He had compassion on him and ultimately healed him.

Your life on mission will require that you "go to the other side" for people. The people who need your help are not necessarily going to show up on your doorstep, so you have to identify them where they are and move toward them.

I (Aaron) met Kevin when I signed up for a group fitness class when I lived in New York City. This particular class had some intense requirements: For three months, I had to attend the class six times a week and I agreed to a strict fifteen hundred-calorie-a-day diet. If I stuck to the plan, the meals and the class were free. I just had to give a video testimonial about it at the end of the three months.

I didn't much care for the grueling process or the packed schedule or the lack of cheesecake and pizza, but it did allow me to meet a lot of people I wouldn't normally hang around. One of those guys was Kevin. He was an actor/director and had experienced many ups and downs. As we hung out in the class he opened up about the emptiness he felt, and he ultimately admitted that the path he was on was leading nowhere fast. As I and others in our church ministered to him, he eventually placed his faith in Jesus.

The fact that Kevin came to Christ was a group effort. Kristen, a member of our church, invited my wife and me to participate in that fitness class. Many people in the church went to great measures to show love and care for Kevin. Freddy, one of our other pastors, spent hours counseling and working with him. The truth is that none of us would have met him if we had been sitting still.

KNOW YOUR NEIGHBOR

As followers of Jesus, our job is to identify people in our sphere of influence and share the gospel with them. Do you know your neighbors? Do you know their names, their stories, their background, and their

spiritual beliefs? A staggering 28 percent of Americans do not know a single one of their neighbors, while 29 percent know just "some" of their neighbors.[1] Essentially more than half of Americans honestly do not know their neighbors at all. In Mark 12:31, Jesus told us to "Love your neighbor as yourself." If we are called to love our neighbors, then without excuse, we must *know* our neighbors.

In some cases those people will be from the same cultural background as us. In many other cases the cultural context may be different and it will be up to us to establish some common ground so the message of the gospel is clear.

I (Dustin) live in the suburbs of Atlanta where barbeque restaurants, sweet tea, and church buildings seem as numerous as sand on a beach. However, the range of spiritual beliefs is exceptionally diverse. On our street alone, my wife and I are the only ones who believe Jesus is the only way to a relationship with God. Our neighbors are a collection of everything from atheists to Muslims. That may cause fear with some Christians, but my wife and I see it as a blessing that God has favored us with our immediate area of influence. And that influence started by simply identifying who our neighbors are.

Though the gospel has to be foundational in the way we connect with those around us, if we don't think through how we communicate then we run the risk of people not hearing the message. The apostle Paul said that his goal was to "become all things to all people, so that I may by every possible means save some" (1 Cor. 9:22). This doesn't mean that he became a cultural chameleon and just blended in to his surroundings. No, he found ways to communicate the central truth of the gospel to different audiences.

GOSPEL THREAD

By nature we are all self-absorbed. It's easy to become consumed by ourselves, only to think about how situations affect us, to make friends and pursue relationships based solely on what they have to offer us.

In Greek mythology we find a sobering example of what self-obsession leads to. The legend of Narcissus tells of a man who stumbled

upon a pool of water, and upon seeing his reflection, he fell in love with his image. So enamored with himself, he was unable to leave the beauty of his own reflection, and Narcissus eventually died by the pool.

Like Narcissus, sin causes us to have eyes only for ourselves and whatever fleeting pleasures we believe will satisfy us. At the heart of this self-obsession is a form of idolatry. We set ourselves up as idols by expecting people and situations in life to give us joy, meaning, and approval. Meanwhile, all around us are people in desperate need of the gospel who go unnoticed. Our self-absorption blinds us to them.

When we meditate on the gospel, however, we realize that in Jesus we've already been given everything we are searching for. He offers us all the satisfaction, purpose, and validation we could ever need. Jesus not only gave everything *for* us, He also gave everything *to* us.

There is an unimaginable amount of freedom in understanding this. If our souls are satisfied in Jesus, we can stop being self-absorbed and move beyond ourselves and into God's mission.

As we spiritually mature, the Holy Spirit will turn our gaze outward. We will begin to see with new eyes, to have an accurate perspective on the world around us. We will notice that God is at work everywhere. Our eyes will see the needs we encounter every day and the people who are desperate for Jesus. Instead of wanting to *take* from others, we will want to *give* the hope we have.

In which areas do you tend to be self-absorbed? In what ways do you need the gospel to free you from self-absorption?

Pray and ask the Holy Spirit to reveal to you where He is already at work around you and how you can join Him. Write down anything He reveals.

GETTING PRACTICAL

So where do you join God in His work? The short answer is to start where you already are. Go where you already go. Just go with new eyes.

What do you do in life? Do you work? Your workplace is likely a

great mission field where God is already at work. Do you go to school? People on your campus need the hope of Jesus.

In Acts 17:26–27, we learn that God has placed us in distinctive places at exact times so that those around us may come to know Him.

"From one man He has made every nationality to live over the whole earth and has determined their appointed times and the boundaries of where they live. He did this so they might seek God, and perhaps they might reach out and find Him, though He is not far from each one of us."

What about your community? What about your city? Are there neighborhood meetings you can attend, sports teams you can coach, or other rhythms you can be part of to get to know those around you? What about your hobbies or interests? Where do your gifts and passions lie? What makes your heart beat faster? What do you look forward to? Perhaps all are things God will use to connect you with others.

COMPASSION, CONVERSATION, AND COFFEE

Smitty worked for a small local real estate company. The company's offices were only a few miles from his house, and most of his coworkers were already Christians. Smitty wanted to live out God's mission, but it seemed his normal rhythms didn't place him around others who didn't know Jesus.

There were two things Smitty enjoyed immensely: coffee and sleep. The coffee shop Smitty liked the most was on the opposite side of town and, considering traffic, going there would mean waking up an hour earlier than desired. In this circumstance, sleep won over the favorite coffee shop. That jaunt would not become part of Smitty's normal rhythm.

One morning Smitty overslept and was running late for work, and to make matters worse, when he got into his car, he noticed he was low on gas. He couldn't chance running out of gas so he stopped at Stu's to fill up. Stu's was an old, run-down gas station where you couldn't even pay at the pump. This meant Smitty would have to go inside and interact with an actual *human*.

Since Smitty had overslept, he hadn't made his morning cup of coffee. As he hurried into Stu's store, he smelled the heavenly aroma of

freshly brewed coffee. Smitty paid for his gas and asked the older lady behind the counter, Miss Helen, how much the coffee cost.

"Honey, the coffee is not for sale. I brew it fresh every morning for myself, but I'll pour you a cup if you'd like."

"Nah, that's okay, I'm good," Smitty said, though deep down he really wanted that cup of coffee. But Miss Helen insisted. Smitty glanced at his watch. He was already going to be late, so he accepted. As he watched her pour the coffee, he asked the simple question, "So how are you doing?"

"I'm doing okay," she said in a quieter voice. "Not great, but okay." The tone of her voice gave away the pain she was experiencing. And Smitty recognized that this woman needed someone to ask a few questions and offer a little time to listen.

God used that moment on a Wednesday morning when Smitty was low on gas and late to the office to help him identify the person God wanted him to eventually share the gospel with. The truth is, Smitty stopped at that gas station a few times every month. This was a normal rhythm for him. It's amazing what can take place when gospel intentionality is woven into the fabric of our everyday rhythms.

Start with whatever your natural rhythms are, because it's not by mistake where God has placed you. Maybe for you it isn't as much about where you are as it is *who* you are—how God has distinctly wired you. Maybe you enjoy biking, fishing, knitting, hockey, or painting. Whatever your passions and interests, they can often help you identify the people God is moving you to share the gospel and your life on mission with.

When we combine our natural rhythms or passions with the gospel and use them to build relationships, powerful things can happen. Our passions or placement (where we live, where we go) can help us identify opportunities for sharing the gospel.

List the people or groups you interact with in your normal rhythm of life. What on your list could be an opportunity for mission?

What are your specific passions and gifts? What opportunities for mission could lie there?

THE ECONOMY OF JESUS

To identify where God is at work, look first at the glaring needs around you. These may be physical needs among the poor, or maybe you live near a high concentration of single mothers or at-risk youth. On the other hand, needs may be more relational or spiritual than physical—people struggling with loneliness, depression, addictions, or even the hopelessness of greed and materialism.

A good rule of thumb is: Look in the margins of your world. Who are the people others tend to shy away from or avoid? Who are the "untouchables"? This doesn't have to be a homeless person asking for loose change. It's just as likely to be a person who struggles socially at work or school and who doesn't have many friends. Often being an everyday missionary requires stepping out and over social boundaries, looking for opportunities to identify the marginalized as you seek to put the gospel on display. Consider how Jesus identified the lonely and the marginalized people of His day.

- Jesus had an in-depth conversation at a well with a promiscuous woman who had been married multiple times and who was currently living in an adulterous situation. This woman had been ostracized by her community (see John 4:1–42).
- Jesus had supper at the house of a tax collector—someone completely despised (see Matt. 9:9).
- Jesus touched a leper no one would even think about getting close to (see Mark 1:40–45).
- Jesus protected a woman from being stoned to death who had just been caught in bed with a man not her husband (see John 8:2–11).
- Jesus identified ordinary, unschooled men as the ones he would pour his life into during his three years of earthly ministry (see Acts 4:13).

Jesus' economy is different from the world's economy. In the world, people are all about ascending—doing whatever they can to step up whatever ladder they are interested in. It's all about getting something they don't have.

Jesus' social economy is completely the opposite. It's about descending, not ascending. It's not about looking to see what you can get from others, but identifying how you can give to others. It's about pressing out toward the margins—to the people who need love and friendship.

Which people around you are marginalized or avoided by others?

What social boundaries could you step over to be a witness to the social economy of Jesus?

IDENTIFYING THE NEEDS THROUGH PRAYER

A central part of identifying people and their needs is through prayer. Ultimately we want to identify those whom God wants us to identify. If you want to know whom God is specifically calling you to love and care for, ask Him.

Pastor Charles Spurgeon was often asked about the secret to his church's success (Metropolitan Tabernacle in London, England). The church was seeing record numbers of people come to Christ and was known as one of the largest churches in the world (during the 1800s). Christians and young pastors would visit the church to try to figure out this amazing feat. When they came, surprisingly Spurgeon would not take the visiting leaders into the two-tiered grand sanctuary but rather to the basement. There the leaders found people praying for God's direction and His grace for the work of His church.

This was the secret to their success, or as Spurgeon called it, the "powerhouse of the church."[2] The powerhouse of a great move of God starts with prayer. The fuel of our mission is prayer. One of the best activities you can do as an everyday missionary is to walk or ride through your neighborhood and ask God to show you what He sees.

Ask God to help you identify the people and needs that you can help meet. Why not even stop reading this book now and pray before moving on?

IDENTIFYING THE NEEDS WITH OPEN EYES

Josh and his roommates were in their early twenties, living in a neighborhood where they were all part of the same church. After hearing a sermon about being on mission in daily life, they were convicted to look for opportunities for mission work in their context. But what could they do? They felt overwhelmed, not knowing where to start.

After praying, Josh had the idea that they should bake a bunch of cookies and deliver them to their neighbors and introduce themselves. Yes, a bunch of twentysomething guys baking.

One Thursday evening, after they successfully baked and stuffed baggies with cookies, the fellas started their trek. They introduced themselves to more than forty neighbors and overall received a warm reception. Afterward, they went home and discussed what they'd learned. They were amazed at how clear their direction was moving forward.

Simply put: Their eyes were opened to a massive need. Out of the forty or so homes they visited, almost half were single mothers raising children. And what do single mothers often need? A break.

> Identifying who God is leading you to may be as simple as taking a short walk with your eyes open.

It was such a simple, commonsense idea that the guys were blown away by how easily they saw the need after they opened their eyes and took a short walk.

Identifying who God is leading you to may be as simple as taking a short walk with your eyes open. Of course, it might involve much more than that, and God could lead you to a place farther from home physically or culturally. But no matter where He leads, it all starts with prayer and opening your eyes.

What are some practical things you can do to identify the needs around you?

List three different groups of people (neighbors, coworkers, etc.) you feel God is leading you toward with the gospel.

Stop now and ask God to reveal to you who He is burdening you for. After praying, write down the group or individuals He reveals.

LIFE
ON MISSION

*Invest your life in others
as you share the gospel.*

INVEST

After identifying where God is at work around you, the next step is to take action and invest in those to whom God has led you. Paul made this part of the missionary process clear when he wrote to the church in Thessalonica: "We cared so much for you that we were pleased to share with you not only the gospel of God but also our own lives, because you had become dear to us" (1 Thess. 2:8). Paul is making the declaration that, of course, we must speak the gospel to those we identify, but we must also invest our lives—our time, our resources, our gifts.

So what did investing look like for Smitty and Josh, the two stories from the previous chapter?

For Smitty, it was an incredibly simple process:

1. Go to Miss Helen's gas station on the way to work every morning to get a cup of coffee.
2. Ask her how she is doing.
3. Pray for her.

Smitty discovered a lot about Miss Helen over the next several months as he stopped every morning for a cup of coffee and conversation. He would stand (no seats in the place) and listen as she talked about her four sons and all the grandchildren she was having to raise. Smitty was able to identify story after story of heartache and would say a simple prayer for her and be on his way. Smitty was able to display

compassion and grace to this woman and eventually to her family, but it all began with identifying the opportunity on a morning when he was running late.

Investing turned out to be simple for Josh and his roommates as well—it simply took time, energy, and the willingness to do a little yard work. Josh and his roommates devised a plan to serve the obvious abundance of single mothers raising children in their neighborhood. After praying and talking, they decided that by cutting grass and taking care of the yards of these mothers' homes, they could begin to build relationships with both the mothers and their kids.

So they began doing just that. A couple of times a month they gathered lawn tools (they had to borrow some from friends at their church—"poor college students" after all) and worked on as many yards as they could on that given weekend.

From there on occasion some of the girls from their church would offer free babysitting, so the moms could have a break and a night out without kids, a rare occasion for any mom, but especially single moms. The girls would play games, help with homework, and share a Bible story with a related craft. They realized they didn't have to wait for a magical vacation Bible school week in the summer to share the Bible with those kids. All of these modest investments led to great relationships with the mothers and their kids. If these moms needed anything, they knew a group of college guys and girls were willing and ready to help.

> Jesus not only modeled sacrifice through His death but also through His life.

Both Smitty and Josh understand that those who have been made right with God through Jesus will disadvantage themselves for the advantage of others.

GOSPEL THREAD

The gospel tells us that Jesus sacrificed everything for us. He laid down His very life as a ransom for many, not to be served but to serve (see

Mark 10:45). Jesus not only modeled sacrifice through His death but also through His life. Over and over throughout the Gospels, we see that while Jesus consistently poured His life into the people closest to Him, He sacrificially served all those whom His life intersected.

Mark 6:56 illustrates how Jesus' reputation to help those who were hurting and to meet their needs preceded Him: "Wherever He would go, into villages, towns, or the country, they laid the sick in the marketplaces and begged Him that they might touch just the tassel of His robe. And everyone who touched it was made well." And in Luke 6, we even see Jesus, on the Sabbath, stop in the middle of His teaching to heal a man whose hand was paralyzed. Jesus' heart for serving others was rooted in compassion—He sympathetically entered into another person's sorrow and pain. Another example shows that as Jesus traveled with His disciples He arrived upon a crowd and His first reaction, as recorded in Matthew 9, was to have compassion for them, because they were weary and worn out. Interestingly enough right after that, Jesus told His disciples that humanity was in great need and to pray that the Lord would send out compassionate servants to meet the needs of the world (see Matt. 9:37–38).

We live in places that are full of pain, whether we can see it tangibly or not. The homeless person is in great discomfort because of the cold and his tangible need for shelter, while the wealthy CEO in the gated community searches endlessly for worth and value. Their conditions are completely different but nonetheless both need someone to forsake passivity and have compassion for them. Sacrificially investing in others is anchored in the ability to have a care for them that drowns out our own ability to focus on self. And when believers join as a community and together invest their lives in those around them, they reflect Jesus in a more powerful way than they could ever imagine.

How is your view of mission and investing in the lives of others motivated by the gospel or something else? How is your view of mission influenced by the grace that Jesus has shown you?

INTENTIONALITY AS A WAY OF LIFE

If you are familiar with church activities, the first thing you think of when you hear the word *mission* might be a mission trip or an offering. While those things are certainly valid aspects of being a biblical community, they are, by definition, short-term with limited involvement. Being on mission is not always about going to a specific place—it's about being intentional where you are. That's investment. And investment is always intentional. It's a lifestyle choice.

> Being on mission is not always about going to a specific place—it's about being intentional where you are.

A missional lifestyle is rooted in the knowledge that God is already on mission around you, and He has placed you in your environment because He wants to use you to reach the people around you. It's a mistake to think that you will be intentional as soon as you move somewhere different or take the next step—if you're not on mission where you are now, you won't be on mission where you're going.

The great thing about intentionality as a way of life is that it goes where you go. If God calls you to move, you will already know how to be on mission to anyone around you. Your location may change, but your intentionality won't.

In what ways are your normal, everyday surroundings your mission field?

How can you grow to be more intentionally on mission where you are?

GETTING PRACTICAL

Once you've identified where God is at work around you and noticed opportunities for spreading the gospel, it's time to put intentional effort in investing into the lives of those people. In other words: Share your life with people. Make friends. Ask them to lunch. Throw a party.

Have a cookout. Invite them bowling. In short, build relationships.

As modeled by Jesus, another great way to build relationships is through serving. Learn the needs of the person or group and how you can help fill that need. If you were to get on a plane and fly to Rwanda, you would quickly discover the need for clean water. Identifying this need would move you toward figuring out how to dig wells and provide sanitary water. It's similar for your people: what are the "wells" that need to be built within your community and how do you build those "wells"? Remember Josh and the guys serving the single moms? They saw a "well" that needed to be built in the form of yards that needed to be cut. Their venture was a big investment, but the reward came through the relationships they and the girls from their church formed with the moms and their kids.

> Whatever you have to do—do whatever it takes to invest in the lives of others.

Of course fulfilling a need doesn't always have to be as big as a year-round neighborhood lawn service and free child care. It can be as simple as offering to help a neighbor make a one-time home repair. Whatever you have to do—do whatever it takes to invest in the lives of others.

Why wouldn't you just tell them about the gospel and move on? Because, while there is certainly room for telling someone you barely know about Jesus (see Rom. 10:14–15), it often works best to build a relationship with them first. (We'll talk more about this in the next chapter.) In general, people don't like to feel they are a project, or that they are receiving a sales pitch, and they may have the wrong idea about why you want so badly for them to become a follower of Jesus.

Just like any friendship, as a relationship grows deeper, you will naturally get to the things that are important. If Jesus is important to you, then as your relationship grows He will naturally come up in conversation.

INVESTING: BOTH/AND

The methods you use to intentionally invest in relationships may differ depending on the person and situation.

Some situations will look like a somewhat normal friendship because the person you're investing in is fairly similar to you culturally. He or she may be a coworker with whom you share common interests, such as golf. In other situations, though, God calls us to cross significant cultural barriers. Investing in these scenarios may require a concerted effort since it might be difficult to discover common ground. It's not either/or—it's both/and.

For example, Paul and Jennifer felt a strong call to be missionaries to the Hispanic community in their city. This direction reoriented their lives in many ways. They learned Spanish. They looked for like-minded believers to join them, and they even moved into a predominantly Hispanic neighborhood.

Depending on where God has you and whom He has led you to identify, your methods of investment may look different from those of other people pursuing the same missionary process, and that's okay. The important thing is that we are all joining God in His mission to seek and save the lost.

A HELPFUL TIP

If you're having trouble figuring out how to invest in those around you, try this simple tool: Ask people how you can pray for them. When you're building relationship with neighbors, coworkers, or friends, simply say, "Hey, this may seem weird to you, but I'm a Christian so I pray for people. Is there anything I can pray for you about?"

Even non-Christians will oftentimes gladly accept prayer and respond to this question with genuine things that are going on in their lives. Many times this question leads to great conversations and a deeper relationship.

A Christian couple moved to a new neighborhood and after meeting some of the neighbors they eventually asked that question: "Is there anything we can pray for you about?" Late one night several

weeks later, they heard a frantic knock at their door. Upon opening the door, they saw a distraught young woman on their porch weeping. The young woman's first words were, "Are you guys the ones who pray for people?"

If you're stuck, try this and see if God doesn't use it to lead you to just the people you're supposed to invest in.

RELATIONAL EVANGELISM

This act of investing in relationships to spread the gospel is called *relational evangelism.* The reason it works well is because we are more likely to listen to and trust something a friend tells us than something a complete stranger communicates to us. It is much more powerful when we share the gospel with people with whom we also share our lives. We see Jesus do this very thing with His disciples—taking time to invest on a deep level. They spent an extraordinary amount of time together, and church history reveals that it was time well spent.

> The Great Commission calls us not simply to make converts but to make disciples.

The Great Commission calls us not simply to make converts but to make disciples. So as we invest in people's lives, we help them continue to take the next step toward Jesus (refer back to chapter 8), with the hope that one day they will become a reproducing everyday missionary as well. (We will dig deeper into this concept in chapter 12.)

How often do you spend quality time with people who don't know Jesus?

Look back at your answers from the "Identify" questions. What would it look like for you to invest in the people God has helped you identify?

Whom could you invite to come alongside you to invest in the community and people you identified?

WELL WORTH IT

Guess what Josh and his friends discovered early on in their efforts? Seriously investing in the lives of others takes a lot of time and energy.

> Seriously investing in the lives of others takes a lot of time and energy.

They had to learn to sharpen a mower blade. They had to edge many corners and turns of sidewalks, and rake leaves in the autumn as they watched more leaves falling where they'd just raked. They had to sacrifice other things in their schedules and show up ready to work, even during times they'd selfishly rather be doing something else.

But do you know what else they discovered? All of their sacrificial investments were worth it. They got to see the look of relief on the faces of those moms. They got a chance to talk about Jesus when asked over and over, "Why are you doing this and not charging me?" They got to witness and hear about the bonds that the kids formed with the girls over the months, asking their moms when the girls were coming over again. Did all the moms come to Christ and begin serving all the other single moms in one instantaneous swoop? No, but the gospel was made clear both through words and their selfless serving.

Investing our lives isn't easy and often we may wonder why we don't see a return on our investment. Yes, we want to see transformation, but remember we are moved toward compassion because we have been shown much compassion. Give it time. Be patient. Pray a lot and allow God to work in His timing. Remember that ultimately our mission is to actively display the gospel while offering the opportunity to be saved by Jesus, but God is the only one who can ultimately transform a heart.

What would you have to give up or sacrifice in order to tangibly communicate Jesus to those whom you have been able to identify?

List three tangible ways you can invest your life in those people you have identified.

Invite people into disciple-making relationships.

CHAPTER 11

INVITE

Jesus was all about the invite. Jesus invited people to eat with Him, surrender to Him, give up their possessions, walk with Him, follow Him, be healed, rest, and the list goes on. Jesus was not even above inviting Himself over for dinner either. In Luke 19, we learn that Jesus entered Jericho and started to teach. The crowd was overwhelming, pushing and shoving, trying to hear and see Jesus. To get a better vantage point, a man named Zacchaeus climbed a tree nearby. Zacchaeus was a rich tax collector who not only collected taxes but essentially cheated people out of money, so the people hated him. As Jesus worked His way through the people, He stopped and singled out Zacchaeus, asking him to get down from the tree. What Jesus did next not only shocked the on-looking crowd but also the most hated man on the block, Zacchaeus. Jesus invited Himself to be a guest at the tax collector's house. The invitation went beyond just hanging out and maybe sharing a meal together; Jesus essentially invited the man to leave his life of lies and possessions to experience salvation. A man who was hated as a result of his sin experienced an unmerited love and acceptance that he had never felt before.

This is Jesus' invitation to our world. Jesus concludes His time with Zacchaeus by clearly and concisely stating His mission: "The Son of Man has come to seek and to save the lost" (Luke 19:10).

God Himself is on a rescue mission as He invites people into right relationship with Him. Joining God in His mission will require that we become willing to extend the invitation to others.

GOSPEL THREAD

Ephesians 2:11–22 beautifully expounds upon the fact that Jesus has reconciled us to God through the cross and made us into one family, or one household, with God. The passage starts off by reminding us of what God has carried us from and then moves on to explain what He has delivered us to. Verse 12 states: "At that time you were without the Messiah, excluded from the citizenship of Israel, and foreigners to the covenants of the promise, without hope and without God in the world." So why do we remember? Because we didn't always have the hope we presently have in Jesus. Once we were orphans outside the family of God. We were desperate and hopeless in our sin.

The gospel calls us to remember this fact because, as we once were, many others still are separated from God. Many hopeless spiritual orphans are still lost in their sin and need to be invited into God's family. Remember what it was like to be on the outside, and that remembrance will strengthen your desire to see those on the outside brought in.

But we don't present the gospel to them and once they accept it, leave them there. Instead we invite people into a deeper, discipling relationship with God. As Paul stated, "We proclaim Him, warning and teaching everyone with all wisdom, so that we may present everyone mature in Christ" (Col. 1:28).

Who has made a major investment in your spiritual growth? How have they helped you become more like Christ?

INVITING: BOTH/AND

Just as methods of investing in relationships may look different depending on the situation, the same is true for methods of inviting. Inviting people into discipling relationships will look different in different contexts.

Think back to Paul and Jennifer's story in chapter 10. They moved to a Hispanic community and began to invest their lives in the people

there. They invited other like-minded people from their church to join them in the mission and, while no one else actually moved there, they did get some help.

Slowly but surely, Paul and Jennifer began to see results. Several people became willing to explore Jesus with them, so they invited them into their home where they explored Christianity. Two of them eventually came to know Jesus, an incredible experience, but Paul and Jennifer soon realized something: They were unsure of what to do next. Because there wasn't a nearby church that contextually fit the Hispanic neighborhood, they began their own Bible study, where they answered questions, worshiped, prayed, and encouraged one another toward spiritual growth. In other words, they made disciples.

They soon discovered that pursuing these disciple-making relationships eventually led to genuine biblical community among the new believers. They became a family. And in the midst of this happening, the disciple-making environment provided a context for more people to meet Jesus, because people invited their friends and relatives, who were skeptical about Jesus, to come and investigate Him. Paul and Jennifer had no idea that something so beautiful could happen in a community they never would have placed themselves in without the Spirit's prompting. For Paul and Jennifer, the disciple-making relationships created biblical community where it formerly didn't exist. And as they learned, the universal principle here is strong: As we invite people into disciple-making relationships, biblical community is formed.

> As we invite people into disciple-making relationships, biblical community is formed.

For Patrick, the invitation looked different from Paul and Jennifer's experience. For years Patrick led a small group of men and noticed that the group was growing spiritually stale. So he prayed and decided that they needed to use their community as a tool for mission.

Several of the men enjoyed playing disc golf, so once a month, instead of having their usual small-group meeting, they played disc golf and invited friends they were investing in to join them.

Steve, one of the men's coworkers, played a few times. Steve enjoyed hanging out with them, and eventually he figured out that they met at other times during the month as well. Even though he wasn't a Christian, he expressed interest in hanging out during their small group time. During the meetings he was amazed by the way the men treated one another like family. They fought for, supported, and even confronted one another in love when necessary. Steve observed the men modeling Jesus' words: "By this all people will know that you are My disciples, if you have love for one another" (John 13:35).

After a few months of hanging out with the guys every week, Steve became a believer in Jesus. Not long after, he started to invite some of his other friends who didn't know Jesus to hang out with the group. One by one, several of his friends also came into the group and eventually a number of them took next steps toward Jesus.

The last thing we want this to sound like is an infomercial for mission with the idea, "If you follow this ninety-day plan of *Life on Mission*, you too will see everyone you know come to Christ." Of course it doesn't work that way. But biblically speaking, this process can lead to great possibilities among your friends and in your community. Try it and plead for the Holy Spirit to work in the hearts of those you have identified and are investing in.

> As we invite people into biblical community, disciples are made.

For Patrick, the small group leader, the biblical community that already existed formed the perfect environment for disciple-making relationships. As we invite people into biblical community, disciples are made. Again, it's not one or the other; it's both/and. Like a two-headed coin, the results should be the same either way you flip it.

MAN ON A HILL VERSUS CITY ON A HILL

Make a concerted effort to be on mission in community with others. Too often the road of evangelism and mission is one people attempt to travel alone. But we need the encouragement, support, and account-

ability of community as we live on mission.

In Matthew 5, in what has been termed the "Sermon on the Mount," Jesus gave great metaphors for what mission could and should look like. One of the specific ideas was comparing the idea of our mission and message to light.

> You are the light of the world. A city situated on a hill cannot be hidden. No one lights a lamp and puts it under a basket, but rather on a lampstand, and it gives light for all who are in the house. In the same way, let your light shine before men, so that they may see your good works and give glory to your Father in heaven. (Matt. 5:14–16)

One of the keys to understanding this passage is to recognize that Jesus was addressing a community of people, and He illustrated the carrier of this great hope as a city.

There has never been a city that had a population of one. One person on a hill does not qualify as a city no matter how hard he or she may try. A city is a city because it has a large number of people who make up its population. We are called to invite people into biblical community so they can experience the "city"—the family of God.

People need to see the grace of God lived out among a group of people. They need to see other believers repenting, confessing, rejoicing in God's grace, and forgiving others. They need to see the gospel applied to life. People desperately desire to belong to something bigger than themselves, and despite being more connected than ever (social media), many people are incredibly lonely.

You are not meant simply to show off the light that you have as an individual, but rather you are meant to display the light of the gospel through a community of people who are unified in Jesus. Biblical community is like a city on a hill that emits a great light to those who are wandering around in a dark, desolate desert.

GETTING PRACTICAL

If you are like Paul and Jennifer, pressing out on mission into the fringes where biblical community is not readily available, you need to have a laser focus on discipleship. Invite those you are investing in to meet with you as often as possible and pour into them. Invite them to study the Bible with you or in a small group environment, teach them the basics of the faith, and talk about the gospel continually, showing them how it applies to their lives.

Within the North American church, evangelism is too often reduced to inviting someone to a church service in hopes that the preacher's message that day is engaging, states all the right ideas, and in the end leads to your friend walking an aisle, filling out a response card, or raising her hand. Please understand us clearly, there is nothing wrong with investing for the sake of inviting a person to a church service, but know that seeing someone move closer to Jesus is going to take much more than that. If we are going to reach people where they are, we have to be bold enough to speak the gospel where they are and not wait on the "professional" to do what every believer has been explicitly called to do.

When reading Romans 10, for many of us, we have the tendency to get excited about verse 13—"Everyone who calls on the name of the Lord will be saved"—and verse 15 (NIV)—"How beautiful are the feet of those who preach good news." Both verses communicate amazing truth and are without question something that we should celebrate. Unfortunately, I (Dustin) believe one of the most unapplied and overlooked verses in the Bible is sandwiched between verses 13 and 15: "But how can they call on Him they have not believed in? And how can they believe without hearing about Him?" (verse 14).

The good news of God's grace cannot be mimed; it must be spoken. Other than one's own salvation there may not be a greater joy than explaining the gospel and watching God do what only He can do: save people.

INVITING PEOPLE TO JESUS

We've talked extensively about the gospel, but before moving forward we want to give a clear way to explain the gospel in conversation and invite someone to surrender his or her life to Jesus.

The Starting Point: Brokenness

As you invite someone to Jesus, you need to start with something they can relate to. We live in a broken world, surrounded by broken lives, broken relationships, and broken systems. This brokenness is also seen in the poverty, hunger, violence, crime, pain, suffering, and death around us. Everyone has experienced or witnessed this brokenness and everyone has at one point or another tried to find a way to make sense of that reality. Even the most stoic of characters has tried to put the pieces of life together. This is a perfect place to begin your invitation. You can say something as simple as, "Have you ever thought about the reality of how broken our world is? Do you ever see or experience this in your own life?"

God's Design

When people endeavor to make sense of life, their attempts often end up being an exercise in futility and ultimately lead to more brokenness. Many will say, "I believe that everyone is on their own path." But they know deep down their path too often goes nowhere. It is at this point you could begin to talk about God's perfect design for humanity. God originally designed a world that worked perfectly. Creating a man and woman, God placed them in a world where everything and everyone fit together in harmony. He wanted them, and you, to worship Him and walk with Him. Originally, things were the way they were supposed to be. So what happened to God's perfect world?

Wanting to be in charge, humans rejected God and His original design. The Bible calls this sin. Like a virus, sin is passed down from generation to generation, distorting the original design. The consequence of sin is brokenness and separation from God.

Gospel

At this point we need some good news. Because of His love, God did not leave us in our brokenness. Jesus, God in human flesh, came to us and lived perfectly according to God's good design. Jesus also came to rescue us—to do for us what we could not do for ourselves. This is the good news—this is the gospel.

Jesus took our sin and shame to the cross, dying to pay the penalty of our separation. Jesus was then raised from the dead. His death and resurrection provide the only way for us to be rescued from our brokenness and restored to a relationship with God. Jesus wants to rescue us by His life.

Invitation

Simply hearing this good news isn't enough. We must repent of our sinful brokenness and stop trusting in ourselves. We must put all of our trust in Christ's death on the cross and resurrection from the dead.

This is when you could ask if they want to trust Jesus. I (Dustin) will never forget going to lunch with a classmate, Travis, my senior year of college. Travis wanted to talk about some frustrations he was dealing with and he heard I would be someone good to talk with. In the middle of his monologue about the disaster his life had become (a sign of brokenness), I stopped him and said, "Hey, man, you need Jesus. It's as simple as that, and you need to become a Christian *right now.*"

I'd never been that bold just to interrupt someone in midsentence and invite them to follow Jesus, but I felt the Holy Spirit prompt it and so I acted.

What happened next blew my mind. Travis said, "You're right!" He then dropped his head and started praying. He told God his sin in great detail—right there over a rack of ribs and corn on the cob.

To be fair, I've had similar conversations since then and most of the people didn't give their lives to Jesus. But the point is simple: When God prompts, speak the gospel.

They may or may not accept, but you've done what God asked you to do: offer the invitation. In whatever way you can, be intentional

about helping people take steps toward Jesus. Continually ask yourself (and the Holy Spirit in prayer):

- What can I do to help this person take the next step toward Jesus?
- How can I serve them and encourage growth?
- What do they need to hear or learn?

Share yourself with people so they can see how you handle situations and apply the gospel to your life. Allowing people to see that you do not have it all together will give way for them to see God's grace applied in your life. Too often, as Christians, we see it as our duty to present ourselves as having it all together, nice and neat. When we live this way, we do not give an opportunity for people to see God's grace at work in us and to grasp that following Jesus is possible for them too.

Humbly and openly repent of your sin to testify that your righteousness is in Jesus and model that Christians are not perfect, but covered in grace. Apologize when necessary and don't let yourself become a puffed up, prideful, "super Christian" who is above doing anything wrong. Remember: You can teach people what you know, but you are going to reproduce who you are.

Is your life highly visible to those you are discipling? Are they able to see you grow, repent, and change?

What steps can you take to be more intentional with those you are raising up?

How can you foster biblical community with those you are discipling?

If you're like Patrick, investing in people whom you can invite directly into your biblical community, you are set up to use your existing community as an instrument for discipleship. Talk to your community

about being on mission together. Cast the vision of being a city on a hill that you invite others to join. Have a discussion about the people in whom your group is investing. How can you invite them to become part of your community? Are any of them interested enough in Jesus to want to come to your group meeting? If so, invite them.

Some people might not be interested in taking that step yet (or might be uncomfortable being around people who pray and talk about the Bible), but there are other great ways to invite them into relationship. One way is to establish relational rhythms for your group, such as planning a weekly "nonthreatening" activity that a skeptic would be interested in participating in and that would still build community. For example, your group could grab lunch together every Wednesday. The options are endless—you can turn anything your group enjoys doing into an opportunity to invite others into relationship.

Name a person(s) you have been investing in who you could invite into your biblical community.

Who is in your life who needs to hear the gospel message? What's stopping you from sharing?

How can you cultivate an environment in your community that accepts new ideas and people?

What rhythms could your church establish to serve as relational avenues to invite others to join?

LIFE
ON MISSION

Increase disciple-making by sending people out.

INCREASE

The goal of the mission is not just to have an awesome church, small group, or discipleship group. It's not to keep only the same people around you forever because you like doing life with them and ministering to them. It's not to selfishly keep what you have.

The goal is to see a movement! To see the gospel spread, new people come to know Jesus, and new disciples made. It's to see more people groups reached, more small groups launched, and more churches started in order to enfold the lonely into biblical community. Spreading, sending, and multiplying movements—these are the goals for the good of people and the glory of God.

MULTIPLICATION IS THE HEART OF A MOVEMENT

A simple way to see a movement of new believers is to raise up the new disciples in strong biblical foundations and to send them out to repeat the missionary process of identifying, investing, inviting, and increasing. The previous statement is not a job description for a pastor but rather the intent given to every believer of the gospel.

The most effective thing you can do for the mission is to reproduce yourself as many times as possible, so that there are more everyday missionaries out in the world speaking and displaying the gospel of Jesus.

Jesus testified to this truth in Matthew 28:18–20 when He gave His disciples the Great Commission: "Then Jesus came near and said to them, 'All authority has been given to Me in heaven and on earth. Go,

therefore, and make disciples of all nations, baptizing them in the name of the Father and of the Son and of the Holy Spirit, teaching them to observe everything I have commanded you. And remember, I am with you always, to the end of the age.' "

He mentioned it again in Luke 10:1–3 when He sent out seventy missionaries in pairs to testify about Him: "After this, the Lord appointed 70 others, and He sent them ahead of Him in pairs to every town and place where He Himself was about to go. He told them: 'The harvest is abundant, but the workers are few. Therefore, pray to the Lord of the harvest to send out workers into His harvest. Now go; I'm sending you out like lambs among wolves.' "

The harvest truly is abundant—we showed this at length in chapter 2. Millions upon millions all around us desperately need Jesus. Together, we must pray for God to send out workers, with the understanding that we become part of God's answer to those prayers.

GOSPEL THREAD

As you follow the timeline from Jesus to the early church and throughout history, you can trace the path of disciple-making all the way to your own life. Think about it: Jesus poured Himself into His disciples, the disciples raised up others in the faith, they sent out others—and so on until the chain eventually got to you. How crazy is that? You are part of a huge family tree of discipleship and mission that reaches all the way back to Jesus Himself. If you actually take a moment to reflect on that, it really is miraculous.

> That kind of gospel reflection will make you want to give away what you have instead of grasping tightly to it.

And what an honor to think that your life on mission continues that gospel thread into the future. That kind of gospel reflection will make you want to give away what you have instead of grasping tightly to it. That's why even though you may want them to remain in your small group, church, or city, you'll eventually grow to a place where you'll have a great desire to see people reached for

the gospel, and you'll grasp that you are part of making that desire a reality. Love for Jesus and His mission will compel you to discover the leaders around you, develop them in the gospel, and deploy them to reach more people with the good news.

How does the gospel motivate you to continue that "gospel thread" into the future?

SPREADING AND SENDING

Think back to Paul and Jennifer, the couple who wanted to reach a Hispanic community in their city. As their small group continued meeting, several new people came into the group and eventually became believers. The first believers were growing and showing a lot of spiritual fruit and maturity. So Paul and Jennifer began to pray about how they could equip them to spread the gospel, and even began to ask questions about it while teaching through the whole idea of discipleship.

One man, Alberto, had many friends who lived across town. He told Paul and Jennifer that God had burdened him for that group of people. They talked about it, and all agreed that God was calling Alberto to start a similar ministry in that neighborhood. So with the group's support, training, and accountability, Alberto made plans to move there and repeat the process that Paul and Jennifer had started years before. This man had been so changed by the gospel that he carried a God-given desire to see another community transformed by that same gospel.

What about Patrick's group—the man who intentionally used disc golf as a means toward pursuing God's mission with his small group? What did "increase" look like for him?

Steve, the new Christian in his group, had already quickly become a missionary, growing in maturity and inviting other men into the group who eventually became believers. So Patrick intentionally equipped and developed Steve, as well as a few of the other men. In essence he followed the apostle Paul's model, in which he told his

disciple Timothy: "What you have heard from me in the presence of many witnesses, commit to faithful men who will be able to teach others also" (2 Tim. 2:2). Within Paul's one statement he lists three generations of disciples: Paul (first generation), Timothy (second generation), and the person Timothy will "commit" to (third generation).

Patrick, our disc golf guy, understanding the 2 Timothy 2:2 principle, and seeing how large his group had grown, sent out a few men to lead new groups of their own—to reproduce what they had seen happen in their group. So Patrick cast a vision for their group to multiply. He taught them that God had made room for them when they were without hope (Eph. 2:11–22), so the gospel should compel them to do the same for others. The men caught the vision, and even though they were close friends and wanted to keep the group they had formed, they all gathered to pray over Steve and the other men, knowing that sending them out was what God wanted.

Look at where you are and ask the Holy Spirit if He may be sending you out of your comfort zone for His sake.

GETTING PRACTICAL

The practical step of increase is all about starting the process again by sending people to identify, invest, and invite their friends and family into new communities. Keep in mind that this will not happen overnight and will require prayer and patience as God matures your community.

As you spend time with those you are discipling, you'll want to begin asking them: "Who are you called and able to reach that I can't or won't reach?" For example, let's say you are a forty-year-old man who grew up playing hockey and there is a professional ballet dancer in your group. Guess whom she is likely to reach that you may not?

You got it—ballet dancers.

Maybe a guy in your group has a background in inner-city gangs. Don't you think that because of his history, he has an incredible opportunity at reaching that community?

Besides common interest or backgrounds, there's an even simpler level to consider: The people you are discipling know a lot of people

you don't know. And of course, since they already know them, they are more likely to reach those people than you are.

Regardless of specifics, being intentional about increasing is just that—being intentional about increasing. It's raising up others and then strategically sending them out to do what you have done for them.

The goal is to train them so well that you could disappear and the ministry would not skip a beat. Let this question guide your disciple-making:

How can you raise up those you are pouring yourself into to take over and do for others what you did for them?

Intentionality in increasing the number of people living on mission is central to seeing the kingdom impacted. This will not happen by itself, and we need to equip and develop people as much as possible.

As far as helping grow and mature those around us, here is a simple illustration that many ministries and organizations use.

- *I do; you watch*. In this stage, you are leading and they are simply being led and discipled.
- *I do; you help*. You see enough growth and desire in them to want to begin equipping them for leadership. You still lead, but you start to let them help however they can. You let them lead Bible studies, mission activities, or discussions.
- *You do; I help*. In this stage, you give them more ownership. You let them lead more consistently while still helping and keeping them accountable, correcting them when necessary.
- *You do; I watch*. This is the stage in which you fully trust them to lead on their own, but they need a little more practice. So you give them the reins as much as possible to lead while you still participate and watch them.
- *You do; someone else watches*. This is where the disciples are actually sent out to lead on their own. They are now the leader and someone else is watching them.

From here, the process is repeated with someone else. And then the person they raise up does it somewhere else . . . and that person they raise up does the same thing elsewhere . . . and . . . you get the point.

This is how a movement is accomplished: by intentionally developing everyday missionaries, sending them out to reach others by the power of the Holy Spirit.

JOINING DAD AT WORK

As we look at the daunting reality of our current state in North America and pressure that comes with being an everyday missionary, we must have a healthy perspective on what joining God in His mission really looks like.

Growing up, I (Dustin) spent a lot of time around construction sites. While I loved all the machinery and the thrill of watching the building process, mostly I wanted to be there because I got to be with my father. My dad was a master carpenter who was well respected among those in and around our community. His attention to detail was bar none and his drive to get the job done right was remarkable. In time I became a "glorified gofer," which meant I retrieved whatever the crew needed (nails, level, 2x4s, water, etc.). I didn't mind that so much, but really I hoped for the opportunity to have my own hammer and join the crew.

I'll never forget the day when I was around twelve years old and my dad brought together the whole construction crew and presented me with my first hammer. He announced that I was now part of the actual crew. I felt like I'd just been knighted, southern style.

"Well, don't just stand there," my dad said. "Get to work." Everyone laughed, and I knelt on the floor to start nailing down the sub-flooring—the base before you install the finely finished floors—as all the other crew stood back to watch this kid take his first official "I'm on the crew" swing of the hammer.

I aligned the nail and took a swing.

Missed. I bruised the floor.

Second swing, contact. But the contact I was hoping to be the nail

was intercepted by my thumb. Now my thumb was pulsating and quickly turning blue. And my face was quickly turning red.

My third swing bent the nail. Now I found myself tapping on both sides of the nail in an effort to straighten the "S"-shaped nailed I had just created. By this point I was so nervous, I wanted to walk off the job.

But then my dad came over and covered my small hand with his large hand.

"We can do this, son."

And next thing I knew, *bam-bam-bam*—the first nail was down. *Bam-bam-bam.* The second nail was down. Nail after nail was going down.

I thought, *Check me out, fellas. I'm a carpenter. It just took me a minute. No big deal. I'm a natural.* And then I feel the pressure of my dad's hand still on top of mine. He was doing the work; he was doing the heavy lifting. He was making it happen.

"We can do this," he told me again.

God speaks a similar idea to us even now. It is His mission. It is His work, and God Himself extends to us the great invitation of getting to go to work with our Dad.

Think about the people you've invited into discipling relationships. Whom are they equipped to reach that you aren't? How can you help them identify people around them who need the gospel?

Whom do you need to raise up and send out? How can you practically develop him or her to be an effective missionary to do for others what you've done for them?

In what ways can you celebrate and support groups you send to reach those who are lost and without the gospel?

MINISTRY STEPS

*An everyday missionary
has a plan of action,
understanding there will
be the battle of pitfalls
throughout the journey.*

PITFALLS AND PLANS

T he goal of this book is to equip you biblically and practically for living out God's mission. We believe as you dig deeper into the gospel and live out this mission, ministry will begin to take place. Pastors, church leaders, and ordinary you and me: We're *all* in this mission together.

Ministry is simply the overflow of the gospel of Jesus in you working itself out into practical terms in the world around you. Being grounded with a strong gospel foundation, paired with the formation that occurs as you join God in His mission, leads to a ministry that allows you to effectively relate to the people in your community. In other words: Effective ministry is the result of a solid gospel foundation and clear understanding of the mission of God. While the gospel and mission of God never change, your ministry practice may look different depending on your immediate surroundings. Inevitably God uses different ministry practices to strengthen your understanding of the gospel as well as the mission you have been given.

In light of this goal, we want to end the book with some reflection questions to help you put everything you have learned together and formulate a ministry plan of action. However, pursuing a life on mission is not without pitfalls, so before we press into making an action plan, we'd like to address some of those pitfalls. Ask the Holy Spirit and your community to help you guard against any of these you may be susceptible to.

PITFALL #1: MISPLACED PRIORITIES

A fairly historical struggle for people who are living on mission is to get their priorities out of order. Many times an unhealthy pace of ministry can lead to burnout and even to the destruction of a family. We can be so blinded by the never-ending needs that we can neglect our more important responsibilities.

As mentioned previously, in the mid-2000s my wife and I (Dustin), along with a few other people, planted a church in downtown Columbia, South Carolina. The first year was incredibly rough. Our attendance was only a few dozen, and most of those were college students, so our offerings were around twelve dollars and a bag of Skittles. In year two we began to see some incredible traction. We were baptizing people, working closely with our city, moving homeless people off the streets, seeing marriages restored, and were rapidly running out of space. I was twenty-seven years old and working overtime alongside some of my best friends to make this mission work. I was preaching numerous times each Sunday, launching what felt like five new small groups a week, interacting with the local news outlets in regard to our involvement with the homeless, and we had hired a couple of staff. Seeing people grasp and live out the gospel was amazing.

Then on a Sunday in November 2007, I stepped off our porch on my way to our church's evening service, where I was set to preach to the overflowing crowd.

"See you there!" I told my wife.

"No, I'm not coming tonight," she said.

What? Her words stopped me mid-step.

"I probably won't be back," she continued. "I don't much like our church." Then she began to cry. "I'm glad this mission is going well, but I don't have any community myself, my relationship with Jesus is dry, and the church we started is *not* helping either one of those."

My response? I thought, *Don't you know I have a sermon to preach? And here you are crying? What are you doing?*

And then God hit me with His own question, *No, Dustin. What are* you *doing?*

Mission is great, but sacrificing your family on the altar of mission is not what God has called us to. The good news is that God changed my priorities that day and my wife didn't leave the church I pastored, but fell deeply in love with the ministry we had been given there. That moment was a wake-up call, which began a journey that I'm still on, in which I'm learning what it means to actively love my family more than I love the high of doing ministry.

The greatest mission effort you will ever participate in is the one that involves the people who sit around your dinner table at night. As you pursue the mission God has for you, never let that truth grow cold to your heart.

Andy Stanley has a great book called *When Work and Family Collide*, in which he says that when faced with a decision to cheat either your ministry or cheat your family—always choose to cheat your ministry.[1] Why? Ministry will always be there and will never be finished—not to mention the fact that God is in charge of it and other people can do it. Your family, however, is a different story. Who beyond yourself is called to love and take care of them? Exactly. No one. Your family is a responsibility given uniquely to you by God, and you are called to make that responsibility a priority. If you don't pursue being on mission *with* your family then the mission you seek is a failure before you even begin.

Please avoid this pitfall at all costs. Love your family more than you love your ministry. If you get this backwards, you are not a faithful missionary no matter what kind of ministry fruit you see.

PITFALL #2: REFUSING TO REST

Because we tend to equate busyness with success, many people living on mission get so caught up in the duties of ministry, work, school, and family that they never take the time to rest. Think about it. How often do you hear people say how busy they are and how they're doing their best to keep it together? It's almost as if getting no rest because of a long to-do list is a sign of success. But here's the truth: Busyness is *not* a badge of honor to wear.

In Genesis 2, God instituted a day of rest, not as a rule to keep us

Busyness is not a badge of honor to wear.

from achieving everything we want but for the purpose of our own health. It is a gift for us, and refusing to receive it is detrimental to our health and to our mission. Without rest, we will eventually burn out physically, emotionally, and spiritually. Our lives will be negatively affected, including the people nearest and dearest to us. It won't be a pretty sight.

I (Aaron) am not a very regimented guy. I tend to be a hard-charger, and taking time to rest can be especially hard for me. In fact, I just spent time with a professional life coach who told me that my energy level ranked near the top of the almost three million people who had used the assessment tool he took me through. His counsel to me served as an affirmation, but also as a warning: I need to take time to rest.

The idea of a balanced life is a myth to me. What I mean is that there are seasons when we have to work really hard, and finding the perfect amount of time to rest in the midst of that may be difficult. However, life has its rhythms. So if we find ourselves running really hard for a season, we need the next season to include significant times to rest.

The way this plays out for me is that my job may require my travel schedule to be heavy for a few weeks. When that is the case I have to be intentional that the following several weeks keep me at home. I may even take a couple of vacation days so I can spend significantly more time with my family.

One last practical example—because most of the people I work with are located all over North America—is that I spend a significant amount of time on my iPhone. I could literally return phone calls and emails 24/7 if I chose to. When it was time for our last family vacation, I decided to leave my phone at home. That break was amazing. I spent focused time with my family, free from the potential worries that email and phone calls can bring. Here is what I also discovered: The world can exist without me being electronically connected to it all of the time.

Working 24/7 and refusing to rest is a telltale sign of works-based theology. The Sabbath reminds us that we are approved, based on Jesus' performance and not our own, and many of us need to apply the gospel to this part of our lives. As you aggressively seek to live on mission, please

be careful to trust God with this area and take the time to rest in Him.

PITFALL #3: WEIGHT-OF-THE-WORLD MENTALITY

Another pitfall is when we attempt to carry the weight of the world on our shoulders. Some people think they are the only ones who can carry out a specific type of ministry. They think they are the *only* people who can reach so-and-so. This stems from the belief that their mission will no doubt fall apart without them leading every facet.

When Carmen and I (Aaron) decided to get involved in foster care/adoption in New York City, it was hard not to take on the weight of the world. We found out quickly that thousands of foster kids needed care and a home. Something in us made us wonder if we were doing enough by only taking two children. Of course, we knew that it was not practically possible to do more than we were doing, but we still fought a sense of guilt wondering if we could do more.

We are indeed called into meaningful ministry, but we are not responsible for every aspect of it. We are not supposed to carry 100 percent of the weight. We must move to a place where we understand who truly carries the weight and actively believe the truth of God's responsibility in this whole mission. As Paul said in 1 Corinthians 3:6–7, "I planted, Apollos watered, but God gave the growth. So then neither the one who plants nor the one who waters is anything, but only God who gives the growth." We work and we toil, but God gives the growth.

This is incredibly freeing, as it takes away an enormous amount of pressure and also teaches us that we can empower others to do the work of ministry and rebuke the lie that we should do it all on our own. Pray earnestly that God will give you the discernment and reasoning to know when to say yes, when to say no, and when to say not now.

PITFALL #4: LONE-RANGER MENTALITY

The lone-ranger mentality is dangerous because it leads us to unhealthy isolation. Referring to chapter 7 on biblical community, we see that no one is intended to be on mission alone. We need not only

the support of community, but also the ability of others to see our blind spots. No one can see his own blind spots, hence the word *blind*.

We have to remember that the church is a body and that each part is expected to carry its own weight in conjunction with the whole. No one part is expected to do everything. In one of my opening stories I (Aaron) talked about how I felt overwhelmed in New York City. I wondered how I was going to make a difference in that vast metropolis. Essentially, I felt defeated because I could not do enough by myself. After a while, I realized that God was calling many people to live on mission and that was how God was going to accomplish His purposes. It was not all dependent on me!

When we seek the mission in and of ourselves we forfeit the idea of the kingdom. We were not called to live out the mission of God alone, and we reflect the kingdom of God when we work with other believers. Together we are better suited to carry out God's mission.

PITFALL #5: MINISTRY IDOLATRY

Any good thing that has turned into an ultimate thing is dangerous, and this can definitely be true of living on mission. It is easy for our ministry motive to turn from being about Jesus to being about personal success. I (Dustin) had a friend who discovered that mission was not just what he did during a summer trip once a year but that his own neighborhood was his year-round "mission trip." I remember he called it his "life trip." It was incredible to watch as God opened his eyes to what it looked like to identify, invest, invite, and increase those who lived right around him. I was so encouraged as I watched God work through and in him. The guy was growing by leaps and bounds, but gradually he began to change. I noticed that all he talked about was, "My neighbor *this* . . . my neighbor *that*" and there didn't seem to be much else going on.

You may think, *What's wrong with that?* But if his neighbors were responding to his efforts to serve them, then he would say, "It was an incredible week." If they weren't responding, then he would say, "This week could not be any worse."

My friend was putting his hope in whether the people were

responding to his efforts or not. At that point his mission had become his "giver of life." Mission will never give you life—only the God of the mission can do that.

> If you don't pursue being on mission **with** your family then the mission you seek is a failure before you even begin.

I (Aaron) can "outdo" Dustin when it comes to his church-offering story. Dustin mentioned earlier in this chapter about receiving an offering that was twelve dollars and a bag of Skittles. Well, the second offering we collected at our church in NYC was six dollars and a gum wrapper (seriously). I will never forget how defeated that made me feel. I went home that night and wanted to cry. After a while, I reflected on why that offering made me feel the way it did. What I realized was that my personal success was tied up on the "success" of the church. I felt that the offering was a reflection of my abilities.

At the end of the day it is natural for a person to want his or her ministry to go well, but what if things *don't* go so well? What if the ministry God calls you to turns out to be difficult and messy and you never see positive results? What if, like Moses, you find yourself wandering in the desert with stubborn people who won't listen to you? If your motive is success in ministry, your joy will quickly dry up. Too often we pursue ministry with our true goal not as pure faithfulness but the fruit we hope to see. Ministry fruit is a great thing, but fruit as motive is fruitless.

The solution to this, of course, is that success in ministry cannot compare to the hope we already have in the privilege of knowing God and will not fulfill us even if we achieve it. God is the true reward, and we get Him no matter what. If we really grasp that on a heart level, then our joy and contentment are secure no matter the outcome of our ministry efforts—because relationship with God never changes. Our deepest affections are designed to be tied to our Creator, not the visible fruits of Him working through us.

We are called to be faithful and trust God with the results. This relieves a lot of pressure and allows ministry fruit to be a thing we celebrate, but not the ultimate goal.

Which of these pitfalls will you need to be on guard against as you pursue life on mission?

PUTTING IT ALL TOGETHER

Can you imagine if millions of Christians in North America came to understand and live out the ideas expressed in this book? What if scores of believers woke to the reality that their lives on mission really do matter and began to live as the everyday missionaries they are called by God to be?

Our schools, workplaces, and neighborhoods would suddenly be captured with hope. Light would invade the darkness in innumerable ways as Christians find an eternal and weighty purpose for their lives.

Needs would be met. Disciples would be made. The lonely would be enfolded into community. The hope of Christ would be tangibly and verbally expressed. Single moms would be taken care of, orphans would be adopted, the broken would find healing, and addicts would be set free. The course of our continent would change forever by a simple idea applied to real, ordinary, everyday life.

This renewal both could be and should be, and it's certainly what we're praying for. But you don't determine what happens to the world—you determine what happens in your own life. You and you alone will decide if these ideas have any impact on your life, or if you'll simply go back to business as usual.

So . . . what's next for you?

Well, that depends on . . . you. But we hope that you will do two things:

1. Grow in the gospel and biblical foundations. We hope you will meditate on the gospel and seek to continually apply it to every fabric of your life. We hope you will pursue maturity, community, and discipleship as lifetime principles.

2. Actively pursue the missionary practices. We hope that the foundations you pursue will compel you toward a biblically

faithful missionary effort. We hope you will identify, invest, invite, and increase.

We believe this book will serve as a helpful tool in your development as a missionary, and we pray that you will consult it often and use it wisely. As you grow in the gospel and the biblical foundations for ministry, you will by grace become the everyday missionary God is calling you to be as you faithfully live your *life on mission*.

So . . . really . . . what's next for you?

QUESTIONS TO SET YOUR PLAN OF ACTION

What has the Holy Spirit prompted you to glean from this book?

What steps do you need to take in order to grow as a missionary?

How can you grow to be more grounded in the missionary foundations (the gospel, spiritual maturity, biblical community, intentional discipleship)?

Very practically, what can you do to pursue the missionary practices in the next three months?

IDENTIFY: Whom has God led you to identify as people who need the gospel?

INVEST: In what ways can you invest your life in those people while you share the gospel?

INVITE: How can you invite them into disciple-making relationships?

INCREASE: In what ways can you send them out to make new disciples?

LEADER'S GUIDE: SIX-WEEK STUDY

HOW TO USE THIS LEADER'S GUIDE

Life on Mission seeks to deliver a solid gospel foundation with everyday mission practices. It offers engaging stories threaded with powerful questions to help people take their next steps to living life on mission.

Ideally, we encourage the reader to discuss and process the content within community. Our goal is for small groups, missional communities, Sunday school classes, church plant core teams, and church staffs to work through the book together and allow it to shape the way they live on mission.

This Leader's Guide is intended to be a helpful resource for any leader or group facilitator. It is based on a six-week discussion of the book (taking a few chapters per week). However, feel free to take this at your own pace and spread the discussion over more weeks if that would be better for your community.

The guide is simple and straightforward, including highlights from each chapter to help focus your conversation, a few helpful questions to guide discussion, and some practical challenges. You may want to read the chapter highlights aloud as a refresher before starting each chapter's discussion. Also, refer back to the questions embedded in the content of each chapter. Your group members should have already worked through those questions during their reading for that designated week.

SIX-WEEK READING PLAN: OVERVIEW

Week 1: The Big Picture
Chapter 1: Everyday Missionary
Chapter 2: The Current Reality

Week 2: The Big Picture
Chapter 3: The Mission of God
Chapter 4: Kingdom Realignment

Week 3: Gospel Foundations
Chapter 5: The Gospel
Chapter 6: Spiritual Maturity

Week 4: Gospel Foundations
Chapter 7: Biblical Community
Chapter 8: Intentional Discipleship

Week 5: Mission Practices
Chapter 9: Identify
Chapter 10: Invest

Week 6: Mission Practices & Ministry Steps
Chapter 11: Invite
Chapter 12: Increase
Chapter 13: Pitfalls and Plans

WEEK 1: THE BIG PICTURE (CHAPTERS 1 & 2)

Chapter 1: Everyday Missionary

CHAPTER HIGHLIGHTS:

- Your life has a mission. If you are a follower of Jesus, then He has a purpose and plan for you.

- An everyday missionary is one who lives life on mission where God has placed him or her.

- The ultimate aim of our lives is to glorify God!

- Understanding that God is sovereign is essential for mission. A missionary must recognize that God is at work in the world and ask His children to respond to that work.

- If you determine the success of mission, then that isn't a God-centered mission. If God directs the success of the mission, however, then you are on the right track.

- The reality of God's love and grace should propel us toward living on mission.

- A weak gospel foundation leads to fragile mission practices.

- The overall goal of all life on mission is to serve the glory of God. That goal in turn provides the necessary fuel and endurance for the mission.

DISCUSSION QUESTIONS:

1. How have you struggled with figuring out what God's will is for you? In what ways is it freeing to think that His primary will is for you to simply glorify Him where you are?

2. How do God's sovereignty and God's love form the correct motivation for mission? How do they take away unnecessary pressure from mission?

3. Which camp do you tend to fall in most?

    a. The "I'm not a professional" camp

    b. The "I'm too busy pondering" camp

    c. The "Why are we doing this?" camp

4. What from chapter 1 stood out to you, and how could this impact your life?

Chapter 2: The Current Reality

CHAPTER HIGHLIGHTS:
- America's evangelical population loses 2.6 million people per decade.

- While many evangelical denominations are on the rise, they still fall woefully behind in catching up with the population growth and cultural changes.

- Entire cities that were once vibrant, gospel-transformed places are now spiritually boarded-up wastelands.

- When things seem bleak and hopeless, God shows up and breathes life into our situation.

DISCUSSION QUESTIONS:
1. Did this chapter change your perspective about the need for the gospel in North America? If so, how?

2. How does understanding the realistic spiritual landscape in North America affect your thoughts toward your everyday life?

3. What from this chapter stood out to you, and how could this impact your life?

WEEK 1'S PRACTICAL CHALLENGE:

Ask God to let you see your community and city as He does.

Spend some time this week examining your city and community and ask God to show you where it lacks gospel influence. As God begins to reveal the current reality, ask Him how you can live on mission where you are.

WEEK 2: THE BIG PICTURE (CHAPTERS 3 & 4)

Chapter 3: The Mission of God

CHAPTER HIGHLIGHTS:

- As we push deeper into what it looks like to join God in His mission, we should take caution not to skip "why" it's important.

- The current reality of our world is certainly a motivation for what we do as everyday missionaries, but the ultimate motivator is God Himself.

- Our missionary God is not waiting for you or me—He is already at work.

- God has always been about forming a gospel people for a gospel mission.

- As we are changed and freed by Jesus, we are compelled to want to be where He is—right in the middle of the greatest rescue mission ever given, led by God Himself.

DISCUSSION QUESTIONS:

1. Discuss the practical challenge from the previous week. How did it go? What did God show you?

2. In what ways does understanding God's mission throughout history affect you?

3. How do you see your everyday life as a part of God's mission to bless the world? In what ways can this truth be something you are constantly aware of?

4. What from this chapter stood out to you, and how could this impact your life and ministry?

Chapter 4: Kingdom Realignment

CHAPTER HIGHLIGHTS:

- God is still King of His kingdom.

- Jesus is a King who gets down into the mess of humanity, who goes to ultimate lengths to seek and save the lost and restore people back into His kingdom.

- In the standard economy of a kingdom, kings are not servants and servants are not kings, yet King Jesus is both.

- Jesus calls us to repent of building our own kingdoms.

- The kingdom of God is the best thing we could ever get swept up in.

- He calls us to repent of chasing after our own fame and glory, and instead pursue His fame and glory. It's the best trade we could ever make.

DISCUSSION QUESTIONS:

1. How does knowing that God is our King strip away any hopelessness that might creep in when we consider the decline of the church in North America?

2. What self-centered kingdoms have you pursued with your time, energy, and resources? What do repentance and getting swept up in God's kingdom look like for you?

3. What from chapter 4 stood out to you, and how could this impact your life and ministry?

WEEK 2'S PRACTICAL CHALLENGE:

Walk around your neighborhood this week and introduce yourself to any neighbors you do not know. Bake some cookies (or something else delicious) and give them as gifts. Be bold. Have fun. Watch God work.

WEEK 3: GOSPEL FOUNDATIONS (CHAPTERS 5 & 6)

Chapter 5: The Gospel

CHAPTER HIGHLIGHTS

- Living out a gospel mission is not a guilt or fear-driven task— it is the good life.

- A missionary who isn't grounded in the good news of Jesus is no missionary at all because he or she does not have good news to proclaim.

- Though we are more sinful than we'll ever truly know, we are *still* loved by God more than we could ever imagine.

- If Jesus is your Savior, the pressure is off.

- The gospel is not based on what you do for God, but what God has done for you. It is not "you do" but "Jesus did."

- The gospel is how we become Christians, but it is also how we grow as believers—through meditating on God's Word and applying it to every fabric of our lives.

- The gospel stands opposed to earning, but it should by grace propel us toward great effort.

DISCUSSION QUESTIONS:

1. Discuss the practical challenge from the previous week. How did it go?

2. How do you struggle to believe that "if Jesus is your Savior, the pressure is off"?

3. In what ways do you tend to believe that God's feelings toward you rise and fall based on your spiritual performance (instead of being secured by Jesus' righteousness)?

4. What from chapter 5 stood out to you, and how could this impact your life and ministry?

Chapter 6: Spiritual Maturity

CHAPTER HIGHLIGHTS:

- As you grow a deeper understanding of your identity in Jesus and submit your sinful nature to the Holy Spirit's work, spiritual maturity will be consistently present.

- The gospel doesn't just free you; it changes you.

- Knowledge does not equal maturity.

- Our world does not need people who know more facts about God, but rather people who are falling deeper in love with God.

- Humility, obedience, and application are far more closely tied to maturity.

DISCUSSION QUESTIONS:

1. Where have you seen Jesus at work in your life recently? How is He growing you toward maturity?

2. Are there areas where you have knowledge but not application and obedience? Are there things you need to repent of in order to grow spiritually?

3. What fruit of the Spirit is less prevalent in your life?

4. What fruit of the Spirit is more prevalent in your life?

5. What from chapter 6 stood out to you, and how could this impact your life and ministry?

WEEK 3'S PRACTICAL CHALLENGE:

Contemplate the ways you try to earn God's love and write those ways down. Then pray each day that God would free you from the performance trap. Ask the Holy Spirit to reveal any areas that you haven't given over completely to Him and ask Him to show you what pursuing health and obedience in those areas looks like in a typical week. Once He shows you, commit to following that. (Example: If you've been convicted about your prayer life, commit to pray for fifteen minutes every day this week.)

WEEK 4: GOSPEL FOUNDATIONS
(CHAPTERS 7 & 8)

Chapter 7: Biblical Community

CHAPTER HIGHLIGHTS:
- Biblical community is built on committed, authentic, and caring relationships that urge one another toward Jesus and His mission.

- Everyday missionaries understand their biblical calling to be anchored to a group of believers, to whom they confess, with whom they repent, celebrate, and live in faith.

- You can't choose Jesus and not choose the church. They are a package deal.

- Biblical community is the group of believers with whom we walk through the good, the bad, and the ugly while digging deeper together into the gospel.

- Community is essential because it is one of the primary ways we grow in the gospel.

- We need one another to carry out the mission of God.

DISCUSSION QUESTIONS:
1. Discuss the practical challenge from the previous week. How did it go?

2. With whom are you walking in biblical community?

3. When was the last time you confessed your sin to another believer?

4. What changes could you make to move more purposefully toward being in consistent biblical community?

5. What from chapter 7 stood out to you, and how could this impact your life?

Chapter 8: Intentional Discipleship

CHAPTER HIGHLIGHTS:

- As followers of Jesus, everyday missionaries understand they are sent, just as Jesus was sent.

- Jesus' ministry strategy was to pick twelve people and spend a ton of time with them.

- Disciple-making happens best in the context of relationships and biblical community.

- Discipleship cannot be divorced from community, because discipleship happens in community.

- As we pursue God's mission we have to focus on following those ahead of us, while at the same time helping those behind us stay on track.

DISCUSSION QUESTIONS:

1. Discuss the practical challenge from the previous week. How did it go?

2. Do you struggle with seeing mission as a "have to" rather than a "get to"? If so, what is off in your perspective?

3. Who has helped you take next steps toward Jesus? How can you encourage and thank them this week?

4. Who has God put in your life who you can intentionally help take next steps toward Jesus?

5. What barriers make it difficult for you to make disciples who make disciples? How can we as a group help remove those barriers?

6. What from chapter 8 stood out to you, and how could this impact your life and ministry?

WEEK 4'S PRACTICAL CHALLENGE:

1. Confess any current sin to another believer in your community, and ask them to remind you of the gospel in response.

2. Write down the name(s) of the person(s) you are going to help take their next steps toward Jesus and call them this week to set up a time to hang out.

WEEK 5: MISSION PRACTICES (CHAPTERS 9 & 10)

Chapter 9: Identify

CHAPTER HIGHLIGHTS:

- If our souls are satisfied in Jesus, we can turn our eyes away from ourselves. By grace we can stop being self-absorbed. Instead we will identify people who desperately need the hope of Jesus.

- Where do you start in your efforts to join God in His work and be a disciple-maker? The short answer is to start where you already are. Go where you already go. Just go with new eyes.

- When we combine our natural rhythms and passions with the gospel and use them to build relationships, powerful things can happen.

- Identifying who God is leading you to may be as simple as taking a short walk with your eyes open.

DISCUSSION QUESTIONS:

1. Discuss the practical challenge from the previous week. How did it go?

2. Who has God placed around you that He may be calling you to be on mission with (coworkers, neighbors, friends, those who share hobbies/interests, etc.)? Mention specific names and pray for them.

3. Are there ways your passions or natural life rhythms may focus God's mission for your life?

4. What group of people is God leading you to focus your mission efforts on?

5. What changes could you make to be more consistently aware of what God is doing around you?

6. What from chapter 9 stood out to you, and how could this impact your life and ministry?

Chapter 10: Invest

CHAPTER HIGHLIGHTS:

- Growing in the gospel will move you from identifying those around you who need the hope of Jesus to investing your life in theirs.

- As an everyday missionary, you are rooted in the knowledge that God is already on mission around you, and the fact that He has placed you in your environment because He wants to use you to reach the people around you.

- Being on mission is not about going to a specific place— it's about being intentional where you are.

- Share your life with people. Make friends. Ask them to lunch. Throw a party. Have a cookout. Invite them to go bowling. In short, build relationships.

- As we invest in the lives of people, we help them continue to take the next step toward Jesus, with the hope that one day they will become a reproducing everyday missionary as well.

DISCUSSION QUESTIONS:

1. Discuss the practical challenge from the previous week. How did it go?

2. What would it look like for you to invest in the people God has led you to identify? How can you consistently build relationships and spend time with them?

3. What changes might you need to make in order to truly invest in people?

4. What practical step can you take this week to invest relationally in someone?

5. What from chapter 10 stood out to you, and how could this impact your life and ministry?

WEEK 5'S PRACTICAL CHALLENGE:

Pray about who God wants you to be intentional with (neighbors, coworkers, friends, people with similar interests/hobbies, etc.). Write

down one to three specific names and pray for them every day this week. Then write out how you will give of your time and energy to invest in them. Then do it.

WEEK 6: MISSION PRACTICES AND MINISTRY STEPS (CHAPTERS 11, 12 & 13)

Chapter 11: Invite

CHAPTER HIGHLIGHTS:

- As we invite people into disciple-making relationships, biblical community is formed.

- Invitation includes making a concerted effort to be on mission in community with others.

- You need the encouragement, support, and accountability of community while you are on mission.

- Invite people to give their lives to Jesus. Speak the gospel.

- People need to see God's grace lived out among a group of people. They need to see other believers repenting, confessing, rejoicing in God's grace, and forgiving others. They need to see the gospel applied to life.

- Biblical community is like a city on a hill that emits a great light to those who are wandering around in a dark desert.

DISCUSSION QUESTIONS:

1. Discuss the practical challenge from the previous week. How did it go?

2. What would it look like practically for you to invite people into disciple-making relationships?

3. Do you have consistent relationships with other believers (biblical community) with whom you could invite others to join?

4. Who do you feel God is leading you to invite into a relationship with Jesus?

5. What conversation might you need to have with someone about the gospel?

6. What from chapter 11 stood out to you, and how could this impact your life and ministry?

Chapter 12: Increase

CHAPTER HIGHLIGHTS:

- Love for Jesus and His mission will compel you to identify the leaders around you, raise them up, and send them out to reach more people with the gospel.

- The goal is to see a movement! The movement includes spreading the gospel, bringing people into relationship with Jesus, and growing them to maturity. We desire to see more people groups reached, more churches started, and more small groups launched to enfold the lonely into community.

- The most effective thing you can do for the mission is to reproduce yourself as many times as possible, so that many more missionaries spread the good news of Jesus.

- The goal is to train them so well that you could disappear and the mission would not skip a beat.

DISCUSSION QUESTIONS:

1. Discuss the practical challenge from the previous week. How did it go?

2. What is the hardest part about making disciples and reproducing yourself as a missionary?

3. How does Jesus' promise in the Great Commission that "I am with you always, to the end of the age" (Matt. 28:20) encourage you in your disciple-making efforts?

4. What does the increase step look like in your setting? How can you be intentional about raising up others and sending them out?

5. Discuss the leadership development process from the end of the chapter. What would this look like in your context?

6. What from chapter 12 stood out to you, and how could this impact your life and ministry?

Chapter 13: Pitfalls and Plans

CHAPTER HIGHLIGHTS:

- Ministry is simply the overflow of the gospel in you working itself out into practical terms in the world around you.

- An everyday missionary has a plan of action, understanding there will be pitfalls throughout the journey.

- Many times an unhealthy pace of ministry can lead to burnout and even to the destruction of a family.

- Busyness is *not* a badge of honor to wear.

- We are called into meaningful ministry, but we are not responsible for every aspect of it.

- It is easy for our ministry motives to turn from being about Jesus to being about personal success.

- Actively pursue the missionary practices.

- Identify, invest, invite, and increase.

DISCUSSION QUESTIONS:

1. Of the five pitfalls mentioned, which one tends to be a problem area for you and why?

2. Discuss the first three personal reflection questions from chapter 13.

3. Summarize and discuss your action plans based on the missionary process you learned in this book. Which one is the easiest? The most difficult? Why?

4. How does what you have learned in *Life on Mission* impact your community/church/group, etc.?

WEEK 6'S PRACTICAL CHALLENGE:

1. Pick one person from your prayer list from Week 5 and intentionally invest in him or her (for instance, invite them to lunch, a dinner party, a local sporting event, a concert, or to coffee). Whatever you do, be sure to ask a lot of questions about their life and show genuine interest. Also, try to involve other Christians from your community.

Tip: During this step, a helpful question to ask people is: "This may sound weird to you, but I'm a Christian and like to pray for people, so is there anything I can pray about for you?"

Many times this simple step opens the door for more intentional conversation as you follow up with prayer requests.

2. Write down the person(s) from your group who need to start new groups of gospel influence and have a conversation with them about moving toward next steps.

3. Share your *Life on Mission* plan with the group and how you have begun the journey of an everyday missionary.

NOTES

Introduction

1. http://www.nyc.gov/html/dcp/html/census/pop_facts.shtml.
2. http://quickfacts.census.gov/qfd/states/28000.html.
3. Lyle Schaller, *44 Questions for Church Planters* (Nashville, TN: Abingdon Press, 1991), 14–26.
4. J. D. Payne, *From 35,000 to 15,000 Feet: Evangelicals in the United States and Canada: A State/Province, Metro, and County Glimpse* (jdpayne.org, 2010), 12.
5. Ibid., 12.
6. Ibid., 9.
7. Ibid. 10.
8. http://www.christianitytoday.com/ct/2012/may/quebec-prodigal-province.html?start=3. Also cited in http://en.outreach.ca/Resources/Research/tabid/5233/ArticleId/6938/Is-Canada-Becoming-a-Post-Christian-Country.aspx.
9. Tim Keller, "Why Plant Churches" (Redeemer Presbyterian Church, 2002), 6. http://sermons2.redeemer.com/sermons/why-plant-churches.
10. Ed Stetzer, *Planting New Churches in a Postmodern Age* (Nashville: Broadman & Holman, 2003), 10.
11. Jim Collins, *Good to Great* (New York, NY: HarperBusiness, 2001), 65.
12. http://www.nycreligion.info/?p=1165.
13. Matthew 16:18: [Jesus said to Peter,] "On this rock I will build My church, and the forces of Hades will not overpower it."

Chapter 1: Everyday Missionary

1. Psalm 46:10, ESV.
2. Exodus 34:14.
3. John Piper, *Let the Nations Be Glad* (Grand Rapids, MI: Baker Academic, 2001), 17.
4. "Westminster Larger Catechism" http://www.reformed.org/documents/index.html?mainframe=http://www.reformed.org/documents/larger1.html.

Chapter 2: The Current Reality

1. John Dickerson, *The Great Evangelical Recession* (Grand Rapids, MI: Baker Books, 2013), 26.
2. http://jacksonville.com/tu-online/stories/063008/lif_296770295.shtml.
3. http://www.pcaac.org/church-search/_Also cited in http://www. usnews.com/opinion/blogs/robert-schlesinger/2011/12/30/us-population-2012-nearly-313-million-people.
4. http://www.efccm.ca/pdfs/WelcomeToTheFamily.pdf.
5. http://www.cmacan.org/statistics.
6. *The Great Evangelical Recession,* 22.
7. http://www.usatoday.com/story/news/nation/2012/12/12/census-whites-us-2043/1763429/. Also cited in John S. Dickerson, *The Great Evangelical Recession*, 33.
8. http://www.reginaldbibby.com/images/Revision_Bibby_CSA_Presentation,_Ottawa_May_09.pdf.
9. http://www.slate.com/articles/life/faithbased/2012/11/re_evangelizing_new_england_how_church_planting_and_music_festivals_are.html.
10. Adam Miller, "Overview of Montreal," http://www.namb.net/montreal/overview/.
11. Ibid.
12. Ibid.

Chapter 3: The Mission of God
1. Genesis 1:26–27.

Chapter 4: Kingdom Realignment
1. Romans 8:28.

Chapter 5: The Gospel

1. Tim Chester, *You Can Change* (Wheaton, IL: Crossway Books, 2013), 15.
2. John Van Diest and Alton Gansky, *The Secrets God Kept* (Carol Stream, IL: Tyndale, 2005), 145.
3. Louie Giglio, in a message delivered at Send North America Conference, July 30, 2012.
4. Tim Keller, "Knowing that we know God," preached 11/13/1994, http://www.monergism.com/thethreshold/articles/onsite/jesusourdefense.html.
5. Dave Harvey, *When Sinners Say "I Do"* (Wapwallopen, PA: Shepherd Press, 2010), Kindle Edition.

Chapter 6: Spiritual Maturity

1. Ephesians 3:18, ESV.

2. Nehemiah 1:5, ESV.

3. Esther 4:14, ESV.

4. Bruce Ashford, ed., *Theology and Practice of Mission* (Nashville, TN: B&H Books, 2011),18.

5. This is a paraphrase of the language that Wayne Grudem uses in his *Systematic Theology*. Wayne Grudem, *Systematic Theology: An Introduction to Biblical Doctrine* (Grand Rapids, MI: Zondervan Publishing, 1994), 214, 337, et al.

6. John 3:16, ESV.

7. Dave Harvey, *When Sinners Say I Do,* Kindle Edition. This is not a specific quote but a theme from the book.

Chapter 8: Intentional Discipleship

1. Walter A. Henrichsen, *Disciples Are Made Not Born* (Colorado Springs, CO: David C Cook, 2002).

Chapter 9: Identify

1. http://www.pewinternet.org/2010/06/09/neighbors-online/.

2. Charles Spurgeon, edited by Robert Hall, *The Power of Prayer in a Believer's Life* (Lynnewood, WA: Emerald Books, 1993), 12.

Chapter 13: Pitfalls and Plans

1. Andy Stanley, *When Work and Family Collide* (Colorado Springs, CO: Multnomah Waterbrook, 2011).

ACKNOWLEDGMENTS

A book is the result of the ideas of countless people. Though two people were given the opportunity to write the book, it would be entirely appropriate to list hundreds of people on the cover who have contributed to its fruition.

In 2010, the North American Mission Board (NAMB), one of the United States' largest domestic charities, endeavored to refocus itself around one central mission: to push back lostness in North America through evangelistic church planting. This was a seemingly impossible task, considering that NAMB is more than 160 years old and has dozens of different types of ministries.

The strategy that was begun in 2010 is called Send North America. The goal of the strategy is to see churches planted at a rate faster than the population is growing (something that has not happened since pre-WWI). In order for this strategy to take root, it has meant the sacrifice of hundreds of people. Our partners had to refine their strategies and budgets to come around these new priorities. Our staff had to shift their functions in order to implement the strategy.

At the end of the day, these sacrifices and changes have been necessary so that thousands of churches can be planted and most important, millions of people hear the gospel of Jesus.

Though every person who played a role in this book cannot be named, a few must be mentioned, because without them, the words on these pages and the Send North America strategy would not be a reality.

NAMB Team Members & Partners. You helped develop and refine the ideas that eventually became *Life on Mission.* Steve Canter, Chad Childress, Greg Murphree, Randy Ferguson, Steve Kersh, Ken Miller, Mike Riggins, Shane Critser, Ryan West, Alvin Reid, and Jimmy Scroggins: thank you.

Brandon Clements. Without your ongoing development of the content, writing, and editing over the long haul, this book would have never been inked. You made this book happen—start to finish.

Ginger Kolbaba. Thank you for your help in the editorial shaping of this book into its final form, while providing the encouragement and humor needed in the ninth hour of our deadlines.

Our staff, friends, and publisher. You have read over manuscripts, inspired ideas, modeled the book's DNA, sacrificed a great deal, and picked up the slack in other areas so that this work could be completed. Pat McCarty, Heather Buck, Darby Hanevich, Adam Miller, Micah Millican, Andrew Kistler, Carmon Keith, Beverly Cooper, the crew at Midtown Columbia who live out this DNA, and our new friends at Moody Publishers: Duane Sherman, Parker Hathaway, and Brandon O'Brien.

NAMB Senior Leadership Team. You have been in the trenches tirelessly strategizing, negotiating, and implementing the Send North America strategy. Steve Davis, Jeff Christopherson, Steve Bass, Gary Frost, Carlos Ferrer, Mike Ebert, Clark Logan, and Al Gilbert.

Kevin Ezell (NAMB President). Thank you for fearlessly leading NAMB to a new day. Without your visionary leadership and winsome style, this mission would not be where it is today.

To the people of the Southern Baptist Convention who support the work of North American missions with passion, zeal, and sacrifice. Thank you.

AARON'S PERSONAL ACKNOWLEDGMENTS

To my family for your continual support along this journey to make the name of Jesus famous across North America and the great cities of this world: Carmen, Ezra, Ella, Joshua, and Harper.

DUSTIN'S PERSONAL ACKNOWLEDGMENTS

To my family for the continued encouragement and sacrifice you give toward this work. My greatest joy is living on mission side by side with my favorite mission team: Renie, Jack, and Piper. To Ma, Pa, Mandy, and Wendy for displaying to me a lifetime of what it looks like to faithfully follow Jesus. I am blessed.